On the Cultures of Exile, Translation, and Writing

Comparative Cultural Studies, Steven Tötösy de Zepetnek, Series Editor

The Purdue University Press monograph series of Books in Comparative Cultural Studies publishes single-authored and thematic collected volumes of new scholarship. Manuscripts are invited for publication in the series in fields of the study of culture, literature, the arts, media studies, communication studies, the history of ideas, etc., and related disciplines of the humanities and social sciences to the series editor via email at <clcweb@purdue.edu>. Comparative cultural studies is a contextual approach in the study of culture in a global and intercultural context and work with a plurality of methods and approaches; the theoretical and methodological framework of comparative cultural studies is built on tenets borrowed from the disciplines of cultural studies and comparative literature and from a range of thought including literary and culture theory, (radical) constructivism, communication theories, and systems theories; in comparative cultural studies focus is on theory and method as well as application. For a detailed description of the aims and scope of the series including the style guide of the series link to <http://docs.lib.purdue.edu/clcweblibrary/seriespurdueccs>. Manuscripts submitted to the series are peer reviewed followed by the usual standards of editing, copy editing, marketing, and distribution. The series is affiliated with *CLCWeb: Comparative Literature and Culture* (ISSN 1481-4374), the peer-reviewed, full-text, and open-access quarterly published by Purdue University Press at <http://docs.lib.purdue.edu/clcweb>.

Volumes in the Purdue series of Books in Comparative Cultural Studies <http://www.thepress.purdue.edu/comparativeculturalstudies.html>

Paolo Bartoloni, *On the Cultures of Exile, Translation, and Writing*

Justyna Sempruch, *Fantasies of Gender and the Witch in Feminist Theory and Literature*

Kimberly Chabot Davis, *Postmodern Texts and Emotional Audiences*

Philippe Codde, *The Jewish American Novel*

Deborah Streifford Reisinger, *Crime and Media in Contemporary France*

Imre Kertész and Holocaust Literature, Ed. Louise O. Vasvári and Steven Tötösy de Zepetnek

Camilla Fojas, *Cosmopolitanism in the Americas*

Comparative Cultural Studies and Michael Ondaatje's Writing, Ed. Steven Tötösy de Zepetnek

Jin Feng, *The New Woman in Early Twentieth-century Chinese Fiction*

Comparative Cultural Studies and Latin America, Ed. Sophia A. McClennen and Earl E. Fitz

Sophia A. McClennen, *The Dialectics of Exile*

Comparative Literature and Comparative Cultural Studies, Ed. Steven Tötösy de Zepetnek

Comparative Central European Culture, Ed. Steven Tötösy de Zepetnek

Paolo Bartoloni

On the Cultures of Exile, Translation, and Writing

Purdue University Press
West Lafayette, Indiana

Printed in the United States of America.

Library of Congress Cataloging-in-Publication Data

Bartoloni, Paolo.
On the cultures of exile, translation, and writing / by Paolo Bartoloni.
p. cm. -- (Comparative cultural studies)
Includes index.
ISBN 978-1-55753-368-5
1. Literature--Philosophy. 2. Philosophy. 3. Translating and interpreting--Philosophy. I. Title.
PN49.B16 2008
401--dc22

2008004332

Contents

Acknowledgments

On the Cultures of Exile, Translation, and Writing was made possible thanks to a series of grants from the University of Sydney, including one Sesqui Research and Development Grant, a Research Institute for the Humanities and Social Sciences (RIHSS) Writing Fellowship and two Faculty of Arts Seed Funding Grants. The School of Languages and Cultures at the University of Sydney and its former and current heads, Tim Fitzpatrick and Jeffrey Riegel, have assisted the process of writing through their generosity and support, both material and intellectual.

Earlier versions of sections in chapters 1, 2, and 4 have been published as journal articles or chapters in collected volumes of essays: "The Paradox of Translation via Benjamin and Agamben," *CLCWeb: Comparative Literature and Culture* 6.2 (2004) <http://docs.lib.purdue.edu/clcweb/vol6/iss2/5/>; "Memory, Translation and the Urban Space," *Literature and Aesthetics* 15.2 (2005): 109-18; "Literature of Indistinction: Blanchot and Caproni," *After Blanchot: Literature, Criticism, Philosophy*, ed. Leslie Hill, Brian Nelson and Dimitris Vardoulakis (Newark: U of Delaware P, 2005): 238-56; "Memory in Language: Walter Benjamin and Giuseppe Ungaretti," *Literature and Aesthetics* 16.2 (2006): 116-24. The permission to reproduce Vincenzo Accame's poem "Nuova Scrittura" was granted by his brother, Felice Accame, and the permission to reproduce the image of Pietro Paolini's *The Fortune Teller* (oil on canvas, Auckland Art Gallery Toi o Tamaki, gift of Mr N.B. Spencer, 1961) by the Auckland Art Gallery Toi o Tamaki.

Librarians at Fisher Library at the University of Sydney, but especially Peter McNiece, have been invaluable, answering bibliographical enquiries with professionalism, care, and promptness. In the last four years I have been a regular visitor at the Biblioteca dell'Orologio in Rome, the home of the former library of poet Giorgio Caproni, and at the Gabinetto Vieusseux in Florence, in which beautiful rooms the manuscripts, letters, and diaries of Caproni are kept. My thanks for the patience and availability of the librarians in Rome and Florence, especially of Luciano Pontecorvo, Marina Girardet, Fabio Desideri, and Roberto Seghezzi. Caproni's son, Attilio Mauro Caproni, and daughter, Silvana Caproni, have been a source of constant inspiration.

The final version of *On the Cultures of Exile, Translation, and Writing* is indebted to many colleagues and readers who, over the various drafts, provided suggestions and comments. I would like to extend a special thank-you to Tony Stephens, Suzanne Kiernan and Andrew Benjamin. Joseph Falsone has been more than a research assistant. His comments and sensibility have greatly improved this book. Kathleen Olive was scrupulous and extremely composed when the time came to get the book ready for publication, checking for consistency of style, and coding the text for the index.

Many of the ideas criss-crossing this book have been tested over the years and several coffees with colleagues at the University of Sydney and other institutions: Vrasidas Karalis, Anthony Dracopoulos, John Gatt-Rutter, Reingard Nethersole, and Ulrike Kistner above all. A special thank-you to the editor of the Purdue Series of Books in Comparative Cultural Studies, Steven Tötösy de Zepetnek. Steven has not only believed in this project from day one, he has also offered ongoing support and attention to my needs and requests. At Purdue, I would also like to thank Dianna Gilroy for her help through the very final stages of the manuscript. *On the Cultures* has found its ideal location within a series that celebrates interdisciplinarity and which is committed to comparative literature as well as cultural studies in a framework that focuses on the relevance of the humanities in today's world. And last but not least, the help and support of Gem, Mia, and Luca is, as always, unquantifiable and, as it ought to be, beyond measure.

Introduction

In a short story by the contemporary Italian author Gianni Celati, "Mio zio scopre l'esistenza delle lingue straniere" ("My Uncle Discovers the Existence of Foreign Languages"; 1985), the protagonist and uncle of the title migrates to France from a small town in northern Italy. He is a bricklayer, who knows of only one language: the one spoken in his village. When he arrives in France, he believes that the local language is merely another dialect, like all the others he has encountered during his journey. As he always has done, the uncle gets by; he marries a French woman and the couple gives birth to a child. When the child is two years old the protagonist must return to Italy, where he remains for two years. Once back in France, he discovers that his child's use of language is such that communication between the two is impossible. Celati tells us that when the uncle discovers the existence of foreign languages it is as if an impassable ocean full of fog ("un mare pieno di nebbia";103) has come between him and his son; it is as if he has woken up from a dream, and he starts crying.

His crying may be brought about by a realization, which is also a liberation, an opening—a sudden freedom from ignorance. These may be tears of joy. But might it not also be that the uncle cries because he is suddenly confronted with a total disintegration of reified possibilities? The inability to communicate brings the uncle face-to-face with a world where ordinary experience counts for nothing. The child's incomprehensible utterance freezes him and empties him of actuality. The uncle cries because all he has learned, all that has held him in good stead until now, has lost, even if only for a moment, its meaning and usefulness. He can do no more nor less than simply observe his being as it drifts out of presence. I recount this story because it introduces the notion and category of potentiality, which is at the very core of the present book. In the case of Celati's story, one could say that the uncle is a man devoid of potentiality. His counterpart might well be Melville's *Bartleby* (1853), the famous scrivener who courteously and humbly declines to carry out the tasks he is asked or required to do. He simply sits at his desk and stares. Bartleby appears systematically to remove actuality from his horizon, but, precisely because of his decision to do so, he also places himself in a position to observe and embrace the entire gamut of possibilities.

Through renouncing actuality, Bartleby becomes a fully potential being; potentially able to do, but also able not to do. Whereas Celati's uncle stands gazing at the gradual disappearance of his actual being, simultaneously failing to glimpse the appearance of his potential being, Bartleby is immersed in potentiality. But exactly what is the philosophical, aesthetic, social, and ethical relevance of potentiality? A first answer might lie in potentiality's openness. The capacity, that is, incessantly to become, incessantly to produce meanings by defying closure. This is the angle from which this book views the modes of translation (defined as language-that-comes); time and memory (memory as the obvious example of temporal translation); exile (living in between places); and writing (especially the works of the Italian poet Giorgio Caproni and the French author Maurice Blanchot, which are celebrations of suspension and indistinction). Potentiality also responds, however, to broader philosophical concerns and preoccupations, which are typically modern. It was by constructing his project on potentiality that Heidegger announced the end of metaphysics and the commencement of a new philosophical mode which is still in the making. Heidegger interpreted Nietzsche's philosophy as the climax of Western metaphysics, the moment at which the experience of ontic being achieved the total oblivion of Being (the origin). According to Heidegger, the disappearance of ontology, and therefore of the origin, determined not only the ultimate celebration of presence but also the exhaustion of metaphysics. Heidegger considered this moment metaphysics's great fulfillment, but also a sign of its inevitable decline and erosion. Through forgetting the relation between the origin (the essence) and the originated (the ontic sphere), Western metaphysics also forfeited the very engines of thought: productivity and creativity. In a sense, Heidegger's philosophical project is an attempt to revive this relation by going beyond metaphysics or, perhaps, by regaining the original essence of metaphysics.

The problem is that the philosophical process toward this goal is not entirely transparent and has given rise to many divergent readings of Heidegger's thought. In *Oltre l'interpretazione* (*Beyond Interpretation*; 1994), the Italian philosopher Gianni Vattimo offers a useful summary of the vast literature on Heidegger, as well as a lucid insight into the internal dynamics at play in Heidegger's work. Vattimo writes that Heidegger's project has been interpreted either as the modern attempt to regain the essence as presence (the "approach from the right") or as the thought that suspends the essence (Being) by withdrawing it (the "approach from the left"; *Oltre l'interpretazione* 18). However (and apart from possible differences between two supposed Heideggers—the Heidegger of *Being and Time* and the Heidegger of the *Kehre* [*The Turn*])—there is no doubt that Heidegger's work resonates again and again with notions such as "becoming," being "underway," "renunciation," "astonishment," "destruction," and "silence," all of which point in the direction of a philosophical place and mode that refuses, and defuses, the idea of presence, be it ontic or ontological. What emerges instead is a philosophical framework founded on the very suspension of presence, on the potentiality of presence. According to Heidegger, this is the necessary mode through which *aletheia* (truth, unconcealment) can be gained and through which being might be opened (unconcealed) to the experience of Being. What is less clear, and less systematically expounded, is the ethical, social, and even aesthetic significance of this mode and the way in which it can affect, touch, and inform us. And while it is true that Heidegger has provided in his writing on Hölderlin, Rilke, Trakl, and George some suggestive interpretations of poetic discourse—reviewing in the process the position and function of art—it is also true that these readings are often fragmented and singular.

This book is an attempt to contextualize notions such as potentiality and suspension by making them react with a series of modes and categories of being (translation, time, exile, and writing) and by comparing a series of key modern and contemporary thinkers and authors under the lens of potentiality. If it is true that Heidegger's is the voice that resonates explicitly and implicitly throughout the book, it must also be stressed that his voice is supplemented, challenged, and integrated with the voices of others, including Agamben, Augustine, Benjamin, Blanchot, Caproni, and Kafka. I wish to stress the methodological and programmatic significance that the singular voices of philosophers and authors have for this project. This book does not enter into the discussion of the differences that mark, say, the philosophical work of Heidegger from that of Benjamin. Rather, it brings their thoughts and ideas to bear on a series of central issues, singularly but also in a way that might suggest continuities as well as discontinuities. I have taken Benjamin's conceptualization of the halo—and his attendant reflection on citation—literally, treating the philosophical and literary figures criss-crossing this book not so much as historical presences but as traces, segments of the Western tradition. These voices coalesce, interlocute, talk to one another in ways and with effects that might otherwise simply remain unaccounted for. The result is perhaps, from a scholarly point of view, heterodox. And yet, this procedure appears to me to be eminently suited to the presentation and discussion of potentiality and the many literary and philosophical possibilities that it invokes.

On the Cultures of Exile, Translation, and Writing is divided into four chapters—"Translation," "Time," "Exile," and "Writing"—which can be read as independent essays as well as parts of a whole. Each chapter presents a particular view of potentiality, offering theses that converge and mutually integrate with one another and pointing to something unique to the respective fields of study. The movement of the book is more circular than linear, with issues and themes returning, but coming from different directions and providing different perspectives. Time is the concept that contextualizes the others, providing the necessary framework for my discussion. "Translation" starts, for instance, with a reflection on the temporal movement that characterizes Benjamin's "Die Aufgabe des Übersetzers" ("The Task of the Translator"; 1923) and continues with a discussion of temporal relations between invention and translation. "Exile" investigates by thinking of memory as suspension (as in the example of the *flâneur*) in order to refocus attention on memory's productivity, as well as on the articulation of literary language. "Writing" focuses on the relation between remembering and forgetting, and on waiting as the locus of a poetics of discovery sought by suspending the conventional experience of discovery.

Toward the end of the first chapter, "Translation," the question is asked: "could the process of translation be one of those instances in which language speaks itself as language? In other words, could translation be the moment when language stays still in order to reach out, in order to become and in order to encounter subjectivity?" This question reflects the general discussion of this chapter as well as the theoretical approach adopted, which is informed by hermeneutical concerns, and deals not only with language but also with subjectivity and ethics. At the root of this theoretical articulation of translation is Benjamin's essay, "The Task of the Translator." Benjamin's reflection on translation is investigated, exposing the paradox and philosophical conundrum of his argument. Benjamin's notion of "pure language" is also closely scrutinized by comparing and contrasting it with Agamben's discussion of voice and with the Heideggerian notion of language as "ringing stillness." The result is the sketching of an epistemological and philosophical function for translation that, while it includes linguistic and literary preoccupations, responds directly and specifically to key ontological and metaphysical issues. The focus of the argument is on the area of indistinction between what Benjamin calls "pure language" and "unsupplemented languages." What is this area? And more importantly, what exactly are its ontological implications? According to Benjamin, translation is the mode that may offer access to the language in between. And yet in Benjamin this access, and to a certain extent translation's purpose, is only alluded to and ultimately remains unresolved. Chapter 1 traces the philosophical and literary significance of the indistinction of language, but it also asks whether the indeterminacy between "pure language" and "unsupplemented languages," the locus, that is, of a potential language—the language-that-comes—can be brought to visibility and experience. Can this visibility be achieved by removing not only the barriers separating the original from the translation, but also those between different translations of the same original? This process of removal enables voices that are saying the same thing differently to merge synthetically. What is arrived at is a language in between—a possible language—indeterminate and yet resounding with a richness that is simply not present in the individual texts and voices from which it derives. The poem "L'infinito" ("The Infinite"), by the Italian Romantic poet Giacomo Leopardi, and two of its English translations are discussed as an example of this process of synthesis.

Time and being are linked inextricably to the extent that their respective readings are also and invariably marked by their relation. This implies that time and being are almost inevitably ontologized or phenomenologized and, in turn, become either transcendental or ontic. By inserting the conjunction *und* between *Sein* ("being") and *Zeit* ("time"), Heidegger emphasized their connectedness but also, perhaps, their separateness. Was Heidegger stressing a fundamental relation or was he also indicating a possible suspension of this relation? In chapter 2, "Time," I follow this potential trace, asking if it is "possible to think time not as an adjective of being, not as a chronology," but as time *as such*—as an event distinguishable from being. If it is true that time and being are inseparable, it is perhaps also true that this inextricable relationship might better be understood by attempting to extricate time and being from each other. "In dismantling the symbiosis between time and being," I argue, "the process of reassembly might give rise to a greater consciousness of this necessary union."

The suspension of the relation time/being, its translation into a potential "to be" but also "not-to-be," is looked for in memory, especially in the articulation of memory found in Benjamin's *Berliner Chronik* (*A Berlin Chronicle*; 1932). Benjamin's articulation of memory as "moments" and "discontinuities" is contrasted with Augustine's dense and still intensely relevant discussion of time and memory in Books X and XI of *The Confessions*. These two texts are integrated with a series of references to and quotations from other texts. The purpose of these asides, which can either run transverse to Augustine's and Benjamin's works or directly interact with them (as in the case of Benjamin and Ungaretti), is to provide a polyphony of intersecting voices which speak of the dynamic subjectivity of the modern individual, the temporality of which—as discussed in chapter 2—at once abandons and returns to him. It is from this temporality that *is* and *is not* with the subject—and as such is a temporality where the conjunction *and* acquires considerable philosophical significance—that fluidity and potentiality flow, and that Heidegger's "existentialism" and static ontology may be questioned.

Explicitly or implicitly, exile brings about a suspension and a relation of time, space, language, and identity. Exile is, like translation and memory, a mode situated at a threshold. Chapter 3, "Exile," begins by interrogating Plotinus's famous formula: "the flight of one alone into one," which is also an enduring model of literary and philosophical exile. The flight from ordinary, quotidian life has been considered one of the necessary steps toward achieving the proper *habitus* in which creativity and philosophical inquiry can occur. This form of exile is nothing other than the attempt to reunite the subject with a perceived lost origin and essence. Exile can also be related in this sense to translation as discussed in chapter 1. The study of exile in this book focuses, accordingly, on the language of exile. Language must be here understood in its broader sense as that which produces texts, and not exclusively literary texts. The main questions asked in chapter 3 relate to memory, but not so much to remembering as to the making of memory. When and how are memories made? Possible answers to these questions are sought in the productive relation between the past and the present, a relation which is articulated at the point of its spatial and temporal suspension. In a sense, this chapter is also the place where the theses of the other three chapters converge. It is exile that, in the end, provides a further reconfiguration of translation, time, and language. Exile is treated as a metaphor and a condition of existence, and not only of literary existence, although the discussion of literary exile is prominent throughout the chapter. Exile is interpreted as an innate condition, which is in no way meant as an intellectual justification or mitigation of the anguish and pain of those who still today suffer political and enforced exile, but rather as a reflection on the absence of mnemonic production that seems to characterize the contemporaneous. I argue that the making of memory is brought about *when* the fracture between the present and the past is so profound—as in exile—that its healing requires a comparison or, as I call it in the book, a "turning back." And yet, this turning back is in reality "looking forward," in that the individual searches for the past by looking to the present, and the ways in which the past might be reflected in the present. In a society that seems to have closed temporal as well as spatial gaps, the action of "turning back," of returning, seems irrelevant and unnecessary. It may be that when there is no "turning back" there is also no mnemonic production.

Chapter 4, "Writing," is the direct continuation not only of my previous book (*Interstitial Writing: Calvino, Caproni, Sereni and Svevo*, 2003), but also of the problematization of potentiality, which in this chapter is studied from the perspective of writing. The question that criss-crosses the book addresses the ontological significance of potentiality. While it is true that potentiality is one of the oldest philosophical notions, it is also true that its articulation remains elusive and underdeveloped. Is potentiality (and the attendant notions of suspension, renunciation, and waiting) the passivity of a cultural state, a *habitus* between action and negativity? Or is it, rather, the deliberate and revolutionary production of a language and a subjectivity that know and experience otherwise? "Writing" engages these issues by probing further into the production of language. This discussion is then contrasted with and brought to bear on the work of two important modern authors, Giorgio Caproni and Maurice Blanchot. The relation between Caproni and Blanchot testifies to a cultural proximity which seems to me to be much more than a poetic and aesthetic affinity. On the manuscript of the poem "Le parole" ("The Words"; 1977), Caproni left a note defining a relation between his work and that of Blanchot. He wrote that he had been ahead of Blanchot by seven years when he had written in 1946 that "words empty things." Caproni, one of the most highly acclaimed Italian poets of the twentieth century, kept a close eye on the work of Blanchot. Thanks to his command of French and the outstanding cultural enterprises of the journal *Botteghe Oscure* (which featured original works by important yet, at the time, little-known international intellectuals), Caproni read Blanchot's *Le Retour*, *Le Calme*, *Comme un jour de neige*, *L'Attente l'oubli*, and *La Bête de Lascaux* in the years 1951-1958 (all of these texts are held in the former library of Giorgio Caproni, now kept in the Biblioteca Cardano in Rome). There is no evidence that Blanchot and Caproni ever met, or that Blanchot read Caproni's work (volumes of Caproni's works in French translation appeared only in the 1980s, although individual poems were translated into French much earlier), and yet their writing shows striking similarities. The two authors stare at each other through their poetic language, which is also the product of a series of philosophical preoccupations shared with their time. More specifically, it is the reflection on language, subjectivity, and temporality mediated through the work of Hegel and Heidegger that takes centre stage in Blanchot's and Caproni's writing. If Hegel led them to think about the relation between sign and thing, Heidegger prompted them to look beyond this relation at the space in which sign and thing are exposed to each other and—astonished and silent, indistinct—open up. Chapter 4 also traces this "coming face to face" of Blanchot and Caproni through a close reading of Blanchot's *L'Attente l'oubli*, Caproni's *Il muro della terra*, and of the interface between these writings and Hegel's and Heidegger's thought. I define the writing of Caproni and Blanchot as suspended between effability and ineffability. Their writing is not so much negative as indistinct. The thing is not annulled—made void—by their words. Instead, it adheres to words, but on the non-linguistic side of words. The thing emerges when words are permitted to experience the nonlinguistic. I argue that in Blanchot and Caproni this experience is achieved over the threshold of sayability and unsayability, at those moments, that is, when sound and silence, visibility, and invisibility coalesce.

At its heart, this book attempts more than I have described so far. It attempts to describe a disposition to listen to some of the central thinkers and authors of the Western literary and philosophical tradition, and, perhaps most importantly, to listen with them to echoes and sounds resonating throughout this tradition. There is a word in Italian that perfectly summarizes this disposition: *acconsentire*. It literally means to allow oneself (the prefix *a* is nothing other than the preposition "a," meaning "to do something for," "to do something in order to") to "feel," to "listen to" (*sentire*) "with" (*con*). In this book I have *acconsentito* (allowed myself to listen and feel with). In other words, I have opened myself to the voices of other thinkers in order to capture, on the one hand, their own singularity, and on the other, the traces that, reverberating in their voices, are the fragmented remnants of the Western aesthetic and philosophical foundation. The wholeness of this tradition is not so much a myth as a space that can only ever be visited—and recounted—in fragments. This book is not without analogy to a diary kept by a traveller during his journeys. I, myself, am not sure if I have ever been "there" or, indeed, if my fellow travellers have been "there." It may well be that their recounting is like mine: an account of an account, a translation and interpretation of actual experiences, or a tale about allegedly authentic experiences. This may be what Walter Benjamin had in mind when he proposed to write a book which was to consist of a collection of quotations from other books, or what Borges alluded to when writing books about books never written. It is no accident that this book is very much about writing and ideas, but also about journeying in time and space, about exile, memory, and translation. Above all, *On the Cultures of Exile, Translation, and Writing* is a book about potentiality, which is the ability simultaneously "to be there" and "not to be there," the disposition, that is, to remain open—*acconsentire*—to an experience that is simultaneously complete (an encounter with the singularity of a given voice) and unfinished (a coming into the presence of traces). As such, it is about the preparedness to wait not so much on the threshold of the indeterminate as on that of the indeterminable: between closure and openness, concealment and unconcealment, wholeness and partiality.

Comparative literature is undergoing further assessments and review, especially in light of the progressive influence and prestige of cultural studies. The need to support comparative literature should not arise from merely maintaining narrow discipline boundaries and specificities, but from the far more significant cultural and social necessity to engage globalization through a cross-cultural, transnational and interdisciplinary approach. The Purdue monograph series of Books in Comparative Cultural Studies, edited by Steven Tötösy de Zepetnek, addresses cultural and intellectual imperatives that are directly connected to the relevance and future of academic endeavors, attempting to link rich theoretical frameworks with practical outcomes in the sphere of society and its increasingly complex mechanisms, including technology, the mass-media, and artificial forms of life. This, as Tötösy de Zepetnek claims, might well be an innovative path for comparative literature or, as he proposes, comparative cultural studies (on Tötösy de Zepetnek's conceptualizations of comparative literature and comparative cultural studies, see, e.g., *Comparative Literature: Theory, Method, Application*, "From Comparative Literature," *Comparative Literature and Comparative Cultural Studies*).

On the Cultures of Exile, Translation and Writing is framed by a methodology that attempts to combine the hermeneutic tradition and interests that have been the precinct of cultural studies (the discussion of exile, for instance), while not directly engaging the notions of comparative literature and cultural studies. This has opened up investigative paths that are at once recognizably literary and philosophical but also, I hope, transdiscplinary in a way that responds directly to Tötösy de Zepetnek's conceptualization of comparative cultural studies. Similarly, while the discussion is firmly grounded in theory, the tone and the overall approach to the topics of this book are intended to stimulate practical reflections on the nature of contemporaneity, providing what I believe is a tangible form of self-awareness.

Chapter One

Translation

The Paradox of Translation

Translation is based, as Walter Benjamin intimates in his essay on translation, "Die Aufgabe des Übersetzers" ("The Task of the Translator"; 1923), on an exhilarating paradox and a fundamental metaphysical conundrum. Benjamin's thesis is that translation is possible, indeed necessary, because all languages are connected to one original language (on language and translation in Benjamin see also Andrew Benjamin, "The Absolute"; Jacobs; and Fynsk). Benjamin calls this original language "pure language" ("die reine Sprache"). But perhaps "related" is a better word than "connected" since in Benjamin's thought there is a strong sense of origin and genealogy—of kinship ("Verwandtschaft"). It is no accident, then, that Benjamin characterizes human languages as languages after the Fall. In positing a before and an after, Benjamin introduces a temporal relation and a direct line of descendency. Pure language exists before languages, and languages are born as a direct result of the Fall. This assumption enables Benjamin to establish a link between pure language and languages, and also to postulate the continued existence of pure language in between the folds (or cracks) of languages.

Time and its passage mark the discourse on translation, as Benjamin articulates in "The Task of the Translator," "in defining the more restricted usage [of kinship] the concept of origin remains indispensable" (*Illuminations* 74; "für die Bestimmung jenes engern Gebrauchs der Abstammungsbegriff unentbehrlich bleiben wird"; *Ein Lesebuch* 49). What is less clear, but potentially more significant, is the lesson one can learn from this movement and from examining how the temporality of the separation between pure language and languages is redescribed in the simultaneous synchronicity and diachronicity of languages or, as Benjamin calls it, in the "suprahistorical kinship of languages" (*Illuminations* 74; "überhistorische Verwandtschaft der Sprachen"; *Ein Lesebuch* 49). Two questions arise as a direct consequence of the linguistic fracture: Is this separation between an elemental language and its many descendants still apparent in languages? If so, how does this separation, and the differences that result from it, manifest themselves in languages?

Benjamin claims that the essential relatedness of languages is predicated on intention. He gives the example of the German word *brot* and the French word *pain*, remarking that both languages intend the same object. The mode of this intention varies, however, and it is this difference that ultimately generates a different meaning and a different experience of the thing called bread. If linguistic kinship is based on the communality of an original intention, configured in the naming of pure language, the linguistic difference is marked by a separation and an estrangement through which the original intention is hidden by cultural and experiential determinants. These differences are nevertheless brought to light *in* and *through* translation. In Benjamin's words: "In the individual, unsupplemented languages, meaning is never found in relative independence ("Bei den einzelnen, den unergänzten Sprachen nämlich ist ihr Gemeintes niemals in relativer Selbständigkeit anzutreffen"), as in individual words or sentences; rather, it is in a constant state of flux ("vielmehr in stetem Wandel begriffen")—until it is able to emerge as pure language from the harmony of all the various modes of intention ("bis es aus der Harmonie all jener Arten des Meinens als die reine Sprache herauszutreten vermag"). Until then, it remains hidden in the languages ("So lange bleibt es in den Sprachen verborgen"). If, however, these languages continue to grow in this manner until the end of their time ("bis ans messianische Ende"), it is translation which catches fire ("so ist es die Übersetzung...sich entzündet") on the eternal life of the works and the perpetual renewal of language" (*Illuminations* 75; *Ein Lesebuch* 50). Translation is the brief moment at which pure language appears on the surface of languages, only to vanish again into inarticulacy. But by the same token, Benjamin also speaks of pure language as that which incessantly signals its presence in the process of *becoming* of languages; at that instantiation, that is, when languages mingle with each other in their constant transcendental leaning towards a reunion with pure language. If on the one hand pure language is the essential, the origin, on the other it is also *becoming*, the fluid, the incessant, and the indistinct. Is the passage from origin to potentiality the result of the linguistic fracture, the necessary tribute that pure language must pay in order to become itself again? If this is the case, then pure language itself, and not only unsupplemented languages, exists in the hope of reunion with itself. While it is a plausible notion that languages' main purpose is to return to the origin, the thinking of pure language as that which wishes to return to itself is ambiguous. Assuming that pure language is indivisible, the idea that pure language might reunite with itself is contradictory and nonsensical. And yet, this is precisely what Benjamin's essay on translation appears to argue. Benjamin postulates two movements toward the same goal; one movement is that of languages toward pure language and the other is that of pure language as it exists after the Fall toward pure language as it exists before the Fall.

If Benjamin is right, the linguistic fracture is then a double fracture, one that also indicates a separation within the origin, and that decrees the divisibility of pure language. This separation introduces the possibility of thinking the origin not as transcendental negativity but as potential presence; a presence within the world of phenomena. Translation is therefore the modality of language that brings the origin into the factual by simultaneously celebrating and withdrawing it. The withdrawal of the origin is achieved by calling it into a potential presence through the becoming of language. It is at this juncture—which is also the quintessential example of philosophical mediation—that a reconsideration of Western transcendence and metaphysics can take place. To posit an entity which is simultaneously ontological and ontic—"What you understand by the phenomenal sense of the word *génesis* we can also label as ontic" (Heidegger and Fink, *Heraclitus Seminar* 8; "können wir auch als ontisch bezeichnen," *Heraklit* 17)—is to challenge the very opposition between sensible and supersensible and between empirical and *a priori*. The thinker, therefore, is no longer concerned exclusively with the task of negotiating the incorporeal and the corporeal, but with engaging the incorporeal, the corporeal, and the mode of their simultaneous occurrence. And the challenge is no longer limited to the analysis of pure language and languages. It must include by necessity the *becoming* of language as well; it must include, that is, the simultaneous occurrence of pure language and languages.

The central preoccupation and argument of this chapter is emphasized in the preceding two periods. However, a more detailed account of the relation between language and languages must be provided before we can enter into discussion of what will be called the "language-that-comes."

Death Masks

Every language is potentially translatable into another and, ultimately, back into pure language. Translation's very existence is based on this principle: "translation thus ultimately serves the purpose of expressing the central reciprocal relationship between languages" (Walter Benjamin, *Illuminations* 73; "ist die Übersetzung zuletzt zweckmäßig für den Ausdruck des innersten Verhältnisses der Sprachen zueinander"; *Ein Lesebuch* 48). The paradox stems from the fact that pure language has been lost—irretrievably, some would argue (Benjamin included). The metaphysical conundrum stems from the postulation that pure language's existence is predicated upon its very ineffability. This assertion is not without analogies to the mystic belief in the centrality of creation, and therefore to the theological assumption that knowledge—in its purest form—can only be knowledge of God, of that which pre-exists nature and humanity. One can understand in this sense the emphasis that has historically been given to the concept of the surface, and the purity of an unadulterated *tabula* as a metaphor of the *Whole*. It is after creation that the *tabula* begins to be inscribed, begins to be narrated in the image of God. In God's image the beginning can be analyzed in order to regain knowledge of the supreme Origin.

The search for pure surface is also the task that the Austrian art critic Ernst Gombrich (see "Psychoanalysis and the History of Art") declared to be the purpose of the art critic, and the function that Benjamin ascribed to the philosopher. Both art critic and philosopher assumed that the essential and purest form of interpretation is that which ultimately obliterates the work under interpretation. As memory undoes the life of a person by exposing its most profound secrets (see also chapter 2), so interpretation strips the work of art of its superfluous *realia*. This amounts to appropriating the work and re-writing it, from its end to its origin.

The interpreter becomes an author, or, perhaps more appropriately, a translator whose task is to undo the work in order to retrieve the essence hidden beneath layers of words and colours, in order to reach—by following to the letter Hofmannstahl's dictum—the depth that lies at the surface of things. If the author starts at the essence and gradually and inevitably leaves it behind in the urge to possess it and know it, the interpreter and the translator start from fiction and erase it to know and possess the essence. These two processes are complementary and necessary; they could not exist without each other. In order to arrive at the essence, one must first disfigure, deface, or exile it. The essence must be banned by its celebration in the work of art. Modern literature, music, and the visual arts are acts celebrating the negativity of that which they have purposefully removed. And yet, it is precisely because of this removal that the essence can become accessible through the act of interpretation and translation. Benjamin's words on translation must be read in this context:

> We may call this connection [between original and translation] a natural one, or, more specifically, a vital connection ("Er darf ein natürlicher gennant werden und zwar genauer ein Zusammenhang des Lebens"). Just as the manifestations of life are intimately connected with the phenomenon of life without being of importance to it, a translation issues from the original ("geht die Übersetzung aus dem Original hervor")—not so much from its life as from its survival ("Zwar nicht aus seinen Leben so sehr denn aus seinem 'Überleben'"). For a translation comes later than the original, and since the important works of world literature never find their chosen translators at the time of their origin, their translation marks their stage of continued life. The idea of life and afterlife in works of art should be regarded with an entirely unmetaphorical objectivity. ("In völlig unmetaphorischer Sachlichkeit ist der Gedanke vom Leben and Fortleben der Kunstwerke zu erfassen"). (*Illuminations* 72; *Ein Lesebuch* 46, translation modified)

The essence will remain without meaning unless it is violated by art and reconstituted by interpretation. "It is as if that which is to be heard," wrote Heidegger in *Holzwege* (*Off the Beaten Track*; 1950), "is compelled to suffer violence" (Heidegger, *Off the Beaten Track* 247; "Gleich als leide das, was hier zu hören und zu sagen ist, notwending Gewalt"; *Holzwege* 328). But this must be a particular kind of interpretation, one that does not talk about the work, and one that does not paraphrase it. In 1945 Georges Bataille wrote a visionary book on Nietzsche, *Sur Nietzsche*, in which we find this remark: "Admitting its inaccessible nature [Bataille speaks of the 'summit,' that is, his personal definition of the essence, of freedom] I approach it only by not setting out for it" (39).

Interpretation is indeed a translation that searches for the essence by stripping the work bare, by going toward the origin and the infancy of the work. Paradoxically, the work of art can only discover the essence by banning the essence. "The work is the death mask of its conception," wrote Benjamin in *One Way Street* (1928; Walter Benjamin, *Reflections* 81).

Giorgio Agamben articulates a similar idea when, in the "Introduction" to *Infanzia e storia* (*Infancy and History*, 1978), he argues that:

Every written work can be regarded as the prologue (or rather, the broken cast ["cera persa"]) of a work never penned, and destined to remain so, because later works, which in turn will be the prologues ("preludi") or the moulds ("calchi") for other absent works, represent only sketches ("schegge") or death masks ("maschere mortuarie"). The absent work ("l'opera assente"), although it is unplaceable in any precise chronology, thereby constitutes the written works as *prolegomena* or *paralipomena* of a non-existent text; or, in a more general sense, as *parerga* which find their true meaning only in the context of an illegible *ergon*. To take Montaigne's fine image, these are the frieze of grotesques ("la cornice di grottesche") around an unpainted portrait, or, in the spirit of the pseudo-Platonic letter, the counterfeit of a book which cannot be written ("la contraffazione di uno scritto impossibile"). (3; *Infanzia e storia* vii)

For Agamben the actual work is nothing other than a "death mask" which represents the *imago* of a non-existent work; the death mask, in other words, of a work that has never been written and will never be written. This is, Agamben argues, the destiny of all written works, whose ultimate essence will never be fully revealed because it is inscribed in and belongs to their illegible counterparts. The *ergon* Agamben speaks of cannot be read simply because it cannot be written. As soon as an attempt is made to write it, the *ergon* is transformed into its death mask and its essence is disfigured. While Borges articulated this thought when he penned stories about non-existent stories and wrote "Pierre Menard, Author of Don Quixote" (1939), Benjamin resolved to confront the artistic *aporia* head on, not by writing about non-existent texts, but by putting on the critical map the ciphers of erasure *par excellence*—the processes of translation and citation. "Citation," writes Agamben, discussing Benjamin's essay on Karl Kraus, "appears as an eminently destructive procedure whose task is 'not to shelter, but to purify, to rip out of context, to destroy.' Its destructive force, however, is that of justice; to the very degree to which citation tears speech from its context, destroying it, it also returns it to its origin" (*Potentialities* 152). If the *ergon* cannot be written, it can perhaps be observed in the process of breaking open its death mask.

Metaphysical conundrum

The paradox of translation and the metaphysical conundrum intersect at the point where ineffability and loss coincide with the impossibility of speaking pure language through what Benjamin defines as unsupplemented languages. It is this impossibility that determines the negativity of pure language. And yet, it is this very negativity that demonstrates the existence of pure language, and that makes its presence philosophically possible. Pure language exists in not being effable. The loss becomes therefore the inability to speak a language that *is* its incommunicability. In other words, for metaphysics, the loss of pure language is simultaneously the beginning of thought and the pretext of thought.

In theological terms, cosmological and psychological knowledge are at the service of theology and can only be predicated on the existence of something prior to such knowledge. While cosmological and psychological knowledge or, as Kant calls it, ontic knowledge, are arrived at through experiencing the sensible, ontological knowledge—the quintessential and all-inclusive sphere of knowledge in which beings and Being are included—is transcendental. The experience of nature and human beings (cosmology and psychology) cannot be conducted, indeed cannot be conceived, without the existence of nature and of beings. How can ontological experience and ontological knowledge be achieved? In other words, is it possible to think of a Kantian *a priori* and to know it through ontic experience and ontic knowledge? The book of nature is the first step. And yet, religion has been quite explicit in saying that knowledge arrived at through cosmological and psychological study, while legitimate, is nonetheless inadequate and incomplete. It is here that the distinction between theology and philosophy must be made. First, philosophy further divides ontological knowledge by asking whether it is possible to predicate an ontology of ontic experience and ontic knowledge as such and not as transcendence. The reflection on language is the centerpiece of this study, and the challenge that Kant poses himself in his analysis of metaphysics. Is there a language that pre-exists language? Furthermore, is there a language that pre-exists a non-transcendental understanding of language?

Benjamin appears to believe so when he distinguishes *in language* from *through language* and when he differentiates between *supplemented languages* and *unsupplemented languages*. Benjamin's thought on translation is the project of defining a potentiality that actualizes itself in between the effable and the ineffable, and of a mode of language that positions itself in the temporal interim of a now that subsumes its appearance in its continuous disappearance. This is the simultaneity of the effable and the ineffable, where the unsayable turns into the sayable as the sayable reverts to the unsayable. But what if the ineffable of language is not that of pure language but rather the quiddity, the essence, of language itself?

Voice

Agamben's *experimentum linguae*, as expounded in *Infancy and History*, is nothing other than the philosophical effort to wrest potentiality from the grip of metaphysics and place it in the realm of the factual. The linguistic split that characterizes the work of Benjamin still drives the work of Agamben. In the latter, however, the split is not so much between pure language and languages as rather a fracture inherent in human language. Agamben sees the locus of this fracture in infancy and conducts his own *experimentum linguae* within the space where, as he says, "the limits of language are [to be found] not outside language, in the direction of its referent, but in an experience of language as such, in its pure self-reference" (*Infancy and History* 5; "i limiti del linguaggio non sono cercati al di fuori del linguaggio, in direzione del suo referente, ma in un'esperienza del linguaggio come tale, nella sua pura autoreferenzialità"; *Infanzia e storia* x). It is necessary to quote a central passage of Agamben's thought on language in its entirety:

> If every thought can be classified according to the way in which it articulates the question of the limits of language ("Se il rango proprio di ogni pensiero si misura secondo il modo in cui esso articola il problema dei limiti del linguaggio"), the concept of infancy is then

> an attempt to think through these limits in a direction other than that of the vulgarly ineffable ("in una direzione che non è quella, triviale, dell'ineffabile"). The ineffable, the unsaid ("l'irrelato"), are in fact categories which belong exclusively to human language; far from indicating a limit of language, they express its invincible power of presupposition, the unsayable being precisely what language must presuppose in order to signify ("lungi dal segnare un limite del linguaggio, essi ne esprimono l'invincibile potere presupponente, per cui l'indicibile è precisamente ciò che il linguaggio deve presupporre per poter significare"). The concept of infancy, on the contrary, is accessible only to a thought which has been purified, in the words of Benjamin writing to Buber, "by eliminating the unsayable in language." The singularity which language must signify is not something ineffable but something superlatively sayable: the *thing* of language ("ma è il massimamente dicibile, la *cosa* del linguaggio"). (*Infancy and History* 4; *Infanzia e storia* viii, translation modified)

The letter to which Agamben refers was written by Benjamin to Buber in July 1916 (*Briefe* Band 1:125-28). It concerns Benjamin's collaboration with the journal *Der Jude*, edited by Buber, and discusses issues of style and language. The sentence, "the pure elimination of the unsayable in language" ("die kristallreine Elimination des Unsagbaren in der Sprache"; *Briefe* 127), is part of a broader linguistic reflection in which Benjamin first hints at a problem he will address more systematically in another essay of the same year, "Über Sprache überhaupt und über die Sprache des Menschen" ("On Language as Such and on the Language of Man"). In the central section of his letter to Buber, Benjamin challenges the idea that language is a mere instrument or tool, a means subordinate to the goal of the signifier. He opposes to this utilitarian language a magic, poetic, and prophetic language; a language, in other words, that Benjamin sees as the essence and true reality of language itself. By eliminating the unsayable from language, Benjamin cannot and does not mean to remove the magical from language. On the contrary, he wishes to celebrate the epiphany of the unsayable, an epiphany attained by causing language to approach that which denies itself to language. If, on the one hand, Benjamin is concerned with eliminating the unsayable by reclaiming the sayability of pure language through the magical immediacy of language—and, subsequently, through translation—Agamben dispatches the unsayable by positing the philosophical reflection on language not on a fracture between a supersensible before and a phenomenological after, but on the fracture of the now of factual language. And yet, the language Agamben speaks of as the connecting link between the thing of language and the ordinary experience of language (the infancy of language) is also a lost language, a mode that continuously loses itself in its inherently interstitial status between semantic and semiotic, between language and discourse, or, in other words, between recognition and comprehension. If on the one hand the metaphysical loss is centered in the utterability of a language that *is* in the presence of its incommunicability, on the other—that is, in the realm of the factual—the loss is the inability to grasp the significance of a linguistic transition and to study the moment at which the essence of language says itself in the very process of unsaying itself. Both philosophical angles on language assume a pre-existing mode of language, but whereas in Benjamin what pre-exists human language is pure language, in Agamben it is the voice.

The voice is firmly ensconced in language, and its actuality is, according to Agamben, the true home of humanity and the cipher of an inalienable communality. Furthermore, the voice has the potential to become language, which is also the potential to translate itself into grammar, writing, and discourse. Agamben locates the transition from voice to language in infancy; and it is in infancy that Agamben chooses to carry out his study of linguistic potentiality.

Non mi viene la parola

A philosophical thought about relatedness, be it metaphysical or factual, necessarily gravitates not only to the principle of origin but also to the attendant one of movement: from pure language to languages, from languages back to pure language and from voice to language. Language is in constant flux, forever moving and changing, never static. But this movement must be characterized and qualified, in that it is, and must be understood as a movement in language by language.

Expressions such as the Italian *non mi viene la parola* ("the word does not come to me") partake of language's dynamism but simultaneously misunderstand the implication of the movement in question. The movement implied by *non mi viene la parola* is from language to subjectivity. Where should the word come from? Is the word supposed to come as we summon it? Moreover, assuming that the word travels, for how long does it travel? Does it arrive safely and unchanged? The traveling invoked by the expression *non mi viene la parola* assumes an origin and a point of departure at which the word is generated or where the word resides and waits for a call. This simple expression, so common in ordinary parlance, tells an important tale about the movement of language and also about language's original home. It implies that language leaves its home in order to reach a destination which is also its situatedness in the world of communication, comprehension, and utterability. And the story is told as if language can only exist by virtue of the subject that utters it. The before of utterance is pure linguistic potentiality. The expression *non mi viene la parola* appears to indicate the separation of an elemental but silent language and its embodiment as uttered language.

What does happen to language as it travels? Does it change? In other words, is the language at the origin, the potential and silent language, different from the uttered language of actuality? If so, how do they differ? Clearly, the difference is between voice and language, but also between pure language and languages. In either case the question "how does language change?" cannot be answered since the origin, be it the voice or pure language, remains undisclosed. The question cannot be answered in and by language but it can allegedly be answered at the moment when subjectivity becomes the primary cause of the change. Language changes as it is spoken by the subject. It would appear, then, that the actuality of language is that of the subject itself. It is as a result of this simple axiom that Saussure could articulate the difference between *langue* and *parole*.

If it is true that there is an origin of language and that the origin of language is something other than the uttered experience of language, then the origin is irreparably lost. The challenge is not really that of retracing the irretrievable origin, but rather that of investigating the nature of, and the reason for, those instances in which language, by defying its own fluid nature, does not move, refuses to come: *non mi viene la parola*. What kind of language is a language that *non viene*? There exists the possibility that this question, together with the investigative perspective from which it derives, is incorrectly formulated. Indeed, it would be plausible to postulate the immobility of subjectivity before that of language rather than the other way round. In this case it is the subject that does not travel toward language, that finds itself caught in the absence of language. This is a realm devoid of language, of grammar, a realm where there are only sounds. In these utterly embarrassing moments of aphasia the subject is plunged into an uncanny and surprising dimension where subjectivity experiences the abandonment of language. These are moments, usually a matter of seconds, after which the banishment from language is resolved. And yet the banishment from language can last longer and can drag the subject into madness or mental and social exile. But if it is true that it is the subject that moves, it is also true that the abandonment of language is a self-imposed exile, a banishment that the subject forces upon itself. It is not language that moves away from the subject but the subject that moves away from language.

Assuming that language does not move, it is then without origin and without difference. It follows that the traveling of language is only apparent, induced by the continuous traveling of subjectivity. It is a deception, an optical trick akin to the apparent movement of a stationary train in which we are sitting, when it is in fact the adjacent train that is in motion. The distinction between *langue* and *parole* would then be the result of such an illusion and would more correctly be restated as the distinction between *the subject within language* and *the subject outside language*. It is in this sense that the expression *non mi viene la parola* ought more appropriately be rephrased as *non vengo alla parola* ("I do not go to the word").

Ringing Stillness

In the chapter "Das Wesen der Sprache" ("The Nature of Language"), of Heidegger's *Unterwegs zur Sprache* (*On the Way to Language*; 1959), one reads: "To undergo an experience with language...means to let ourselves be properly concerned by the claim of language by entering into and submitting to it" (57; "Mit der Sprache eine Erfahrung machen heißt dann: uns vom Anspruch der Sprache eigens angehen lassen, indem wir auf ihn eingehen, uns ihm fügen"; *Unterwegs zur Sprache* 159). Yet in the same book, although in a different chapter ("Der Weg zur Sprache," "The Way to Language"), one also reads: "We, accordingly, listen to language in this way, that we let it say its Saying to us ("Demgemäß hören wir auf die Sprache in der Weise, daß wir uns ihre Sage sagen lassen"). No matter in what way we may listen, whenever we are listening to something we are *letting something be said to us* ("Sich-sagenlassen"), and all perception and conception is already contained in that act.... We let its [language's] soundless voice come to us, and then demand, reach out and call for the sound that is already kept in store for us" (124; "Wir lassen ihre lautlose

Stimme kommen, wobei wir den uns schon aufbehaltenen Laut verlangen, zu ihm hinreichend ihn rufen"; *Unterwegs zur Sprache* 255).

In Heidegger's creative reflection on language, language comes and goes to and from the subject and the subject comes and goes to and from language. Language and subjectivity simultaneously move in search of one other and simultaneously pause in their tracks to hear each other's proximity. One's own silence is the other's voice and one's own absence is the other's presence. We can only hear language if we stop speaking language, if we cease to "merely follows language constantly" (75; "Das Wesen der Sprache"; *Unterwegs zur Sprache* 179). In these moments of pure self-silencing and linguistic abandonment the essence of language can be heard, in that whenever "we speak a language, language itself never has the floor ("die Sprache selber kommt dabei gerade nie zum Wort")...Language speaks itself as language...when we cannot find the right word for something that concerns us" (59; "wo wir...das rechte Wort nicht finden"; *Unterwegs zur Sprache* 161).

We find language when we listen to it by shutting ourselves out of its continuous utterance, by stopping and allowing language to come to us. And yet language cannot find us unless it too holds back in what Heidegger calls *das Geläut der Stille*, "the ringing/resounding stillness" (*On the Way* 108; *Unterwegs zur Sprache* 215); in a state, that is, of pure immobility, of linguistic *quidditas*, where only the existence of an indecipherable breath can lead us to language. Language comes to us at the moment in which we move toward it in the experience of a suspended subjectivity which denies itself in order to find itself (see also chapter 4). The going toward language and the coming of language is, in both instances, a *going forward*, a moving ahead toward the origin. In positioning the origin ahead we are not only following Heidegger's route, we are also challenging his "existentialism" as we conceptualize the movement of language and subjectivity not as a transcendental thrust, but as a propelling force whose philosophical significance rests on its becoming language as such. It is in this sense that the forwardness of the origin is treated here as the necessary source of aesthetic production and labor, but only when the forward movement suspends the impetus to turn production into a static and ahistorical fusion with the origin. Origin is simultaneously the beginning and the end of production, its birth and its death, its genesis and nemesis. Origin is what production tends to and yet must avoid in order to remain active. It is on this premise that the articulation of a "language-that-comes" can be made. But what exactly is Heidegger suggesting when he speaks of undergoing "an experience with language"?

There is a game called "Blind Man's Buff" which children play with enthusiasm. One player is blindfolded, made to turn around a few times and then spurred to catch the other players. The game usually starts with great noise and fuss, with the blindfolded child stumbling and crashing into all sorts of obstacles. In the noise of play the blindfolded child is unable to catch anyone, even risking injury in a futile attempt to find the other players, as if he could actually see and run around with ease. The game takes a turn for the better when the blindfolded child realizes that he cannot actually see and that his only chance of finding anybody rests on accepting his own blindness. The blindfolded child stops breathing, stops calling out, stops moving. He stops being. His immobility is analogous to divesting oneself, although temporarily, of life. In a magical response to this denial of the self, the other players fall silent and stand still and yet they can still see, and it is this seeing that betrays them, in that their being alive is soon manifested through their audible breathing, the minute sounds they cannot help but make. These sounds will betray them and allow the blindfolded child to catch them. What the blindfolded child is seeking in those infinitesimal moments of existence-without-being is precisely a reconnection with existence-with-being that can be achieved by catching another being. The blindfolded child can only be himself again if called by the movement of the other. It is in stillness that movement takes place and that language catches fire.

Reflecting on this simple children's game is the best way of approaching Heidegger's reflection on language, and helps to explain the otherwise obscure statement that "we hear Saying only because we belong within it" (*On the Way* 124; "Wir hören sie nur, weil wir in sie gehören"; *Unterwegs zur Sprache* 255). We can only catch somebody else because we *are* that somebody else. And we hear language because we are in language, because we are language. *Non mi viene la parola, non vengo alla parola*; the negative state of not going can be resolved by halting all movement, both of language and of subjectivity, by suspending and waiting, by ultimately ridding "ourselves of the habit of always hearing only what we already understand" (*On the Way* 58; *Unterwegs zur Sprache* 160).

Mediation

Earlier references to blindness and visual tricks—and their visionary implications—are not accidental. It is worth remembering that for Benjamin the essence of language must be found not in its capacity to communicate but in its ability to speak the spiritual content of things, which is nothing other than the ability to speak the relation with pure language. At the moment in which language reconnects with its spiritual content it becomes language as such. In "On Language as Such and on the Language of Man," Benjamin writes that:

> [Every] language communicates itself *in* itself; it is in the purest sense the "medium" of the communication ("jede Sprache teilt sich in sich selbst mit, sie ist im reinsten Sinne das 'Medium' der Mitteilung"). Mediation, which is the immediacy of all mental [spiritual] communication ("Das Mediale, das ist die Unmittelbarkeit aller geistigen Mitteilung"), is the fundamental problem ("Grundproblem") of linguistic theory, and if one chooses to call this immediacy magic, then the primary problem of language is its magic ("so ist das Urproblem der Sprache ihre Magie"). At the same time, the notion of the magic of language points to something else: its infiniteness ("Unendlichkeit"). This is conditional on its immediacy ("Sie ist durch die Unmittelbarkeit bedingt"). For just because nothing is communicated *through* language ("*durch* die Sprache sich nichts mitteilt"), what is communicated *in* language ("was *in* der Sprache sich mitteilt") cannot be externally limited or measured, and therefore [every] language contains its own incommensurable, uniquely constituted infinity ("wohnt jeder Sprache ihre inkommensurable einziggeartete Unendlichkeit inne"). (*Reflections* 316-17; *Ein Lesebuch* 29)

Mediation is understood here both as that which lies in between, in the middle space, as well as that which simply speaks the essence as it enacts its existence as such.

In the words of Benjamin, *in* language is a medium which is simultaneously in between and magically endowed with the capacity to approach the essence of things. If this is true, *in* language comes to the essence as such without communicating it to anybody for the sake of comprehension; *in* language merely presents a movement without effects. But what is an event without apparent meaning? Benjamin answers this question by drawing attention to the inherent infinitude of language, to its unfathomable and yet elating incommensurability. An event which defies comprehension is precisely that which cannot be measured in the enclosure of a complete and comprehensive knowledge. It follows that the essence is a world forever open, a few attributes of which can be glimpsed as things as such. The things of language are these words that say, that can perhaps be recognized, and which yet defy clear meanings. What can these things be? Are they simply sounds, smells, memories? How can they connect at all with us just by being what they are? Moreover, how can they remain impermeable to all our efforts at interpretation?

The irony is that the thing of language, its *quidditas*, is pre-eminently interpretable. The essence shows itself ahead *in* language and yet most of the time it remains unnoticed. We are blind to it because a presence without comprehension is not only infinite but also meaningless and, as such, invisible. The incomprehensible is inevitably turned into oblivion and negativity. We can only see what we know: the rest is a great homogeneous grayness. The question is therefore how we can know more in order to see more. Translation, as we shall see, offers one answer to this question. Another answer explored by Benjamin and other modern authors can be found in the attention they give to small things, to apparently banal and ordinary objects, or memories and thoughts behind the seeming puerility of which an elemental and profound truth unfolds as it is watched and grasped. This is the story of Proust's writing, or Baudelaire's baroque banality, or Pascoli's naïve poetic ingenuity. It is also found in the most intimate autobiographical writings of Benjamin, such as *A Berlin Chronicle* and *One Way Street*. In Proust, Baudelaire, Pascoli, and Benjamin the central purpose is to sharpen sight and remove a self-imposed blindness caused by varying degrees of cultural conformity and ingrained cultural, linguistic, and philosophical values and beliefs. These authors narrate what is present before their eyes and yet invisible to everyone else. Their complexity is nothing other than the result of their tremendous simplicity. It is not even a form of highly sophisticated or bizarre imagination but a pure seeing in a language that closely follows events in the realm of small things.

Whenever we have language we also have things: language cannot exist alone. It is in this sense that, when thinking of *in* language as the mode of the pure taking place of language, we inevitably assume that its saying is only apparently meaningless. In reality we believe that *in* language speaks to be interpreted and that its saying might be meaningless for *in* language and yet full of meanings for the interpretations which might occur through language. In this instance, *in* language is only a conduit, a mere vehicle connecting and mediating between two worlds. But in assuming this, do we not revert to an understanding of language, be it *in* language or *through* language, as an instrument for communication only? If this were the case, what would then be the difference between *in* language and *through* language?

In language would be the instrument of pure language and the necessary passage through which pure language can reach the possibility of communication and comprehension. Conversely, *through* language would be the instrument to give voice, form, and structure to this comprehension. The difference would be one of functionality. This does not appear, however, to be the philosophical view taken by Benjamin and, after him, by Agamben. For these authors there is no point in defining *in* language as that which speaks without understanding, simply because behind the essence of language there is nothing but language. *In* language is not just a medium linking two separate zones. It is itself a zone and not merely an empty vessel that speaks through itself about something else. *In* language says nothing else but itself and its status of potentiality.

The incommensurability and infinity of languages are decreed by the negativity residing within them. It is the fact that pure language inhabits languages without being uttered *through* languages that generates languages' inherent openness and essence as *becoming in* language. Languages will be forever incomplete in their *through* mode—which is also the accepted normative mode of utterance and communication. Their spiritual essence, which is also the coming toward pure language (and toward the origin), is to be looked for in the mediation that operates in the crevices that from time to time open within *through* language. It is in the visionary suspension of literature, or in translation, that *in* language presents itself in images and visions of a language-that-comes.

For Benjamin the ciphers of this infinite and incommensurable language were sacred texts, the Bible above all. As Brian Britt has noted in *Walter Benjamin and the Bible*, "from at least 1916 onward, Benjamin posited an ideal language, the only access to which is found in texts, particularly sacred texts like the Bible. Sacred texts do not, however, provide a magical key to the recovery of pure language. Rather, they paradoxically gesture toward pure language through narratives of its loss" (Britt 13). Britt goes on to clarify that "sacred texts, especially the Bible, represent archives of lost pure language, which it is the task of philosophy to restore. As such, sacred texts, primarily the Bible, reveal the foundational nature of pure language" (15). The revelation is predicated upon the absence of its object, which equates with saying that the retrieval of that which has been lost (pure language) can only take place as a visionary experience. The becoming of pure language will strike the philosopher as an image and will embed itself in the mind of the philosopher whose task, like that of the translator, will be to think of a language that presents itself as visionary revelation. It is in this messianic state, and sense—so characteristic of Benjamin's writing on language—that mediation is synonymous with vision and, above all, meditation.

Meditation

Meditation is at the base of monastic orthopraxis. Orthopraxis sets the rules for the proper learning of sacred texts based on the mastery of certain monastic practices (for a discussion of orthopraxis, see Carruthers). As such, orthopraxis is not so much about accepting and conforming to the exegetical interpretations of sacred texts as it is about imitating the spiritual exercises of recognized masters as the necessary route toward revelation. Meditation is the centerpiece of these spiritual exercises. It is through meditation that the hidden truth contained in sacred texts can be revealed. Furthermore, this truth, which in Benjamin's terms equates with pure language, manifests itself not through language but through images. The articulation of this experience can only be attempted by arriving at a language which is the result of a mediation between *through* language and images. A clear example of this mediation and combination is offered by illuminated texts. Illuminated texts strive to fill the gaps left by the disappearance of pure language by supplementing language with iconic supports, whose function is to say the unsayable, to make visible that which is invisible. Translation follows the same principle. A translation can be thought of as the illuminated text of a preexisting text. Translation is the meditation/mediation conducted with the purpose of a revelation, which in the end will enrich the text by bringing to the surface its invisibility. Like meditation and mediation, translation is the continuous and uninterrupted process of *coming to the invisible*.

According to theology, this task is impossible without faith. It is at the threshold of faith that Benjamin's messianism and monastic orthopraxis part ways. The revelation of pure language, which according to Benjamin is the task of the philosopher, cannot be predicated on faith. It is rather a question of method and of modes of language. Assuming that pure language exists in some form, and that translation is inextricably linked to it, translation can act as a guide toward pure language. If translation and translatability are predicated upon the communality of languages and one common origin, translation and translatability are also the result and the effect of the unsayability and negativity of the origin. It follows that translation and translatability are possible only in the face of an absence which is also their cause. Translation and translatability imply in this sense a return to the origin, and the demand placed upon them is simply that of making that origin visible and able to be experienced again. Experience is here understood in the sense of being in the presence of something sensible. In other words, to experience the origin would mean to return to the Edenic state and to life before the Fall. And yet, if the original language were to become effable (or transform itself from supersensible to sensible) then translation would also cease to exist, as would imagination and invention. If ever there was something irreducible to sensibility, it must be the Edenic state. It is as if the Fall introduced an irreparable fracture, dividing two states of being, the supersensible and the sensible. This fracture cannot be resolved in the realm of the factual through the recuperation of an extraordinary life before the Fall. The only possible passage to the Edenic state is through the end of ordinariness and the end of the factual. To be at the origin would also mean to be out of history. Extraordinariness can only be achieved by trading it for ordinariness. The ontological can only be arrived at by removing the ontic, and Being can only be achieved by removing the state of being.

Translation cannot be the pure language until it negates itself, and yet this negation cannot take place in the ordinariness of human language. What translation can do is to invoke pure language in its potential becoming, in its status as detritus and rubble. That is the greatness and the magic of language; after it there is only the void of nothingness or the extraordinary myth of bliss. Language is destined to remain in language—underway—and its transcendence is only apparent as a result of the continuous movement within its borders.

Kafka's "Before the Law"

But here, following Benjamin, a question arises: are the borders of language infinite? In other words, is language limitless? Language is limitless in our belief that it says something other than itself. It is at this juncture that the inextricable link between language and subjectivity becomes evident in all its philosophical and metaphysical implications. The subject that speaks language, the subject that *is in* language, believes it is in the presence of something else, and believes that its ultimate task is to go outside of itself. In doing so, the subject does not realize that this venturing outside of itself will also decree its end, together with the erasure of language.

In 1919, Kafka wrote a short story, just two pages of text, titled "Vor dem Gesetz" ("Before the Law"). "Before the Law" is perhaps one of the simplest and smallest (in the sense given to small by Benjamin), but also one of the most enigmatic stories that Kafka ever wrote. It tells the story of a man from the country who embarks on a journey to enter into the Law. As he arrives before the door of the Law (or the border between his country and the country of the Law), he is met, as one would expect, by a guard, a doorkeeper. To the traveler's request to enter, the guard replies that, although the door to the Law is always open, this is not the right moment to pass through it. The man from the country waits. The years go by but the right time to enter never arrives. The story ends with the death of the man from the country as he still waits for permission to enter. "Before the Law" is the story of an apparently meaningless journey and of a futile waiting; it might be a tale about the injustices and inequality of the Law as well as a story about the blindness of subjectivity. While "Before the Law" appears to narrate a man's waiting *outside* the Law, it may also narrate his waiting *in the presence of* the Law. The journey could be interpreted as fruitful, a journey which actually delivers the man to his destination. And yet the man does not notice that he has arrived; or rather, he does not recognize the changes that have taken place and that distinguish the new country from the old country. Either way, "Before the Law" tells an ever more subtle tale which is peculiarly similar to our discussion of language and subjectivity.

It is clear that "Before the Law" is not a story about entering or crossing. In fact, it is, if nothing else, a story in which entering and crossing are deferred continuously until the end of life. What Kafka's character experiences is precisely the impossibility of translating extraordinariness into ordinariness on the plane of the factual, and the impossibility of being in the transcendental state of purity, even if that purity is intrinsically his own.

Imagination and Translation

In antiquity, imagination was understood as that which mediates between the corporeal and the incorporeal. Imagination was perceived as a cognitive tool—a concrete and legitimate way of arriving at knowledge. Imagination was not concerned merely with fable or fiction, but was rather an epistemological tool comparable to reason or experience. In this way, according to Agamben (see *Stanze*; *Stanzas*), medieval troubadours and *stilnovisti* could fully experience possession and knowledge of their object. Only when object and subject coalesce into a single body can the union of experience and knowledge be arrived at. Imagination, as a concrete tool, could guarantee that union. What would it say about translation if translation truly were comparable to imagination?

If translation mediates between pure language and languages, and assuming that the process of translation can be experienced as real and present, translation will then represent a full union of subject and object. More importantly, translation will become the central goal of the coming philosophy if it is true that, as Benjamin claims, the task of the philosopher is first and foremost to reclaim for knowledge and experience the archives of pure language. Translation, like sacred texts, is one such archive. The philosopher becomes a kind of archeologist excavating language with infinite care to search—and this is fundamental—not so much for the essence but for a trace of the essence. In order for this to take place, however, the very concepts of imagination, language and visibility have to be revised.

In the first instance, imagination must be brought back to the plane of tangible epistemology. Translation must similarly be brought to a stage of concrete existence in its own right. This means wresting imagination from the erroneous labels of unreality and hallucination that have gradually adhered to it in Western culture, and to reclaim it from the realm of the oneiric and unconscious to that of the empirical. It also means bringing the process of translation back to light by undoing the translated text as well as the original, by stripping them both bare and returning to their inception, to the elemental grain of artistic imagination and linguistic magic.

Play

The proximity of imagination and translation is evident not only in what has been discussed so far but also in the act of creation itself. Imagination and translation build something new from something old, erecting the unknown on the solid foundation of the known. It is, however, this very construction that must be dismantled as the thing of knowing. In other words, the act of thinking does not wait for the building to be finished in order to think it. Thinking happens incessantly, defying and postponing completion and deferring the concept of arrival both in time and space. Imagination and translation must be transformed from products into processes as such; they must retain their potential diachronic essence.

Benjamin was alluding to something similar when reflecting on children's innate interest in rubble and ruins. In *One Way Street* he wrote that "children are particularly fond of haunting any site where things are being visibly worked upon. They are irresistibly drawn by the detritus generated by building, gardening, housework, tailoring, or carpentry. In waste products they recognize the face that the world of things turns directly and solely to them. In using these things they do not so much imitate the works of adults as bring together, in the artifact produced in play, materials of widely differing kinds in a new, intuitive relationship" (*Reflections* 69). Detritus, rubble, and ruins become thus the focus of children's enjoyment and play. Such stuff is also the material with which the archeologist works to bring to light a glimpse of lost worlds, the stuff of precious archives. Translation is the quintessential detritus of literature: the ruins of a work undone.

We usually turn a blind eye to the ugliness of the unfinished, incomplete, or ruined, without realizing that perhaps it is precisely in the apparently unsettling state of potentiality that the essence lies. Children, as Benjamin saw, are not deterred so easily by the mess of incompleteness. On the contrary, they are attracted to it, finding within it the propelling force which allows their imagination to flourish. To children there is nothing more exhilarating than the unfinished or indeed the invisible, the purely imaginative, with which they establish a strong and lasting connection—more enduring than the relationships they build with perfectly polished toys. Why is it that the perfectly functional and desirable toy gleaming from the shop window besots children only until the moment they possess it, and that they forget it after a few hours of play? And why is it, by contrast, that the malfunctioning objects found in second-hand stores, or imaginary friends, can accompany children faithfully throughout their childhood?

New toys promise immediate happiness. They are the ready-made objects that can be used instantly to achieve the desired effect. But it is precisely because of this perfect attunement of desire and fulfillment that the shine has a short duration. In order to be fulfilled, desire must be rekindled continually, and imagination is an essential spark to desire. An object is destined to be left behind if it cuts imagination short. Only that which has the power to renew imagination can last. An object counts only insofar as it keeps imagination active.

Invention and Translation

One might arrive at the conclusion that translation exists in order to negate itself in the face of a rediscovered and practicable purity and originality. But this is only the case if translation is understood as oriented toward the past. In fact, this is the sense that translation has traditionally assumed: a process which invariably moves backward. What are the implications of this assumption for translation? First and foremost, translation has been understood as the opposite of invention. Invention is axiomatically directed toward the future as it leans inevitably to the new and the unexplored. Even when invention is the result of meditation conducted on the past—as in the case of medieval rhetoric—its intention and motivation are inherently directed at the future. While invention has been related to the future, translation has been linked to the past.

It is worth pausing to interrogate further this conventional understanding of translation and invention. Is invention necessarily directed forward? Could it not go sideways, go backward, zigzag? Could invention not lose itself? Might it not be the case that in losing the way new territories could actually be discovered? Forwardness in time is strictly correlated with forwardness in space. And yet, it is precisely by connecting invention and forwardness that spatial and temporal trajectories—as well as our way of living time and space—can be reconstituted into alternative modes of spatial and temporal being. To move forward in time cannot mean simply to proceed linearly, as if time were a succession of calendar dates. Similarly, to move forward in space cannot simply mean to arrive at a predestined location after having covered a certain amount of ground. No invention is required to adapt to and comply with prearranged temporal and spatial itineraries. Invention takes place in dialectical opposition to that which preexists it.

If this is true, invention would appear to be the antithesis of the concept of knowledge described at the beginning of this chapter. Invention would be the necessary step preceding knowledge of the unknown. If it is true that knowledge can only be predicated on the experience of that which preexists it, it is also true that knowledge is inherently knowledge of the already known. In order to be transformed into knowledge, the already known must be given a structure and a form, an image and a language; in a word, it must be made comprehensible. The passage from the known to the knowledge of the known is, as we have seen, based on the existence of an unformed and unstructured known. The known is present among us as a part of our ordinary life. And yet, it lacks a discourse without which it cannot become common knowledge. This is something different from postulating the knowability of the unknown. How can that which is outside our ordinary experience, the simply unknown, be turned into knowledge? This is the task of invention and imagination.

Imagination is nothing other than that which fills the gap in our understanding of the unknown and which goes some way toward translating the unknown into the known. Invention is propelled by imagination and can only be so when directed exclusively toward knowledge of the unknown. That is why invention is creation. The simple fact that it exists as a result of a void is the cipher of its inherent creativity. It is in this sense that invention is simultaneously transcendental and immanent. It is transcendental because it tends toward something outside of itself, and immanent because it creates this something from within itself. The transformation of the unknown into the known (and subsequently into knowledge) is nothing other than invention's giving birth to imagination by shaping it into a structured form. Invention both includes and excludes the unknown; it includes it as it produces it, and excludes it as it yields the unknown to knowledge.

Translation is a journey in time as well as in space, but it is above all a journey into language. And it is a journey in which the familiar and unfamiliar are always intermingled. In translation, unknowability is the search for pure language, and the known is the pre-existent. Therefore, the journey of translation is a journey into the familiar, during which, from time to time, translation is plunged into the unknown (into its coming to pure language). But even the coming to pure language cannot be the unfamiliar since languages consist, in essence, of pure language. It is, however, a familiar that has lost its memory and its identity; which does not remember itself, but which merely appears as itself in language.

Textual Movements

Much of modern literature believes that invention arises from a suspension of experience. This is discovery through creation. An image described by Renaissance author Francis Bacon comes to mind: the unknown is approached simply by lighting a lamp and proceeding in the dark (see Agamben, *Infancy and History* 17; *Infanzia e storia* 10). This image is easily connected to the work of the Italian poet Giorgio Caproni and his continuous reference to candles and darkness. In the poem "Perch'io..." (1958), we read: "perch'io, che nella notte abito solo, / anch'io, di notte, strusciando un cerino / sul muro, accendo cauto una candela / bianca nella mia mente—apro una vela / timida nella tenebra, e il pennino / strusciando che mi scricchiola, anch'io scrivo / e riscrivo in silenzio e a lungo il pianto / che mi bagna la mente" ("because I, who live alone in the night, / even I, at night-time, scraping away a match / on the wall, cautious, light a white / candle in my mind—open up a shy / sail in the darkness, and the scraping / nib that creaks back at me, even I write, / and rewrite in silence and at length, the weeping / that soaks my mind"; Caproni, *L'opera* 185, trans. Brian Fitzgerald; see also the discussion of poetry and darkness in Stewart 1-57).

If, conventionally speaking, invention goes ahead, translation proceeds by turning back. The great error that has been made in the history of translation theory has been to interpret this proceeding backward as a journey into the past. Benjamin is one of the first theorists and philosophers to attempt to correct this theoretical myopia. One of the kernels of Benjamin's philosophy is his conception of time and memory as testified most clearly in his *Berlin Childhood* (1932/1938), *A Berlin Chronicle* (1932) and the unfinished *Arcades Project* (1935/1939). Benjamin's reading of *Erinnerung* (the internal analysis of the past built on the framework of present networks and contingencies) is of great importance and significantly influenced his reflection on translation. For Benjamin, memory is the quintessential temporal translation, the spatialization of time (see also chapter 2). It is the mediating historical and psychological mode, the mode of connection. But what is it that memory wants to translate? What is the original of memory? In the conventional understanding of memory, the original is the past, which memory translates into another form and brings into a new context. Memory translates the foreign language of the past into the comprehensible language of the present. Here, as in the conventional understanding of translation, we have a passage from a source language (the past) to a target language (the present). But as we know—and we know this much more clearly for time than we do for translation—memory fills the invisible gaps left by an intangible past by inventing. In the context of creation, memory reconnects with the function it had in monastic and patristic experience and thought (on this see also Carruthers, especially 60-115). Memory is not so much interested in recalling for the sake of recalling as in recalling for the sake of discovering. This is recalling to go forward. *Erinnerung*, as Benjamin uses it, must be understood as the internal predisposition and desire to renew the self by conjuring up images and states whose priority is to move forward rather than backward.

Thresholds

Erinnerung's images proceed by turning back. But their turning back is only pretextual. It is a homage to the natural predisposition to suspend disbelief that allows us to invent. Only in the ambiguity generated at the threshold between truth and untruth, reality and fiction; only in the zone of indistinction between being and non-being can creation and invention take place and flourish (see also Agamben's discussion of temporality, *Infancy and History* 73). This is also true for translation, which turns back not to reconnect with the past but to use, in a calculated sense, the past as a pretext to invent new territories for exploration.

What we face when looking at invention and translation are two only apparently opposed routes. In fact, they are destined to connect. Their interaction, or better still, their coming together, occurs in the zone of indistinction where invention and translation—backwardness and forwardness—become blurred. This threshold is also the only possible reality of the process of translation (and also of invention) as it aspires to move toward pure language. Whereas the directions of translation and invention might appear to be opposite, their goal is exactly the same: to approach the origin. But pure language, the origin, is also a pre-text: it is another clever concession to our creative desire. Pure language is a gesture toward our infinite greatness as self-deceiving beings. We make pure language exist in order to search for something else that we do not know and cannot know. In one of his most beautiful poems, "Un posto di vacanza" ("A Holiday Location"), in *Stella variabile* (1982), the Italian poet Vittorio Sereni writes the stunning line, "sapendo di non sapere" ("knowing of not knowing"; Sereni 248, my translation). And in the posthumous collection of poetry by Giorgio Caproni, *Res amissa* (*The Amissed Thing*; 1989), we read: "C'è / soltanto il non c'è" ("There is / only that which there is not"; Caproni, *L'opera* 839).

The paradox of translation, with which I opened this chapter, is generated by the unknowability of pure language which, in the process of the birth of all other languages, dissipates itself by obscuring and annulling its utterability. As I stressed earlier, the existence of pure language is based upon the impossibility of speaking it through languages. It exists by excluding itself from the existence of languages. If it is true that all languages are made in the image of the original language, it is also true that this link cannot mean that the essence of the original is the same as those of languages. To ascribe sameness on the basis of genesis would be a fundamental mistake as well as an ontological and epistemological dead end. Languages, translation, and invention exist and flourish because of this innate (and mythical) fracture, which is also a rule and a law, a commandment that forbids mimetic representation.

The Prohibition

The very existence of human knowledge is based on an exclusion that humanity has accepted as its destiny. The exhilarating potency of this exclusion is that it contains the very thing that is excluded. Pure language is outside and yet simultaneously inside all languages. It is unreachable and yet without it there would be no language at all. The invisibility of pure language is the result of the visibility that it generates. It is in this sense that one must read not only Benjamin's reflection on the task of the translator, but also his work on the task of the philosopher, and in which one must interpret Heidegger's reading and discussion of poetry.

One finds in Benjamin's "The Task of the Translator" and "On the Program of the Coming Philosophy" (1918) on the one hand, and in Heidegger's "The Way to Language" on the other, a similarity and convergence of thought between the work of the two philosophers. Both write of pure language, emphasizing its incommunicability through ordinary language and simultaneously arguing that pure language can appear at times as an echo, a halo, a sound within the fold of languages. What they both insist upon is that languages are not pure language but rather an archive in which elements of pure language can be heard resonating. It is Benjamin, however, who takes further the discussion of the relation between pure language and languages by introducing translation and its relation to the original.

Understanding Benjamin's distinction between the original work and its translation is essential to interpreting his thought on translation. To understand the distinction, it is necessary to quote at length a central passage in Benjamin's "The Task of the Translator":

> The task of the translator consists in finding the intended effect upon the language into which he is translating which produces in it the echo of the original ("Sie besteht darin, diejenige Intention auf die Sprache, in die übersetzt wird, zu finden, von der aus in ihr das Echo des Originals erweckt wird"). This is a feature of translation which basically differentiates it from the poet's work, because the effort of the latter is never directed at the language as such, at its totality, but solely and immediately at specific linguistic contextual aspects ("weil dessen Intention niemals auf die Sprache als solche, ihre Totalität, geht, sondern allein unmittelbar auf bestimmte sprachliche Gehaltszusammenhänge"). Unlike a work of literature, translation does not find itself in the center of the language forest but on the outside facing the wooded ridge ("Die Übersetzung aber sieht sich nicht wie die Dichtung gleichsam im innern Bergwald der Sprache selbst, sondern außerhalb desselben"): it calls into it without entering, aiming at that single spot where the echo is able to give, in its own language, the reverberation of the work in the alien one. Not only does the aim of translation differ from that of a literary work—it intends language as a whole, taking an individual work in an alien language as a point of departure—but it is a different effort altogether. The intention of the poet is spontaneous, primary, graphic ("naive, erste"); that of the translator is derivative, ultimate, ideational ("abgeleitete, letzte, ideenhafte Intention"). For the great motif of integrating many tongues into one true language is at work. This language is one in which the independent sentences, works of literature, critical judgments, will never communicate—for they remain dependent on translation; but in it the languages themselves, supplemented and reconciled in their mode of signification, harmonize. If there is such a thing as a language of truth, the tensionless and even silent depository of the ultimate truth

which all thought strives for, then this language of truth is—the true language ("Wenn anders es aber eine Sprache der Wahrheit gibt, in welcher die letzten Geheimnisse, um die alles Denken sich müht, spannungslos und selbst schweigend aufbewahrt sind, so ist diese Sprache der Wahrheit—die wahre Sprache"). And this very language, whose divination and description is the only perfection a philosopher can hope for, is concealed in concentrated fashion in translations ("Und eben diese, in deren Ahnung und Beschreibung die einzige Vollkommenheit liegt, welche der Philosoph sich erhoffen kann, sie ist intensiv in den Übersetzungen verborgen"). (*Illuminations* 77; *Ein Lesebuch* 52)

The original cannot escape the confines of the unsupplemented language which, by necessity, it inhabits. The echoes of pure language that may be present in it are suffused, hushed by its very narrowness. It is in the original's encounter with its translations that the unsupplemented language of the original meets with a variety of other unsupplemented languages; it is this meeting that recreates and fashions, through reciprocity and communality, a semblance of pure language and its possible presentation.

As we have already indicated, pure language is a pre-text, understood here both as that which precedes the text and that which inspires the text. In the first instance, pure language can be considered as a linguistic mode prior to communication; in the second, as the elemental mediator between the ineffable and the effable. It is in the latter understanding of pure language that assimilation with the myth takes place, in that pure language becomes the creative highway and the philosophical analytical tool used to construct a series of narratives about the domain of the incorporeal and the supersensible. Pure language is therefore not so much the supersensible as a vehicle to the supersensible and one of its many attributes. It is a myth, the making of which allows the story of the supersensible to commence. As such, pure language is the pure transcendental, both literarily and philosophically, and the necessary passage toward the unsayable. And yet, the notion of the pure transcendental remains contradictory: purity, like pleasure, cannot proceed beyond itself but is perfect in itself. Pure language is thus simultaneously the cipher of transcendence and immanence; a process toward, but also a self-sufficient entity. We can take this reflection even further by stating that the mythical nature of pure language is predicated upon its simultaneous existence as the transcendental and its negativity as the immanent. As that which precedes textuality, pure language is also an analytical and literary category and linguistic index, the purpose of which is to define the linguistic split so characteristic of human language: the split between semiotic and semantic or, in other terms, between language and discourse.

The questioning of language as monolithic is indebted to the French linguist Saussure, who was the first to divide language into two distinct parts: *langue* and *parole* (see *Cours de linguistique générale*, 1922). According to Saussure, *langue* stands for the universality of language while *parole* marks the individual usage and performability of *langue*. Saussure posits a general language that is common to everybody but spoken by no one, and a particular language that is unique to the subject but remains unspoken by the community. Another French linguist, Emile Benveniste, takes Saussure's distinction a step further when he argues that the difference is not located in the opposition of "general vs. individual" but in that between the sign and the sign in context (see especially *Problèmes de linguistíque générale*, 1966). Accordingly, the difference is not external to language, depending on who uses it and how this subject uses it, but intrinsic to language. It is the inherent nature of language that marks subjectivity and not the other way around. Benveniste shifts the focus from the speaking "I" to language, redefining the linguistic but also philosophical premise that thought precedes language, and the concomitant assumption that the human precedes language. If this is true, the assertions follow that there is nothing before language and that beings are made of language.

The question is therefore not so much to look for the origin of language, because there is no before language, as to study the grammatical and structural development of language. This approach implies a temporal shift, in that the focus is no longer on genealogy or historicity, on returning to the origin. The attention turns to purely social and cultural determinants which are simultaneously diachronic and synchronic. According to Benveniste, everybody is born in language (that is, in sounds), which does not however mean that everybody is born into discourse (that is, in the combination of sounds for the purpose of communication). The difference between language and discourse, which is the same as the difference between the semiotic and semantic, is also that between recognition and understanding. Language—that is, sounds or even individual words—can be recognized and yet remain without narrative meaning. The passage from language to discourse is also the passage from naming to narrating.

It is interesting to reflect at this point on the hermeneutic distinction between knowing and telling of which Paul Ricoeur speaks (see, for instance, the essay "On Interpretation," 1983). According to Ricoeur, the function of the *hermeneus* (e.g., the novelist, the poet) is that of translating knowledge into narrative. This is a didactic role by way of which the writer is bequeathed the responsibility of teaching and/or disclosing the results of his or her searches. The distinction between knowing and telling appears to be based on the Husserlian belief (see especially *The Phenomenology of Internal Time-Consciousness*, 1928) that thought is essentially mute because it implies a passage from a silent reflection to a vocal indexation of that silent reflection. The differences between knowing and telling and between language and discourse are explained against the backdrop of a historical perception on the one hand, and a cultural perspective on the other. If the difference between knowing and telling is based on the recovery of the origin of thought and the origin of thought's silent language (it must be clear that thought and silent language are the same) through its translation into spoken/written language, the difference between language and discourse is both genetic and cultural. Language is handed down genetically but it develops culturally.

If it is true that the origin of discourse is found in language, it is also true that the origin of language is found in discourse. In other words, if the potentiality of language is that of translating itself into discourse, the potentiality of discourse is that of remaining language (as in the cases of aphasia discussed by, among others, Roman Jakobson, 1941; and Sigmund Freud, 1891). There cannot be discourse without language (which is genetic) just as there cannot be language without discourse (which is cultural). And how could language exist without the presence and the potentiality of discourse? If pure language is the pre-text, one could assume that pure language equates with Benveniste's semiotic or language. In the garden of Eden, Adam named objects but did not negate them through their generalization into discourse. As Hegel saw, language becomes negativity when it passes into discourse, in that, by constructing the normative yet culturally arbitrary understanding of life through language, life disappears behind language. In telling life, language betrays life. For Agamben the purity of language is not so much to be looked for in language but in the area of indeterminacy between language and discourse. In other words, at the moment in which the passage is announced but not yet complete. The question that must be asked now is: "could the process of translation be one of those instances in which language speaks itself as language? In other words, could translation be the moment when language stays still in order to reach out, in order to become and in order to encounter its own being as 'language-that-comes'?" The difference between Benjamin's articulation and the one we propose to explore is that the area of indistinction—what Benjamin refers to as the meeting of unsupplemented languages in translation—*can* be communicated. An example of this occurs when two or more translations of the same work are juxtaposed and compared. Although the space one would appear to occupy is that of unsupplemented language, the reality is rather different. The differences in interpretation, lexicon, style, and intention that are inscribed in any comparison of different translations of the same work are the markers of those echoes from the forest of language to which Benjamin refers to in his essay.

The cohabitation of these differences in the same language points to other, possibly infinite, interpretations and supplementations, ultimately challenging the meaningfulness of a given language, its reliability and truthfulness, its existence among the plurality of languages.

"L'infinito"

"L'infinito" ("The Infinite"; 1819) is one of Giacomo Leopardi's most renowned poems. Over time "The Infinite" has become the emblem of Italian romanticism, and it is often cited as an example of essential Romantic poetic themes and preoccupations, chief among them the sweet elation of the subject before an unfathomable universe. But let us read "The Infinite" in its entirety: "Sempre caro mi fu quest'ermo colle, / E questa siepe, che da tanta parte / Dell'ultimo orizzonte il guardo esclude. / Ma sedendo e mirando, interminati / Spazi di là da quella, e sovrumani / Silenzi, e profondissima quiete / Io nel pensier mi fingo; ove per poco / Il cor non si spaura. E come il vento / Odo stormir tra queste piante, io quello / Infinito silenzio a questa voce / Vo comparando: e mi sovvien l'eterno, / E le morte stagioni, e la presente / E viva, e il suon di lei. Così tra questa / Immensità s'annega il pensier mio: / E il naufragar m'è dolce in questo mare" (*Canti* 103; "I always did value this lonely hill, / And this hedgerow also, where so wide a stretch / Of the extreme horizon's out of sight. / But sitting here and gazing, I find that endless / Spaces beyond that hedge, and more-than-human / Silences, and the deepest peace and quiet / Are fashioned in my thoughts; so much that almost / My heart fills up with fear. And as I hear / The wind rustle among the leaves, I set / That infinite silence up against this voice, / Comparing them; and I recall the eternal, / And the dead seasons, and the present one / Alive, and all the sound of it. And so / In this immensity my thought is drowned: / And I enjoy my sinking in this sea"; *The Canti* 53, translation 1).

The key words in Leopardi's poem are *ermo*, *ultimo orizzonte*, *guardo esclude*, *pensier*, *spaura*, *sovvien*, *s'annega*, and *naufragar*, which are strategically located in order to emphasize the metaphysical opposition between the corporeal and the incorporeal, as one might expect from a truly Romantic viewpoint. The clear separation of the two realms—which are also two separate ontological levels—is reinforced through the juxtaposition of the demonstrative adjectives *questo* ("this"), standing for the corporeal, and *quello* ("that"), marking the incorporeal. The Romantic subject, the Leopardian "I," mediates between the corporeal and the incorporeal, a mediation arrived at through imagination. The ultimate Romantic apotheosis is affirmed by the subject's willingness to renounce his corporeal self in the blissful and complete embrace of the supersensible. The subject's mediation is also the enactment of a journey which, in the end, will deliver the "I" from one zone to another. The movement, so characteristic of Leopardi's poem, is reinforced by the strongly hypotactic structure of "The Infinite," in which sentences are linked by a rhythmic occurrence of the conjunction *e* ("and")—in "The Infinite" we count eleven repetitions of *e*. It is this temporal and spatial dynamism that is so vital to the understanding of "The Infinite," testifying to the complexity and intricacy of a poem that is all too easy to take at face value. Let us now return to those key words and linguistic images underpinning Leopardi's poem and read them within the context of the journey. But most importantly, let us also interpret them in conjunction with two different translations into English of "The Infinite." The second translation I would like to quote for this particular purpose reads as follows: "I always loved this solitary hill, / This hedge as well, which takes so large a share / Of the far-flung horizon from my view; / But seated here, in contemplation lost, / My thought discovers vaster space beyond / Supernal silence and unfathomed peace; / Almost I am afraid; then, since I hear / The murmur of the wind among the leaves, / I match that infinite calm unto this sound / And with my mind embrace eternity, / The vivid, speaking present and dead past; / In such immensity my spirit drowns, / And sweet to me is shipwreck in this sea" (<http://www.geocities.com/leopardileopardi/p.html> translation 2).

My intention is not to provide an evaluation of the two translations. Rather, I wish to coalesce the three texts (the original, translation 1, and translation 2) and to read them as if they were part of the same unfinished narrative. In other words, I wish to use the translations to strip bare the original and then, together with the translations, to listen to the language as it makes itself as language. By questioning language, by confusing its speaking in the mingling of languages, I want to try and catch its saying as showing; in a word, language's "ringing stillness." If the subject of language, in this case Leopardi, could even for a moment be disoriented in an encounter with the translators' subjectivities, the coming of language to the subject could be suspended. In its place we will have the coming of languages to subjects at the moment in which they cease to be languages and subjects and become the process of language and the process of subjectivity.

Leopardi's poetic experience on Mount Tabor (the hill in the poem "The Infinite"), near his birthplace Recanati, is inevitably facilitated by the conscious abandonment of quotidianity and the commerce with other individuals it demands. The poet must be alone on Mount Tabor. It is only because of the total absence of other presences that the "solitary hill," the "lonely hill" can turn into a place of ascetic transcendence. The *ermo colle*, *questo* ("this") *ermo colle*, can thus be understood as a metonymic exchange in which nature acquires and speaks the condition of the subject that comes to rest there. Eremitic, lonely, solitary are not only metaphysical adjectives, they also hint at an ascetic experience which, since Plotinus, has become the quintessential trait of idealist narratives, including Romantic narratives. In Leopardi's poem, Plotinus's famous dictum, the "flight of one alone into one"—that is, the plunging of the physical self into the deep recesses of his soul as the only means to reach a sense of the ultimate transcendental experience, and to approach as nearly as possible the "prime mover"—is employed to the letter. It is no accident that Leopardi devoted one of his most intense *Operette morali* (*Moral Tales*) to Plotinus and his pupil Porphyry (*Operette* 272-87; 1827). Nature devoid of other human presences enables the subject not only to experience solitude, but to turn solitude into an ascetic and cognitive process. The hedge that "takes so large a share" (translation 1) "of the extreme horizon's out of sight" (translation 2) limits the possibility of knowing through seeing what is actually there; in other words, of knowing empirically. *Escludere lo sguardo* equates with excluding the outer layers of knowledge and also barring the outward self, the body and physical senses, in exchange for an internal, inward search. The impeded *guardo*, "view" (translation 2), "sight" (translation 1), on an *ermo*, "lonely," "solitary," hill, facing *l'ultimo*, the "far-flung" (translation 2), "extreme" (translation 1), horizon. How do these words resonate and meet, how do they mingle with and adjust to each other? How does a language come to us in which words such as "view," "sight," *guardo*, "far-flung," "extreme," *ultimo* are inter-penetrated? How can we access it?

One views a landscape and takes in what is seen. To view, and not only in its verbal but also in its nominal form, means to absorb, to ingest that which is outside us and to process it and be nurtured by it. In viewing we grow, not only intellectually but also physiologically, in that viewing is imbued with history and chronology, with time: we grow as we view and it is by viewing that we grow. *Guardare* ("to view") is as hypotactic as the structure of "The Infinite": *guardare* demands a continuation of viewing, which is why we view "this" *and*, after "this," "that," and so on. *Lo sguardo* ("sight")—differently from *un'occhiata* or glance—is static, fixed; it does not absorb, it rather penetrates and goes deeper and further away from its origin, remaining simultaneously connected to the origin by means of a temporal stasis, and a holding back of time. *Lo sguardo* makes us smaller, nearly invisible to ourselves. *Nello sguardo* ("in sight") we lose the sense of being there and can only continue to breathe and exist in making the other, on which we gaze, also breathe and exist. In sight we grow only in the moment of our vanishing.

If viewing is hypotactic, sight is paratactic. It is indeed interesting that translation 2 of "The Infinite," which employs "view," is intensively paratactic and that translation 1, in which "sight" is used, is uncompromisingly hypotactic. The Leopardian *guardo* is both "sight" and "view," as the Leopardian *ermo* is both "solitary" and "lonely," and yet, it is only in recuperating the two meanings as separate and distinct that *guardo* and *ermo* can come to us as we approach them. Leopardi's *guardo* absorbs and penetrates, folds in and fans out as a heart that pumps to live and make live. It nurtures the self and enlarges the self by simultaneously annulling it before the other that grows as the self vanishes. It is in this sense that the great antinomy of "The Infinite," in which the "I" disappears into his epiphany, can be best understood ("E il naufragar m'è dolce in questo mare"; "And I enjoy my sinking in this sea").

If the hedge impedes the actual gazing—that is, the actual penetration of sight into the object of observation—it also triggers a mental gazing (the Leopardian *mirare*), in which the act of viewing is aided and brought about by imagination. It is this *guardo* that fixes itself on an imaginative plane, which turns it into much more than gazing. To open one's eyes before the realm of imagination means to contemplate. Contemplation, like the *sguardo*, implies abandoning the self in an a-temporal zone where past, present and future coalesce ("e mi sovvien l'eterno, / E le morte stagioni, e la presente"; "and I recall the eternal, / And the dead seasons, and the present one"), and in which the self gradually slips out of sight, merging with the object of contemplation. It is this mentally conjured reality (*nel pensier mi fingo*) that allows the "I" to return the *ultimo orizzonte* ("extreme horizon," translation 1; "far-flung horizon," translation 2) to the meaning with which it was identified in an early draft of "The Infinite": "Confine celeste" ("Blue/Celestial Border"). If the *ultimo orizzonte* pertains to the corporeal, it is also the borderline between the corporeal and the incorporeal. It is the *confine* ("border)" beyond which one can experience *gioia celeste* ("a celestial blissfulness"), as we read in another of Leopardi's poems, "Il pensiero dominante" ("The Dominant Thought" *Canti* 156-60; 1833-1835). Leopardi's correction is instructive and poetically significant, in that *l'ultimo orizzonte* cannot be associated with *gioia celeste* unless imagination and contemplation observe it: *ultimo orizzonte* can only be "celestial" once the mode of gazing changes.

Mirando is alternatively translated as "gazing" (translation 1) and "in contemplation lost" (translation 2). The combination of *mirare*, gaze, and contemplate is powerful and fitting, pointing simultaneously to the process of observation but also to an essential ontological shift. The ontological shift announced by the transition from *guardare* to *mirare* is reinforced a few lines after by the clear separation of the self into body and soul, more explicitly characterized in the poem as *cor* ("heart") and *pensier* ("thought, mind, spirit"). Whereas the "heart" is disoriented, fearful in the midst of the process of fusion between subject and object, "thought" (translation 1), the "spirit" (translation 2), rejoices in this supreme annihilation and in the vanquishing of the physiological and least pure attribute of the self. "Spirit," "thought," and *pensier* coalesce against the "heart" and they sink it before allowing themselves gladly to be sunk in the "immensity" of the metaphysical sea. "And I enjoy my sinking in this sea" says translation 1; to which translation 2 replies: "And sweet to me is shipwreck in this sea." Next to the translations we hear "E il naufragar m'è dolce in questo mare." The "I" of poetry is in and out, appearing and disappearing among the waves of an imperious sea, happy to incessantly sink by remaining alive. "I'm sinking" implies a process that is still becoming; the blessed smile on the face of one who is happy to be taken away, shipwrecked without destination, but, above all, without a body to direct and command.

The hypotactic translation (translation 1) is also the one that speaks in the passive voice: "And this hedgerow also, where so wide a stretch / Of the extreme horizon's out of sight"; "Spaces beyond that hedge, and more-than-human / Silences, and the deepest peace and quiet / Are fashioned in my thoughts." Where is the "I" of "Spazi di là da quella, e sovrumani / Silenzi, e profondissima quiete / *Io* nel pensier mi fingo" (emphasis added)? It can be found in "*My* thought discovers vaster space beyond / Supernal silence and unfathomed peace" (translation 2; emphasis added), where *profondissima quiete* is "unfathomed peace," that is, incomprehensible, ungraspable. This *quiete* is both cognitive and spatial, temporal and buried. "This" and "that" is not the only juxtaposition in "The Infinite"; it is complemented and accompanied by an ambiguous "I" who is simultaneously in and out of agency, at once passive and active; "my thought discovers" what is "fashioned in it" by the *that* that my imagination conjures up because *that* makes my imagination exist. We are listening to three different languages and subjects saying the same thing differently, and we see possibilities. We might, in fact, intuit the stillness of language in all its many possible outcomes: "E come il vento / Odo stormir tra queste piante, io quello / Infinito silenzio e questa voce / Vo comparando..." "And as I hear the wind rustle among the leaves, I set / That infinite silence up against this voice, / Comparing them..." "since I hear / the murmur of the wind among the leaves, / I match that infinite calm unto this sound, / And with my mind embrace eternity." Translation 2 constructs a victorious celebration of the mind which, with a grand gesture, embraces eternity. But this eternity (the eternity of translation 2) is a kind of anthropomorphous time which is not only introduced by the "murmur" of the wind. It also arrives with a "speaking present" and a dead past.

But is speaking the same as "sound," *suono*? *Suono* is the eternity of language—that is, the resounding silence of which we will speak in chapter 4 with regard to Blanchot's work. But it is here, in Leopardi's voice, and those of his translators, that one might find a trace of a speaking language whose body is pure sound, pure stillness. Might we call the former language (the one which is the sum of Leopardi's language and the language of his translators) the "language-that-comes," and that brings with it the traces of the other language which is invariably the language that cannot be? Was not Blanchot alluding to something similar when he claimed that: "The original is never immobile, and all that a language contains of the future at a particular moment, all that there is in the language that points to or summons a state that is other, sometimes dangerously other, is affirmed in the solemn drift of literary works. Translation is tied to this becoming; it 'translates' and accomplishes it. Translation is possible only because of this movement and this life" (Blanchot, *Friendship* 59; "L'original n'est jamais immobile, et tout ce qu'il y a d'avenir dans une langue à un certain moment, tout ce qui en elle désigne ou appelle un état autre, parfois dangereusement autre, s'affirme dans la solennelle dérive des œuvres littéraires. La traduction est liée à ce devenir, elle le 'traduit' et l'accomplit, elle n'est possible qu'à cause de ce mouvement et de cette vie"; Blanchot, *L'Amitié* 71). This is also, perhaps, the place that Heidegger had in mind when he wrote that language is the "house of being" (*On the Way* 63)—the home in which presence is illuminated in the present and where true and proper stillness exist—the abode that is simultaneously original and unchanged despite an uninterrupted coming forth. The home, the elemental dwelling, is that which must be left incessantly if one truly wishes to return to it. And yet, the return is also and inevitably an incessant departure from it (for a further discussion of return see also chapter 3). It is in this sense that one must read Heidegger's interpretation of "farewell" (*Abschied*; *On the Way* 54; *Unterwegs zur Sprache* 154) as the coming of what has been. If language is the home of being—Bataille once wrote: "I live, and in me is life (language)" (44)—then being can abide in it only by holding language back and by experiencing it in its making as language. And if it is true that the twofold Heideggerian equation ("The language of being: the being of language") is the quintessential testament of an unbreakable unity, it follows that the original home of language is also that in which the subject keeps on "farewelling" itself into presence. The process of translation may not represent the original home of language and subjectivity, but one might well imagine it as its living-room.

Active recollection

In *Was ist das—die Philosophie?* (*What is Philosophy?*; 1956) Heidegger writes: "Tradition ("die Überlieferung") does not surrender us ("liefert uns nicht aus") to a constraint by what is past and irrevocable ("Unwiderruflichen"). Surrendering amounts to being delivered into the freedom of discussion with what has been. If we truly hear the word and reflect upon what we have heard, the name 'philosophy' summons us into the history of the Greek origin of philosophy" (33-35). This is not only a summary of Heidegger's conceptualization of tradition, it is also a rather interesting and instructive rephrasing of Husserl's reflection on memory and its productive energy.

In a significant passage of "The Origin of Geometry" (1939) Husserl wrote that "if the originally self-evident production, as the pure fulfillment of its intention, is what is *renewed* (recollected), there necessarily occurs, accompanying the *active recollection* of what is past, an activity of concurrent *actual production*" (*Crisis* 360; emphasis added). This is nothing other than the productive energy brought about by the will and desire (the availability) to move toward the origin. But the present's "surrender" is far from being passive. It is rather a performative act, a moving forward, as it were, which is the result of the encounter of present and past in the space of potential discourse. That is why I believe that to translate "Überliefern" and "Ausliefern" as "surrendering" is misleading. Heidegger's "Überliefern" is rather an allowing; that is, the consenting to give oneself up to the experience of an exchange with the other.

This reflection is of considerable importance for a conceptualization of translation and translating. Indeed, the central purpose of this book is to revisit translation theory through the dynamic relations between the act of translation and memory, and between exile and writing. I contend that it is precisely by opening up translation to a productive discourse with other issues and concerns revolving around the polarities of the origin and the copy that a further theoretical perspective on translation can arise. This is why I believe it is essential to investigate further Husserl's remark about "active recollection" as a way of leading the discussion of translation to a temporary close, as well as opening the way to subsequent chapters.

"The active recollection of what is past [involves] an activity of concurrent actual production." The emphasis of Husserl's statement on recollection is, without doubt, on the idea of production. More importantly, it is an emphasis on production that takes place in the present, in the now of life. Only this present construction of memory can be called, according to Husserl, "active recollection." Husserl's notion of active recollection is positive, in that it entails an actual intervention of the present. As mediator, active recollection influences and perhaps manipulates the past in a process of making that resembles an ongoing, dynamic, and ever transforming production. Was Husserl implying that memory is never fixed, but always moving in time as well as in space? If this were the case, memory would not be a crystallized image staring immobile from the depths of time to catch us as we grope around in the present; to fix us in the eye as a monitor, as a "memory" and remembrance of what we used to be. Rather, it would be something like an event in which we are only a singularity, albeit a conspicuous singularity, within a crowd of other singularities. Husserl's statement on active recollection thus dramatically shifts the perspective on the traditional and conventional understanding of memory, and provides a new plane on which memory is remodeled as life, instead of life's death mask.

The postulation of active recollection invites the conceptualization of its opposite: passive recollection. What exactly does it mean to recollect actively as opposed to recollecting passively? The first answer is provided by Husserl himself when, as we have seen, he pairs the adjective "active" with the adjective "actual." The distinction is in the first place temporal: a memory that resides exclusively in the past is passive, while a memory that resides in the present is active. But the temporal distinction introduces by necessity a further one, this time one of definition. What do we mean by "past" and "present"? An agreement arrived at by simply accepting ordinary and conventional interpretations of past and present would probably fail to see through the complexity of the issue and its implications for a deeper conceptualization of memory and its impact on life.

In preface to the question of definition, I could refer to previous remarks, and say that while a passive recollection could be defined as "memory," an active recollection could be defined as the "making of memory" (see also chapter 2). As it turns out, the difference is not so much temporal *per se* as ethically temporal, or, as I would prefer, one of labor. By labor I mean the actual production of an event, be it written, visual, concrete, or imaginative. As a consequence, the difference is not between an absolute past—dead, crystallized, gone—and an absolute past in the present (the Hegelian temporality)—but between the temporal relation and production of the past in the present as well as of the present in the past. The difference is also between an act of memory that entails the interpretation of an object (a memory) by a subject (the present subject), and a memorization in which subject and object are synthetically interconnected.

Heidegger, as we have seen, was one of the first thinkers to warn us about making a simplifying distinction between past and present from a chronological perspective. His reflections on origin and beginning are still essential to thinking fruitfully about memory. Heidegger is best known as the philosopher of "existentialism," and there is no doubt that his work is characterized by an indefatigable quest to capture the events of the origin and essence, their meanings and philosophical implications. What is perhaps less well known and less well articulated is the extent of Heidegger's problematization of origin (*Ursprung*), which, in the German philosopher's work, is never a static, temporally encrusted event. The opposite is in fact closer to the truth. For Heidegger, the origin—which in his case is often looked for among the fragments of pre-Socratic thinking, especially the thinking of Anaximander and Heraclitus—is never located *behind*. It is always already forward, invariably preceding and informing the present: it is here and yet already ahead. The origin is, according to Heidegger, the very essence of becoming and the very *thing* of philosophy. The origin, paraphrasing Heidegger's mentor Husserl, provides the actualization of productive thinking. It is in this sense that Heidegger seeks the origin through placing the present—and present thought (his philosophy)—at the service of tradition. But in doing so, tradition leaps ahead, turning from past to future (on this see also Derrida's remarks on memory, *Points* 383).

If it is true that for Heidegger the event of the origin (*aletheia*) remains the ultimate goal of philosophy, for Walter Benjamin the origin turns into a philosophical mediator, whose presence is indispensable, not as such, as an absolute value, but in relation to the beginning of its own disappearance. The significant difference between Benjamin and Heidegger is found in their distinct treatment and conceptualization of production. Whereas for Heidegger, production is instigated by the origin in order to rejoin the origin in a forward movement, for Benjamin, production, although still driven by the origin, becomes the thing of philosophy and the house of thinking. What assimilates these two very different (and yet in certain respects similar) thinkers is a firm belief in the impossibility of returning.

Returning must be understood here as going back to the original home. In Benjamin and Heidegger, there cannot be any return simply because the home that one looks for is either ahead (Heidegger) or firmly embedded in the now-time (*Jetzt-Zeit*, Benjamin) of the present event. There is no home to be found if one looks for it through memory—through passive recollection in Husserl's terminology. A slightly better chance can be had by looking for home through the *making* of memory—through active recollection.

The language-that-comes

As one departs, as one begins to be, the origin disappears into the beginning or leaps ahead. Returning has no meaning because nothing is left behind. The notion of returning is one of the great misnomers of language and thought, unless one understands returning not as a movement backward but a movement forward. And if it is true that departing implies a return, this return can never be a simple reversal. It is rather a process that takes the traveler even further ahead, away from himself in order to catch himself or, in the second hypothesis, to catch the production that encapsulates the singularity of the self.

In *Cahiers 1894-1914*, Paul Valéry wrote that "Foreignness is the true beginning. In the beginning there was the foreign" (my translation; "L'étrangeté est le vrai commencement. Au commencement était l'étrange"; *Cahiers* 85). Valéry points to the beginning as the locus of an irredeemable fracture which brings about not so much a loss as a sense of estrangement and inauthenticity. In other words, the beginning—which must not be confused with the origin—is not the authentic place, is not home. Turning back to it as if it were true home, the authentic space of the subject's *quidditas*, can only provoke nostalgia and melancholia. Should the beginning be confused with the origin, with singularity as such, it would then present the absence of the origin—its foreignness—thereby plunging the observer into passive nostalgia and a sense of impotence: the observer confronting the impossibility of returning. This impossibility is determined by not finding the desired object where it was thought to reside. In its place there is only dispossession, the feeling of not-feeling-at-home. Nostalgia, passive recollection, is a memory that turns back, believing that what is missing has been left behind.

The Italian philosopher Aldo Giorgio Gargani, one of the most attentive readers of Heidegger's philosophy, once wrote of "an original that is only the effect of the copies that preceded it" ("un originale che è soltanto l'effetto delle copie che l'hanno preceduto"; 65; my translation). Heidegger's influence is obvious, as is the influence that Benjamin's reflection on translation might have had on Gargani's thought. As in Heidegger, the original is located forward, it has leapt ahead of its copies. But most importantly, the original is thought through the copies that inform it, as in Benjamin's understanding of translation as that which catches the originality of language—pure language (*die reine Sprache*)—through the synthesis of unsupplemented languages.

Translation comes after the beginning of the original and yet it precedes the origin, as the origin leaps ahead of the beginning and, consequently, ahead of translation. If this is true, the entire theoretical tradition of translation must be revised. Should translation turn back to look for the origin in order to compare its validity as a copy, it would only find nostalgia, dispossession, and failure. Conversely, should it look forward to see the origin, it would catch its event as becoming and potentiality. It is within its very nature as the language-that-comes that translation can glimpse the origin. If passive recollection is memory, passive translation is the copy; if active recollection is the making of memory, active translation is the language-that-comes.

Chapter Two

Time

"The time of being: the being of time"

Time slips away, time stops; it goes fast, proceeds erratically, it even stays still. Time keeps changing and yet never changes. We often speak of old time and new time, of present time, past time and future time. And yet, whenever we do this we do not talk about time: we talk about ourselves in time. What ages in time is not time itself but subjectivity. Calendars do not measure the passing of time, but the passing of lives in time. History is the site of this peculiar metonym through which what is measured and saved is, in reality, not time but the intricate relationship between time and humans. In fact, what history measures is the cosmology of human life as it unfolds; a cosmology that is nothing other than an ideal body, which is born, grows, decays, dies, is reborn, and so on *ad infinitum*. History is for this reason more than a chronicle of human achievements, misdemeanors, and horrific crimes. It is also an emblematic narrative that staves off death and celebrates humanity's collective immortality. Time is an essential part of this narrative, an indispensable ingredient (for a discussion of temporality and life, see also Malpas). What sense and meaning would time have without subjectivity, without nature and all the creatures that inhabit the world? Who would measure it? Who would employ it as an agent of order and clarification? It is in this sense that time becomes chronology, which is ultimately a strategy for cataloguing and rationally assembling the otherwise obscure and easily forgotten events of life. Whatever we do with time, we do it to evaluate ourselves and the surrounding world. Time is our faithful companion and savior. It is also, ironically, our nemesis. Is it possible to think of time not as an adjective of being, not as chronology, but as an independent entity or presence whose essence is distinguishable from being? If it is true that time and being are inseparable, it is nonetheless also possible that this intricate relationship could be better understood if one were to try to extricate time from being and being from time. In dismantling the symbiosis between time and being, the process of reassembly might give rise to a greater consciousness of this necessary union. By placing the conjunction *und* between being and time in the title of his seminal book *Sein und Zeit* (1927; *Being and Time*, 1962), Heidegger emphasizes at once their separateness and their inevitable conjunction. Being can only be understood in temporality: time can only be understood as the locus of the ontology of being.

Heidegger's work prompts us to consider an interesting analogy between time and language. If it is true, as Heidegger claims in *Unterwegs zur Sprache*, that the interconnectedness of language and being is founded on the formula "The being of language: the language of being" (*On the Way* 94; *Unterwegs zur Sprache* 200), a similar relation can be postulated according to the analogous formula: "the time of being: the being of time." The "and" separating being and time in Heidegger is also their necessary and unavoidable encounter, a threshold which separates by connecting and which unites by keeping apart. Let us imagine a crowded pedestrian bridge, on which the traffic is so intense that the path of each traveler is difficult to follow, and each traveler's point of origin and direction cannot easily be ascertained. The route connecting being and time would appear just as complex: time is so indistinguishable from being that time appears as being and being as time. The threshold of their encounter has been the stage where most of the reflection on time and/or on being has taken place in Western culture. To dismantle the bridge would mean to enter a domain of pure abstraction and potentiality. It would also mean, as Heidegger saw clearly, to deny being the dynamism which is so vital to its understanding. Or would it? What would happen to time if it were stopped on the path of its natural becoming to being? To sever the relationship between time and being would mean to break the circularity of their referential existence, to transport them to the plane of pure Platonic ideas; it would mean, to quote Agamben in *La comunità che viene* (*The Coming Community*, 1990), to confront the "irreparable" (*l'irreparabile*; 89; *La comunità* 63). The irreparable of time is eternity, and the irreparable of being human is, according to different philosophical schools, either God, being-as-such or the "I think" of Kant: "a transcendental subject which cannot be given substance or psychologized in any way" (Agamben, *Infancy and History* 31; "soggetto trascendentale che non può essere in alcun modo sostanziato o psicologizzato"; *Infanzia e storia* 26).

Bringing down the bridge connecting being with time might also illuminate the process of the reconstitution of the bridge, that is, that moment at which the connection is only potential—at once possible and impossible. This chapter is intent on foreshadowing this potentiality, and it does so by reinterpreting the Augustinian time of the soul as the relation between the potential being outside time and the potential time outside being. The reconstitution of the ontological severance is also looked for in the discussion of memory as temporal halo, especially in Benjamin's *A Berlin Chronicle*. Like the time of the soul in Augustine, Benjamin's *Erinnerung* presents a temporality and a being whose reciprocal connectedness is indeterminate. This approach, should it be successful, will emphasize the significance of the philosophical category of potentiality as the main affirmative means and cause of creative thinking and action. In doing so, it will at once highlight the limitations of Heidegger's thought as well as its potentially constructive richness. What follows is a gradual process of disclosure, the purpose of which is to clarify my project by placing it against the background of selected works on time and being.

Kant's ontology and original celebration of metaphysics rest on the clear distinction between an ontology of essence and an ontology of experience, and between an essential time and being and an actual time and being. Temporality, for Kant, is one of the most powerful introductions to the essence, but it is so only through its intuitive attributes. Kant reinstates in this sense the Augustinian connection between soul and time, between spirit and temporality, granting this connection new scope and ontological life.

If, on one level, time can be known empirically and ordinarily through the calendar, on another level time can be perceived intuitively in the depths of the "I think" (some would claim this level to be the more profound and truthful). The postulation of an intuitive time existing somewhere in the topographical *habitus* of the "I think" automatically introduces a distinction between the measurable time of existence and the experienced time of the "I think." This distinction is also, and more importantly, a distinction between an external and an internal time, the time of the calendar on the one hand and the time of the soul on the other (on this, see also Castoriadis). External, calendrical, or clock time is a mixture of circularity and linearity: it is historically linear and naturally repetitive. Calendars and clocks mark the passing of time by pointing forward and obliterating what is left behind. We dispose of individual pages in a calendar either by throwing the past in the bin or by folding it out of sight; by deleting the past either physically or visually. And yet, this pushing and deleting, this throwing and folding, take place in the midst of an inevitable repetition and continuation.

Calendars keep coming back from the ashes and returning to bins in repetition of the same ritual. The names and numbers of the days and months, always the same, are used and dispensed with only to be used and dispensed with once again. Only the change of the year upsets this cozy, reassuring continuity and perpetual return. The quasi-perfect symmetry of numbers and words is anamorphosized by an imperceptible nudge forward that could well be missed or ignored were we not so intent on celebrating it. Life without calendars, without their benumbing motion, would be intolerable since the assurance that the same will recur is our only antidote to the inevitable approach of death. "Life goes on," people say to assuage the pain of life—which is usually the pain of death, in all its variegated forms: debts, sudden unemployment, heartbreak, the death of friends and relatives. What we mean by "life goes on" is that the repetition of the same will calm the pain, will anesthetize it. The monotony of repetition is soothing, as it erases memories and reminds us that we continue to exist. "Life goes on" only because it literally "goes on" in repeating itself. Without calendars as a stable reminder that we will (potentially) be here again tomorrow, next month, and next year, we would be constantly and unbearably exposed to internal time or, worse still, to a time entirely outside us. Through ritualizing time, calendars and clocks invite us to celebrate our magical return, our individual forgetfulness, and our collective immortality.

New Year's Eve

Repetition (*Wiederholung*) is also the key term employed by Heidegger in *Being and Time* to think the authenticity of *Dasein*. Heidegger's conceptualization, however, moves in the opposite direction to the temporal narrative of repetition as immortality described above. For Heidegger, the authenticity of *Dasein* rests in its capacity to come to itself in the awareness of "being toward death." This awareness is based on the knowledge of the "having been" that Heidegger links with the "be-coming" through the social and temporal stamping of heredity (*Erbschaft*) inscribed and directed by temporal repetition. It is the repetition of mortality that bestows on *Dasein* its authenticity. And it is through this authenticity that *Dasein* takes possession of its being-toward-death. Heidegger did not consider the possibility that this fulfilling experience of mortality might be nothing other than the redemption of individual finitude through the continuation of the species: the collective immortality of repetition meets and sublimates individual mortality. The irony of our being with ordinary time is that we celebrate return by pushing the same forward. There is no more paroxysmic celebration than New Year's Eve. The New Year's Eve celebration is a carnival compressed into a day. Everything appears possible and permissible: a sense of proportion, of ordinary and sensible caution, is lost. ("Ordinary" and "sensible" must be understood here as pertaining to acceptable and normative day-to-day business.) Ordinariness and sensibility are the quintessential ciphers of groundedness, of being in tune with the world around us, of getting on with life sensibly. "Being sensible" means nothing other than being here, now, the mind focused on quotidian affairs. The opposition sensible/supersensible puts forward the two levels of ontological knowledge on the stage of empirical as well as psychological occurrence. And it is precisely because of this opposition that the supersensible is associated not only with the essence but also, rather paradoxically and perhaps mistakenly, with the unconscious, the uncanny and the deviant.

On New Year's Eve we are allowed to take time off from being sensible and to break, if only for a few hours, the cycle of sensible life, which is also the cycle established by the return of calendrical time. New Year's Eve is the moment when the return is marked by a change, imperceptible but tangible, as we add a new digit to the year. The collective frenzy that ensues testifies to a fracture, to a brief moment of collective "supersensibility," when the comfort of repetition and the reassuring idea that "life goes on" is momentarily put on hold. It is then, on New Year's Eve, that calendrical time and subjectivity play a game of hide-and-seek and that the subject experiences, for a brief moment, its departure from clock time. Calendar time exposes an intricate and inherently cultural mixture of circularity and linearity, in which two distinct concepts of temporality meet: the ancient Greek and the Christian. The cyclical understanding and articulation of time expounded by Plato and Aristotle, whose pivotal center is nature and its uninterrupted repetition, encounters Christianity's rectilinear interpretation of time, which proceeds from the juxtaposition of a before and an after, of Genesis and Apocalypse, of Creation and the Last

Judgment. The calendar facilitates this meeting, and serves as a living testimony to the fine balance between nature and the world mastered by a pagan community in its shift to monotheism.

Distentio and potentiality

What is internal time, or the time of the soul, and how does it differ from external, calendrical time? To introduce this level of temporality I have used Augustinian and Husserlian terminology (the time of the soul, see Augustine; internal time, see Husserl, *The Phenomenology*). I could equally have used the Ricoeurian distinction between "ordinary" time and "narrative" time (see *Temps et récit*; *Time and Narrative*), or Heidegger's differentiation of "authentic" from "inauthentic" time. This diverse terminology testifies to a history of variegated yet similar reflections on a temporality that appears—by entering into an original rapport with subjectivity—to defy its external counterpart. Kant has in mind this temporality when he speaks of time as the prime example of intuitive ontology. It is a time whose abstractness is all-encompassing; it is present everywhere and in everything, while remaining untold. A presence that is in everything while remaining untold will affect that to which it relates. It is in this sense that temporality in its relation to subjectivity must be understood and studied.

We are conscious of time's passing and of its repetition, we are conscious of calendrical time. We are also conscious, though more dimly, of a time that escapes linearity and circularity, a time that lingers, that leads us in unexpected directions, that knows countless detours. We usually associate this time with memory and with the return of the past. But we know that it is not the return we are used to through calendrical time. It is rather a haphazard returning, as much a repetition as a novelty. This lingering temporality of memory, which is not destined to be discarded (unlike the used pages of a calendar), remains untold despite our continual attempts to recount it. Memory draws a faint halo around us, marking our being in time with the vague presence of an untold story. It allows us to re-enact ancient rituals and games, to translate the past, and to be in time both consciously and in a way that is profoundly unconscious, at once sensible and supersensible.

A time suspended in temporal indistinction is not exclusively related to the past. It also proceeds ahead of itself toward the future. The delicate balance between memory and expectation grants the time of the soul its comprehensiveness and also its a-temporality. Augustine called this kind of temporality *distentio*, a term that indicates the elasticity and compression of a dynamically active present, one that regains presence and vitality through the potentiality of an absent, inchoate past and future. In *distentio* it is not only the present that actualizes and rescues the "now" from oblivion (from Hegelian negativity); the past and the future also enact their own potentiality, which can be understood, following Agamben, as the "rather" (*il piuttosto*; *The Coming Community* 103; *La comunità* 76). The alleged negativity of the past and the future is turned, in this sense, into potential actuality, not as "past" or "future" but rather as "potential past" and "potential future." We can at this point venture the tentative conclusion that the time of the soul is nothing other than the time of potentiality, and that the "time of being: the being of time" is located in the overarching ontological realm of potentiality.

"The face-to-face of things"

Expectation, as Heidegger consistently argues in *Being and Time*, is strongly characterized by openness; in other words, by the subject's availability to wait for the future to appear. This "openness to waiting" is both an act of will—which in this context must be interpreted as synonymous with Heideggerian *care*—and a process of forgetfulness, understood as a temporal and a psychological detachment.

Eugen Fink, in conversation with Heidegger in *Heraklit* (*Heraclitus Seminar*), proposes that "The spiritual movement that releases us to the matter that merits being named the matter of thinking" ("die geistige Bewegung zu kommen, die uns selbst zu der Sache befreit, die als Sache des Denkens bennant zu werden verdient") is indispensable to enable the "furthest [to become] near" (3; *Heraklit* 10). This movement is the "nearness" or the "face-to-face" that Heidegger speaks about in *On the Way to Language*: "In order to experience this face-to-face of things with one another ("Um das Gegen-einander-über der Dinge so zu erfahren")...we must, of course, first rid ourselves of the calculative frame of mind" (104; "müssen wir freilich zuvor das rechnende Vorstellen fahren lassen"; *Unterwegs zur Sprache* 211).

The self actively predisposes itself to encounter the future, and so the process of expectation must be seen as both a journey and a meeting. The subject moves toward the future as the future itself moves toward everything that cares to meet it. The future does not go toward the self, just as language does not come to the self—rather, it meets the self at the crossroads of potentiality. It is the self, though, that must depart, that must care and will for an encounter with that which moves constantly with the sole purpose of being met. A clear example of this encounter—of the self "catching fire" in the sphere of ontological and temporal potentiality—is provided by the creative process. The "catching fire"—this expression so loved by Kafka ("everything can be expressed, that for everything, for the strangest of ideas a great fire is ready in which they perish and disappear"; *The Diaries* 73) and after him by Benjamin—may best be understood if placed in the context of Heraclitus's fragments, as interpreted by Fink. The Heraclitian *pyròs tropaí* implies that in the "transformations of fire ("Die Wandlungen des Feuers")...everything goes over into everything ("daß alles in alles übergeht"); so that nothing retains the definiteness of its character but, following an indiscernible wisdom, moves itself throughout by opposites" (*Heraclitus Seminar* 11; "und zwar so, daß nicht das Bestimmte in seiner Prägung bleibt, sondern sich nach einer unerkennbaren Weisheit durch Gegensätze hindurchbewegt"; *Heraklit* 22).

The self-exile from day-to-day life that artists and authors are so willing to submit to as a necessary step toward creation is nothing other than the will and care to bring about a meeting. The artist and the author must retreat—to the private studio or study, or to a public space allowing anonymity, a restaurant, a café, even a busy underground or bus—it does not matter where the abandonment of the quotidian takes place as long as it does. In the solitude of the self, expectation is encouraged, invited, evoked by "ridding ourselves of the calculative frame of mind," which is also the heightened availability of the self to catch and retain what is ahead of the self. The ability to create arises through suspending oneself, temporally and spatially. In the ontological space of potentiality expectation manifests itself to tell the untold and articulate that which belongs to the future. Memory must similarly be cared for, must be willed through the readiness to wait for a meeting. There is no difference between the movement toward expectation and that toward memory, no different route or direction to take, no arrow pointing forward or backward. The future discloses itself in showing the past on the plane of an open and dynamic present. The future re-writes the past and, in doing so, projects the subject into a temporality which is quintessentially human and elemental, original and immanent—a temporality in which language, time, space, and subjectivity intermingle, transforming and translating each other as they "catch fire." This temporality is neither eternity nor history; it is neither linear nor circular, neither spatial nor calendrical. How can one define it? The answer to this question, if there is one, can only be attempted after a careful analysis of the different temporal adjectives listed above and their connections; after having thought a time separate from being and being separate from time; and after reconstituting the union between time and being in view of their individuality as such.

Scattering: A Berlin Chronicle and "The Buried Harbor"

On 7 April 1932, Walter Benjamin boarded the steam freighter *Catania* in Hamburg en route to Barcelona. From Barcelona, he made his way to the island of Ibiza, where his friends—the Noeggeraths—were waiting for him. In 1932, Ibiza appeared to Benjamin archaic and pristine: "The most remote of places...cut off from the world and civilization...("die Insel wirklich seitab des Weltverkehrs und auch der Zivilisation"). Just as farming and animal husbandry are still carried on here in an archaic manner ("Wie Ackerbau und Viehzucht hier noch archaisch betrieben werden")—there are not more than four cows on the whole island, as the peasants keep to their tradition of goats, no agricultural machinery to be seen and the irrigation of the fields is done as it was centuries ago with water scooped up by wheels turned by mules ("die Bewässerung der Felder wie vor Jahrhunderten durch Schöpfräder geschieht")—so the interiors are also archaic: three chairs against the wall opposite the entrance confront the visitor with aplomb and gravity, as if there were three Cranachs or Gauguins on the wall; a sombrero hung on the back of a chair creates more effect than precious Gobelin tapestries" (*Briefe* 548, trans. Anthony Stephens). In the tranquillity of the house that he rented for "one mark and eighty" (549) Benjamin found the space and serenity to start sketching one of his most illuminating reflections on time: *Berliner Chronik* (*A Berlin Chronicle*).

The late 1920s and early 1930s had proven quite taxing and traumatic for Benjamin. He had recently divorced from his wife Dora and, as a result, he had lost virtually all of his material property, including most of his beloved library. He moved from rented flat to rented flat and his famous love of traveling, which continued incessantly even in these troublesome years, increasingly became a form of escapism. In traveling, Benjamin was not only finding refuge from a personal life in disarray but also from a highly volatile and menacing political situation. It is rather fitting and quite just—in a life otherwise characterized by gross miscalculations and bad luck—that the money Benjamin needed to travel to Ibiza came to him thanks to Goethe's anniversary celebrations and the work Benjamin produced in honor of the occasion. In effect, Benjamin's life as a wandering, exiled intellectual began to take shape and form in those early years of the 1930s. Far from coincidentally, Benjamin felt the need to pause during this unsettled period and to write once again about his childhood and Berlin. He conceived of this work not only as a gift to his son Stefan but also as a kind of intellectual and spiritual will. Language—writes Benjamin in *A Berlin Chronicle*—

shows clearly that memory ("Gedächtnis") is not an instrument for exploring ("Erkundung") the past ("Vergangenheit") but its theater. It is the medium of past experience ("Es ist das Medium des Erlebten"), as the ground is the medium in which dead cities lie interred. He who seeks to approach his own buried past must conduct himself like a man digging ("Wer sich der eigenen vesrchütteten Vergangenheit zu nähern trachtet, muß sich verhalten wie ein Mann, der gräbt"). This confers the tone ("Ton") and bearing ("Haltung") of genuine reminiscences ("Erinnerungen"). He must not be afraid to return again and again to the same matter ("Sachverhalt"); to scatter ("auszustreuen") it as one scatters earth ("Erde ausstreut"), to turn it over as one turns over soil. For the matter itself is only a deposit, a stratum, which yields only to the most meticulous examination what constitutes the real treasure ("wahren Werte") hidden within the earth: the images ("die Bilder"), severed from all earlier associations ("aus allen früheren Zusammenhängen losgebrochen"), that stand—like precious fragments or torsos in a collector's gallery ("wie Trümmer oder Torsi in der Galerie des Sammlers")—in the prosaic rooms of our later understanding ("unserer späten Einsicht"). True, for successful excavation a plan is needed. Yet no less indispensable is the cautious probing of the spade in the dark loam ("dunkle Erdreich"), and it is to cheat oneself of the richest prize to preserve as a record merely the inventory of one's discoveries, and not this dark joy ("dunkle Glück") of the place of the finding itself ("Ort und Stelle des Findens selbst in seiner Niederschrift bewahrt" [note that reference to the "writing down," *Niedershrift bewahrt*, of the dark joy is omitted in the English translation]). Fruitless searching is as much a part of this as succeeding, and consequently remembrance must not proceed in the manner of a narrative or still less that of a report, but must, in the strictest epic and rhapsodic manner ("sondern im strengsten Sinne episch und rhapsodisch"), assay its spade in ever-new places, and in the old ones delve to ever-deeper layers. (see Benjamin, *Reflections* 25-26; *Ein Lesebuch* 372)

In a poem written in the trenches of World War I, on 29 June 1916, the Italian poet Giuseppe Ungaretti wrote: "Vi arriva il poeta / e poi torna alla luce con i suoi canti / e li disperde / Di questa poesia / mi resta / quel nulla / d'inesauribile segreto" (*Il porto sepolto* 26; "The poet goes there / then returns to the light with his songs / and scatters them / Of this poetry / there remains to me / that nothing / of inexhaustible secrecy"; *The Buried Harbour* 26). The title Ungaretti gave to this poem is emblematic of his poetics, and bears a profound resemblance to Benjamin's imagery:

"Il porto sepolto" ("The Buried Harbor"). "Scattering" (*disperdere, ausstreuen*) is the key verb in Benjamin's understanding of memory and in Ungaretti's description of an experience which is both mnemonic and metaphysical. The poet in Ungaretti, like the archeologist in Benjamin, makes his way in the darkness of a spiritual as well as temporal suspension. The diving evoked in the title "The Buried Harbor" suggests a suspension of breathing and the a-temporal silence and stillness of human life enveloped in the depths of water. And it is the re-emerging to the surface—the returning to the light—that restores the subject to temporality and life and, at least in Ungaretti's poem, to language (the scattering of songs).

Memory, the theater of the past, is the exhibition in the "prosaic rooms of our later understanding," of those "fragments" and "torsos" that the excavator found as he dug. Memory brings to light the ruins of the past and sets them on the stage of the present. What is left of poetry (the past with all its spiritual and metaphysical attributes) are poor remains. And yet, as remains, they are rich with an "inexhaustible secrecy." The interpretation of Benjamin's and Ungaretti's texts may appear simple, direct, obvious. Yet it would be an incomplete interpretation that falls into the trap of focusing on some textual aspects, leaving others in shadow. Does not Benjamin himself invite us to dig deeper and to tire not in returning "again and again to the same matter"?

Memory in language

"Language shows clearly that memory is not an instrument." With this remark Benjamin draws our attention to the relation between language and memory; to memory as a performance in language. It must be remembered here that in a series of lectures delivered at Jena in 1803-1804, and subsequently published in 1932 with the title of *Realphilosophie I*, the young Hegel wrote: "the idea of this existence of consciousness is *memory*, and its proper existence is language" (211; English translation in Agamben, *Language and Death* 42). Memory is pure performance, pure production, insofar as its communication and transmission can only take place as a form of narrative, be it through storytelling, music, painting, cinema, poetry, or prose. The most immediate and common way of passing memories down, even in the case of the self bequeathing a memory to itself, is through spoken or written language. Whenever we share our memories, whenever we scatter (*disperdere* to echo Ungaretti) our remembering, we also tell a story. If we attend closely to the process of telling and its scattering, as Benjamin and Ungaretti urge us to do, we are confronted with the image of dissemination. Memory makes sense, memory can be actualized, when it erupts from the cell of the individual and, potentially, enters the collective domain. There follows the related inference that memory can only be memory when it becomes potential.

As we saw when discussing language and subjectivity, the movement of the subject *in* language is also a movement of the subject *toward* language (see chapter 1). Any movement implies a departure, a displacement of the self from itself, be it a hypothetical exit from a mythical existence without language, or, perhaps more appropriately, the continuous movement which brings about the dynamic self-fulfillment and wholeness of the self. The approach of the self to language is not a betrayal of originality but rather a constant struggle for originality. The staging of memory is one such replenishing movement by which the self narrates memories to itself in order to achieve a kind of fullness. By contrast, the present does not need to be told, it can exist as the uninterrupted narration of the past (through memory) or of the future (through expectation). The present needs language only insofar as it needs to narrate its having been or its intention to be. The only reason we move in the present is that we move backward, toward the past, and forward, toward the future. The language of the present is simultaneously a borrowed and a shared language, the linguistic threshold where past and future meet in the language of potentiality, *qua* the language of storytelling.

As the self approaches memory in language, it moves closer to attaining the potential to disseminate but also to dissipate its past—the Italian *disperdere* and the English *scatter* imply both dissemination and loss. As we remember we also place ourselves in a position to forget, to lose memories. It follows that our urge to know better is also marked by an irreparable loss and an inevitable forgetfulness. As we narrate memory we also consign something to oblivion, to darkness. It is perhaps this forgotten thing or things of which the Italian poet Giorgio Caproni was thinking when he gave his last book of poetry the title *Res amissa* (*The Amissed Thing*; 1991). And it may be just this process that Agamben had in mind when, in the introduction of *Infancy and History* he dscribed written books as the death masks of a never penned *ergon* (3-10; *Infanzia e storia* vii-xv). It is what Benjamin was referring to when he spoke of memory as a gallery of torsos and fragments, whose significance is as great as that of their missing parts.

Memory is narration—it is language—and as such it also owes its existence to its negativity, which is ultimately nothing other than memory as the untold, the non-narratable (the potential existence of which lingers in the very potential to narrate memory). And it is because of this negativity that we "scatter" our memories in the hope that someone or something else will be able to translate them, supplementing our narration by filling in the gaps, by adding to our incomplete or maimed images. If it is true that we often lose ourselves in order to find ourselves (on this, see also Hart 32), it may also be true that we expose our forgetfulness to allow it to surface in someone else's narration. The exposure of forgetfulness is its absence, its not-being-there; it is those areas of emptiness which might appear to the eye as part of an incomplete picture. What we see, what we narrate as memory, represents itself, but it also gestures to what is missing. It does so in a continuous performance in which there remains something that can only be implied, evoked, speculated upon, but never seen or articulated. It is no wonder, then, that memory and its representation of the past so closely resemble the language of poetry.

The power of poetry and memory, their beauty, lies in revealing the untold through the told. Language says what it says by digging deep, by divulging the invisible to the surface through the visible: "there remains to me / that nothing / of inexhaustible secrecy." Ungaretti "digs" and then "scatters," remaining in ecstatic contemplation of that plentiful nothing which shows itself so vividly in language.

Rhapsody

The fact that, for Ungaretti, the "poet...returns to the light with his songs (*canti*)" rather than his words (*parole*) is significant and is not without analogy to Benjamin's reference to rhapsodic art. When Benjamin outlines the proper strategy for remembrance he writes that: "Fruitless searching is as much a part of this as succeeding, and consequently remembrance must not proceed in the manner of a narrative or still less that of a report, but must, in the strictest epic and *rhapsodic* manner, assay its spade in ever-new places, and in the old ones delve to ever-deeper layers" (emphasis added).

The word "rhapsody" is derived from the ancient Greek *rhapsodia*. The *rhapsoidos* recited epic poems in public by suturing together (*rhaptein*) various songs (*oide*). In its original meaning, rhapsody signified the recitation of new compositions made by fusing together memories and reminiscences of old, usually popular, songs. This recitation was performed by singing the poem or by alternately singing and declaiming. The original meaning of the word has descended to our time almost unchanged, with the exception that it is now chiefly used to refer to musical compositions. While we have retained the performative and melodic elements of the word rhapsody, we have perhaps lost sight of its mnemonic and linguistic origin. Rhapsody is nothing other than memory in language and, as such, it is a narration of fragments, remnants, odds and ends found by digging deep, then scattered on the surface of the present. Memory, in its original sense and *habitus*, was not spoken but sung; more than language, it was song. It is in this sense that the Ungarettian *canti* is not merely synonymous with "words"; it is, rather, a definite and necessary reference to *rhapsodia* and to the performance of the *rhapsoidos*.

Renunciation

In *On the Way to Language*, and more specifically in the essay "Das Wort" ("The Word"), Martin Heidegger turns not for the first time (see also "The Nature of Language" in the same volume) to Stefan George's poem "Das Wort" ("The Word") and to its last, ambiguous, stanza: "So I renounced and sadly see: / Where word breaks off no thing may be" ("So lernt ich traurig den verzicht: / Kein ding sei wo das wort gebricht"). Heidegger engages fastidiously with these two troubling lines in an attempt to think through and reflect further on the relation between word and thing. What strikes Heidegger is not only the apparently interdependent connection between word and thing emphasized by and in the last line of the poem, but also by the meaning of the "renunciation" of which the poetic "I" speaks.

"The insight into the poet's experience with the word" ("Der Einblick in die Erfahrung des Dichters mit dem Wort")," writes Heidegger, "that is, the insight into the renunciation he has learned ("den gelernten Verzicht"), compels us to ask the question: why could the poet not renounce Saying, once he had learned renunciation? ("Warum konnte der Dichter, nachdem er den Verzicht gelernt hat, nicht auf das Sagen verzichten?") Why does he tell precisely of renunciation? ("Warum sagt er gerade den Verzicht?") Why does he go so far as to compose a poem with the title 'Word'?" (*On the Way* 147; *Unterwegs zur Sprache* 228). Why does the poet continue to write at all after he has learned language's mysterious and unfathomable inadequacy? In order to save from oblivion, one might answer, the little of the world that *is* sayable. If it is true that only those things that can be said can exist, then the logical course of action would be to say as much as possible. But as we know, in saying we also expose what is unsayable, and by viewing we are also exposed to the invisible. It is in this sense that the act of poetry is also and inescapably an act of renunciation before the unspeakable.

In saying, the poet is also confronted by that which is invisible, must also "see" it and renounce it. This is the richness but also the insurmountable limitation of language and knowledge: saying and knowing necessarily cause their opposite. If the limitation is found in concealing through knowing, the greatness lies in generating and exposing, in bringing forth, the unknowable through knowledge. By renouncing the unsayable and, in doing so, exposing it, we can hope to place it on the way toward a state of becoming. Becoming must here be understood in the sense Heidegger gives to it, as that which "comes forth in presence." "When Heraclitus," writes Heidegger in *Heraklit* (1943-1944; published 1970; *Heraclitus Seminar*), "thinks *gènesis* in *ginoménen*, he does not mean 'becoming' ('das Werden') in the modern sense; that is, he does not mean a process ("Vorgang"). But thought in Greek, *gènesis* means 'to come into being' ('zum Sein Kommen'), to come forth in presence" ("in die Anwesenheit hervorkommen"; *Heraclitus Seminar* 8; *Heraklit* 18). The hope to place the unsayable underway must be understood as the possibility of saying it by withdrawing it. In other words, our hope can only be brought about and maintained by renouncing the utterability of the unsayable through its presentation in language. This allows us to grasp Agamben's claim that "we can have hope only in what is without remedy" ("possiamo avere speranza solo in ciò che è senza rimedio"; *The Coming Community* 101; *La comunità* 74).

It is now possible to approach straightforwardly Benjamin's remark that "it is to cheat oneself of the richest prize to preserve as a record merely the inventory of one's discovery." The true significance of memory lies not just in what is visible and communicable but also, and perhaps more importantly, in its halo, in the trace of the missing now engaged in dialectic with that which can be told. It is this dynamic interplay that affords memory its power and fascination, but also its pain. The same is true for language and its engagement with the "no-thing-may-be" at the moment of language's breaking. The renunciation of language is a rhapsodic song in which reminiscence in language exposes not only the stitching together of fragments but also their inevitable gaps. The poet's song is ultimately a celebration of the "irreparable," here literally intended as that which cannot be repaired to its expression. Once again, it is Heidegger who clarifies the meaning of the renunciation of language, and at the same time the renunciation of memory in language: "Saying attains to a different articulation ("Das Sagen gelangt in eine andere Gliederung"), a different *melos*, a different tone. The poem itself [George's poem], which tells of renunciation, bears witness to the fact that the poet's renunciation is experienced in this sense—by singing of renunciation" (*On the Way* 147; *Unterwegs zur Sprache* 228); and again: "The renunciation thus learned is no mere refusal of a claim, but rather the transformation of Saying into the echo of an inexpressible Saying whose sound is barely perceptible and songlike" (*On the Way* 150; "Der gelernte Verzicht ist keine bloße Absage an einen Anspruch, sondern die Wandlung des Sagens in den fast verborgen rauschenden liedhaften Widerklang einer unsäglichen Sage"; *Unterwegs zur Sprache* 231).

"Dark joy"

It is now time to add the last section of that fundamental passage in Benjamin's reflection on memory quoted above: "it is to cheat oneself of the richest prize to preserve as a record merely the inventory of one's discovery, *and not this dark joy of the place of the finding itself*" (emphasis added).

What strikes the reader first is the spectacular oxymoron "dark joy." The adjectival phrase yokes together the lightness natural to joy, its brightening effect on the subject who experiences it and the surrounding space, with darkness, the enveloping quality of loss, disorientation, pain, not knowing. Two opposites are united in a simultaneous exchange of knowledge and lack of knowledge, bliss and pain, visibility and invisibility. This dark joy is either a joy that does not shine and remains blissful in its ignorance (a joy that does not illuminate the causes of its own joyfulness) or a joy that proceeds in the deepest darkness, bringing to visibility only what is immediately adjacent to it. It is a locative, a joy in the dark, or simply a nominative, a dark joy. It is moreover *this dark joy*, the present joy, here and now, that adheres to the language of the speaking "I" as his only true companion. Its genitive, the place to which it belongs, is the "place of the finding itself."

Once again the comparison arises between "this dark joy" of Benjamin and Ungaretti's "this poetry," whose shining light is the "nothing of inexhaustible secrecy." In both Benjamin and Ungaretti, "this" is not only a demonstrative standing for time, the "now," but also and more importantly for space, the "here." It is the joy that "remains" after the journey (of excavation) to the "place of the finding itself." It is the space of the "here" as opposed to the space of the "there"; as such, it implies in Ungaretti a return from darkness to light. But in Benjamin, too, the moment of digging, and the place that this digging has uncovered, is paired with a sequel; both the "inventory of one's discovery" and "this dark joy" are "preserved as a record" of the tillage of memory. Is "dark joy," then, really the mixture of light, knowledge, the known, the familiar, on the one hand, and the unfamiliar, the unusual, on the other? Can we not read "dark joy" simultaneously as a nominative and a locative? Ultimately, memory is the record of an irreparably lost time, a darkness, and the joy of its "singing" in the present. But for Benjamin it is also the locus of a complex, dynamic spatial game in which the "place of the finding itself" is also a potential *torso* and *ergon*, a mnemonic language which, in being "here," can expose the inevitable renunciation of memory. For Benjamin, memory in language is not merely the result of remembering, either voluntarily or involuntarily, in the space of the self. It is also a mixture of a mental and physical journey in which the personal images of the past are matched, confronted and indeed triggered by the space of the past. It is no accident that Benjamin had a passion for collecting postcards of the places he visited.

A Berlin Chronicle is the emblematic example of a mnemonic narrative which recreates the past in and through the spaces of the past; that is, the streets, squares and buildings of Benjamin's Berlin childhood. But even more problematical and fascinating is the feeling that these spaces of the past are not crystallized in any given time. They are instead constantly engaged in a temporal as well as spatial dialogue with different ages, to the extent that the same building is compared through time, emphasizing the intrinsic dynamism of urban spaces. They are caught in their essence as incessant worksites, endlessly developing. Space modifies itself in time as the self transforms itself in time, and the narration of this transformation is also its remembrance shaped by a language that can only emphasize the relevance and the significance of its openness. If memory in language exposes the dark gaps of the past, it also exposes space as a cluster of ruins, half-finished sites, rubble-strewn lots, whose existence testifies to their missing parts and dark gaps. The archeological metaphors that underpin Benjamin's reflection on memory could not be more appropriate and precise, more telling and better suited to his dealing with the past. Memory is in constant flux, moving back and forth, like edited sequences of a film, in which the self exists not only against the backdrop of space but also as a result, as a product of space. It may be that this ever-changing space, this space always under construction, is itself what renders manifest, what brings to being, the self in memory.

"Moments and discontinuities": Benjamin's Erinnerung

In her biography of Benjamin, Momme Brodersen notes that "[Benjamin's] is a particular kind of recollection, in the original sense of the German word *Erinnerung*: observations of the interior—of one's own self and its surroundings, of the city as world and landscape, of time as space" (5). It is the spatialization of time, the memory of space, that drives not only *A Berlin Chronicle* but also the unfinished *Arcades Project*. In the latter, Benjamin's intention was to shed light on the future by describing the urban landscape as he observed it change over time. Benjamin's recollection of his childhood in Berlin, written for his son Stefan, is interspersed with many qualifications and clarifications. The narrative is so often interrupted by haphazard and strategically inconsistent explanations (one would assume that methodological claims should be made at the beginning of a text), that there is no way of knowing whether such provisos are for the benefit of Stefan or Benjamin himself, or whether they are in fact not explanatory at all but rather integral parts of the narrative; memories themselves, fragments of the same rhapsodic song.

One of the most important digressions occurs a third of the way into the narrative and deserves to be quoted in its entirety:

> Reminiscences ("Erinnerungen"), even extensive ones, do not always amount to an autobiography ("stellen nicht immer eine Autobiographie dar"). And these quite certainly do not, even for the Berlin years that I am exclusively concerned with here. For autobiography has to do with time ("hat es mit der Zeit"), with sequence and what makes up the continuous flow of life ("dem Ablauf und mit dem zu tun, was den stetigen Fluß des Lebens ausmacht"). Here, I am talking of a space, of moments and discontinuities ("Hier aber ist von einem Raum, von Augenblicken und vom Unstetigen die Rede"). For even if months and years appear here, it is in the form they have at the moment of recollection ("im Augenblick des Eingedenkens"). This strange form ("Gestalt")—it may be called fleeting or eternal ("man mag sie flüchtig oder ewig nennen")—is in neither case the stuff that life is made of. And this is shown not so much by the role that my own life plays here, as by that of the people closest to me in Berlin—whoever and whenever they may have been. The atmosphere of the city ("Die Luft der Stadt") that is here evoked ("beschworen wird") allots them only a brief ("kurzes"), shadowy existence. They steal along its walls like beggars, appear wraithlike at windows, to vanish again, sniff at thresholds like a *genius loci*, and even if they fill whole quarters with their names, it is as a dead man's fills his gravestone ("wie der des Toten den Denkstein auf seinem Grabe"). Noisy, matter-of-fact Berlin ("Das nüchterne und lärmende Berlin"), the city of work and the metropolis of business, nevertheless has more, rather than less, than some others, of those places and moments when it bears witness to the dead, shows itself full of dead; and the obscure awareness of these moments, these places, perhaps more than anything else, confers on childhood memories ("Erinnerungen der Kindheit") a quality that makes them at once as evanescent and as alluringly tormenting as half-forgotten dreams ("wie halb vergeßne Träume"). (*Reflections* 28; *Ein Lesebuch* 374-75)

The transparency of Benjamin's discourse on the temporal narratives of reminiscence and autobiography, and their dissimilarities, must be regarded with caution. The main difference between autobiography and the peculiar kind of reminiscence Benjamin writes in *A Berlin Chronicle* lies in the contrast between the temporal structure of the former and the spatial structure of the latter. Whereas autobiography is made of a "continuous flow of life" ("den stetigen Fluß des Lebens"), Benjamin's reminiscence comprises "moments and discontinuities." This is clearly true if an autobiography is narrated in a linear fashion consonant with the unfolding of life. In the case of such a narrative, individual segments—the "moments" ("Augenblicke") Benjamin speaks of—are linked chronologically to describe a clear beginning, middle, and end. Such an autobiography is the sewing together of temporal individualities, whose embroidery is a function of the sequential continuity of linear time. Each segment is understood and interpreted in the context of a totality of segments whose very communality is decreed by chronology. Each part makes sense not so much by virtue of its own being as by virtue of its belonging to a greater whole; the essence of the part is measured in relation to what precedes or follows.

In this kind of autobiography, an isolated "moment" is meaningless; what is important is the dependent relationship of the part and the whole. While the part is necessary for the whole, it is also irrelevant without the whole. Autobiography, in the sense given to it by Benjamin, is a narrative that wishes to possess a temporal fragment by knowing it in the context of a community of temporal fragments. An individual fragment is not possessed in relation to the knowing of it *as such*, but to the knowing of the whole within which each fragment sacrifices its own specificity and unique meaning. Is this the price that must be paid to achieve the intelligibility of life and, more generally, the intelligibility of history? Georges Bataille's words, written in *On Nietzsche*, come readily to mind: "The individual—in time—is lost, falls into a movement in which he or she is dissolved" (129; see also Hill 15).

In *A Berlin Chronicle*, Benjamin chooses the opposite path. He narrates segments in their individuality; he narrates moments as such by wresting them away from a temporal continuity and casting them into space. One therefore sees not the whole, unfurling in a ceaseless narrative before the eyes, but rather snippets, glimpses of life crystallized in their spatial masks. Benjamin tells, in other words, nothing other than remnants of time; he dispatches postcards from the past, the incompleteness of which can only evoke their becoming, their coming forward into presence. In possessing these "discontinuities" we must also learn to renounce the whole, in the sense Heidegger gives to the word "renunciation." In saying these moments we renounce the whole by singing it into presence. This possession is also knowledge of the halo, of the "death mask" worn by what is incomplete. Only having arrived at this point can we begin to understand Benjamin's emphasis on the "now" and properly contextualize Agamben's important remark about Benjamin's temporality. "Instead of the nullified present ("il presente nullificato")"—writes Agamben in *Infancy and History*—of the metaphysical tradition, "Benjamin posits a 'present which is not a transition, but in which time stands still and has come to a stop' ("Benjamin sostituisce 'un presente che non è passaggio, ma si tiene immobile sulla soglia del tempo'"). Instead of the social democratic and historicist notion of the historical progress of humankind, which 'cannot be sundered from the concept of its progression through a homogeneous empty time' ("che è 'inseparabile da quella della Marcia attraverso un tempo omogeneo e vuoto'"), he puts forward the revolutionaries' 'awareness that they are about to make the *continuum* of history explode' ('la coscienza rivoluzionaria di far saltare il *continuum* della storia'). Against the empty, quantified instant, he sets a 'time of the now' ('un tempo-ora'), *Jetzt-Zeit*, construed as a messianic cessation of happening, which 'comprises the entire history of mankind in an enormous abridgement'"(*Infancy and History* 102; *Infanzia e storia* 108).

The "past of the now," as narrated in *A Berlin Chronicle*, has exactly the same function as the "time of the now." In fact, Benjamin's critique of the "nullified present of the metaphysical tradition" is really a critique of a nullified time; a time robbed of its moments as independent entities. In this nullified time, moments are forced to roll into each other in the service of the whole; they ultimately vanish into the blur of a temporal crowd. The sacrifice of the moment is a celebration of the whole and its general (because assembled) truth as opposed to the truth of the specific. The long perspective of the whole, its historical longevity, is at the base of its power but also causes profound limitations.

If the whole—the history of Western thought, for instance—provides us with a sense of general grounding, it also betrays the inevitable vulnerability of such a grounding. This vulnerability lies precisely in the potential inaccessibility and unintelligibility of one or more of its originally constitutive parts; the essence of ancient Greek thought, for instance. If it is true that the whole is produced by individual moments and their subsequent sacrifice, it is also true that the whole may continue to be even when one of these moments and its original essence have become blurred, uncertain. Similarly our life "goes on," and autobiography can be written, even in the irreparable absence of some of the individual moments that made it. And yet, as Benjamin reminds us, "it is to cheat oneself of the richest prize to preserve as a record merely the inventory of one's discovery."

Temporal gaps

Heidegger, Fink, and the participants of *Heraclitus Seminar* were confronted by the opposite problem. They possessed fragments of Heraclitus's work but could not fit them into the context of a whole. How could they make sense of what they believed to be one of the key notions in Heraclitus's writing, *tà pánta* ("the universe, everything"), and its relation to being, *en*, if all they had to work on were the remnants of a larger and irretrievably lost narrative? "Participant: If we attempt to make clear to ourselves the meaning of *tà pánta* starting from a fragment, can't we revert ("zurückgreifen") to Fr. 50 in which it is said, 'Everything is one?' ('eins ist alles') Heidegger: But everything we have of Heraclitus's fragments is not the whole ("das Ganze"), is not the whole Heraclitus" (*Heraclitus Seminar* 17; "ist nicht der ganze Heraklit"; *Heraklit* 31).

The frustration and delight evident in Heidegger's sharp yet quasi-exultant reply betray an interesting mixture of despondency and excitement in the face of a typical hermeneutical circularity. The participants' predicament is compounded by the fact that the whole of Western thought is rather tentative in its dealing with this moment of Greek thought: "From Martin Heidegger's dialogues with the Greeks," writes Fink, "in many of his writings, we can learn how the furthest becomes near and the most familiar becomes strange ("wie das Weiteste nah und das Vertrauteste fremd wird"), and how we remain restless and are unable to rely on a sure interpretation of the Greeks ("und wie wir nicht zur Ruhe kommen und uns nicht auf eine gesicherte Deutung der Griechen verlassen können"). For us, the Greeks signify an enormous challenge" (*Heraclitus Seminar* 3; "eine ungeheure Herausforderung"; *Heraklit* 9).

Heraclitus Seminar is interesting and instructive, because it is a practical instance of present thought and present thinkers questioning the partial remains of the past in search of a wholeness that can only exist through and because of its parts. As such, *Heraclitus Seminar* and its methodological approach to excavation shed light on and assist us in our endeavour to understand the difference between the meaning of autobiography and reminiscence in Benjamin's *A Berlin Chronicle*. *A Berlin Chronicle* is not an autobiography simply because it is not supported and subsumed by a given whole present before us, the main traits of which are carefully connected and explained temporal segments, harmoniously united. What the *Chronicle* lacks is the orchestrating subjectivity—as historicity—of autobiographical writings. In its place Benjamin offers discontinuities and fragments. If Heraclitus's philosophical ruins are fragments of thought, linguistic remains, Benjamin's fragments are visual memories. If the transposition of Heraclitus's fragments into contemporary thought and language begins by understanding the "spiritual views" behind them, Benjamin's translation of memories into language must similarly commence with a consideration of temporal gaps and shadows. To highlight once and for all the affinities between the methodology of the *Heraclitus Seminar* and that of Benjamin's reminiscences in *A Berlin Chronicle*, we need to look closely at Fink's distinction between philology and "spiritual view" on the one hand, and, on the other, at Benjamin's distinction between mnemonic matter and the "stuff that life is made of." In *Heraclitus Seminar* Fink writes:

> Our seminar should be an exercise in thinking ("Übung im Denken"), that is, in reflection on the thoughts anticipated ("vorgedachten Gedanken") by Heraclitus. Confronted with his texts, left to us only as fragments ("Fragmente"), we are not so much concerned with the philological problematic ("so geht es uns dabei nicht so sehr um die philologische Problematik"), as important as it might be, as with advancing into the matter itself ("zur Sache selbst vorzudringen"), that is, toward the matter that must have stood before Heraclitus's spiritual view ("zu der Sache, die vor dem geistigen Blick von Heraklit gestanden haben muß"). This matter is not simply on hand ("Diese Sache ist nicht einfach vorhanden") like a result or like some spoken tradition ("irgendeine sprachliche Überlieferung"); rather, it can be opened up or blocked from view precisely through the spoken tradition. It is not correct to view the matter of philosophy, particularly the matter of thinking as Martin Heidegger has formulated it, as a product lying before us ("wie eine vorhandene Sache zu betrachten"). The matter of thinking does not lie somewhere before us ("liegt nicht irgendwo") like a land of truth into which one can advance; it is not a thing that we can discover and uncover ("sie ist keine Sache, die man entdecken und entbergen könnte"). (*Heraclitus Seminar* 3; *Heraklit* 9-10)

Let us recall now the relevant passage in *A Berlin Chronicle*: "Here, I am talking of a space, of moments and discontinuities. For even if months and years appear here, it is in the form they have at the moment of recollection. This strange form—it may be called fleeting or eternal—is in neither case the stuff that life is made of." Benjamin's visual memories are a by-product of the present in which they are remembered and, most importantly, they are not individual parts of an assembled whole. They do not proceed linearly, as life does; they adhere to no chronology. They are rather moments crystallized in their fleeting yet eternal memorability, a series of detailed, unalterable "nows." Their precision, their exactness as such is accompanied by their indistinct and inaccessible surroundings. They are "shadows" of unseen objects, letters on fading "gravestones," haloes of a larger existence which they in turn faintly illuminate. This is a time that looks for being, and a being that searches for time. There is no wholeness here but gaps undergoing narrative fulfillment.

Perhaps the most appropriate metaphor for the fragments of a thinker long gone is that of sound. What perceptible truth remains can be thought of as a sound that once carried a precise meaning made up of space, time, landscapes, language—in a word, life. And yet, the fragment is not life, but a sound imperfectly reverberating in the form we receive it in "now." How could philology, the life of language turned back upon itself, its rewound history, regain the totality of a whole life to us? It may perhaps reveal to us other parts, other sounds, other shadows of the whole. The whole as such remains concealed, but in remaining so it "releases us," in the words of Fink, "to the matter that merits being named the matter of thinking" (*Heraclitus Seminar* 3; *Heraklit* 9). In an analogous way, the concealed past also releases us to the matter that merits being named the matter of memory.

Being now

Kant posits time as the *a priori*, the thing that does not precede but is natural to being, the thing that being brings into existence with itself, naturally, primordially. In *Kritik der reinen Vernunft* (*Critique of Pure Reason*; 1781) Kant first writes that: "Time is a necessary representation that underlies all intuitions. We cannot, in respect of appearances in general, remove time itself, though we can quite well think time as void of appearances. Time is, therefore, given *a priori*" (74-75). Kant subsequently writes that "time is nothing but the form of inner sense, that is, of the intuition of ourselves and of our inner state. It cannot be a determination of outer appearances; it has to do neither with shape nor position, but with the relation of representations in our inner state" (77). This elemental and necessary interpenetration leads Heidegger to argue in *Being and Time* that the ontological meaning of being is its temporality, which means, in Heideggerian terminology, that being brings itself into the world in time, that time is in fact inherently being's own essence in its state of thrownness. In the relation between time and subjectivity there is no derivation, no causality, but only simultaneity of apperception and intuition, whose origin has nothing to do with empirical observation or lived experience. It is the very axiomatic *a priori* of time that, according to Kant, defies its representation. How can we represent something that is not separate from us, whose properties are not those of an observable object lying outside the subject? Kant claims that this innate impossibility has led humans to endeavour to represent time by way of analogies: "We represent the time-sequence by a line progressing to infinity; in which the manifold constitutes a series of one dimension only; and we reason from the properties of this line to all the properties of time, with this one exception, that while the parts of the line are simultaneous the parts of time are always successive" (77).

The impossibility of extricating ourselves from time has demanded a historical representation of time but, interestingly enough, has also given rise to other representations that run contrary to the idea of sequences, perhaps in the attempt to reconnect with a time inside subjectivity and removed from history. The being of memory in language is the remnant, the moment crystallized in its inescapable becoming. As a moment, as a fragment, this "now," or rather, this "being now," is outside historical time. It is no accident that Benjamin calls this strange temporal form "eternity."

Eternity is, in its most common usage and understanding, the a-temporal *par excellence*, the non-time in which time ceases to be by virtue of an excess of time; that is, for the total and inextricable superimposition of individual temporalities, past, present, future, in one blurred and blurring Whole. In the Whole of eternity constituent moments are no longer visible because they are no longer there. It is for this reason that eternity is the end of memory and the death of historical time. If Benjamin's "moments" are eternity as they defy history, as memories, they are just as evidently not eternity. As memories they are moments, *precise* and *defined* temporal instances in which being experiences its coming together with time at the moment in which being leaves historical time. It is in this sense that Benjamin's "being of the now" is reminiscent of but also opposite to Heidegger's "being there," in that the ontological status and meaning of "being of the now" must be looked for outside the temporality of factual life and repetition.

The "now" of Benjamin's "moments," his *Jetzt-Zeit*, is the singularity of time filtered through memory in the language of the self. It is not so much a temporal *a priori* as a presentation of time in language. And what is represented is not a circular, linear, or eternal time but a time-space and, as such, a time outside time, at least in the sense that Kant gave to temporality. Benjamin's reminiscences are not internally determined but are rather, to borrow Kant's words, "represented to ourselves...as outside us, and all without exception in space" (67). In taking time outside us into space, Benjamin turns it into an object of observation, susceptible to description and narration. In doing so he twice contradicts Kant, first by indicating that time can be outwardly located, and second by stating that this location is not a matter of intuition but of presentation. In order to be "sung"—as opposed to "intuited"—time must be objectified and *separated* from the self that "sings" it. It is precisely the spatialization of time that brings about the split between temporality and subjectivity, challenging in turn their interconnectedness. Benjamin's reflection on memory provides the first move toward an analysis of being and time as separate entities.

Suchness

As observed earlier, Benjamin's "moments" ("Augenblicke") and "discontinuities" ("Unstetigen") are the singularity of time. What is meant here by "singularity"? One of the most exhaustive accounts of singularity in contemporary thought can be found in Agamben's *The Coming Community*. Here Agamben does not speak of temporal singularity but of singularity as such. The fact that in Agamben's work singularity is equated with the Latin term *quodlibet* ("the Whatever") should not distract us from pursuing a general as opposed to a specific analysis of singularity in which everything, including time and subjectivity, can be studied from the perspective of its *quodlibet ens* ("being such that it always matters ["l'essere tale che comunque importa"]"; *The Coming Community* 2; *La comunità* 3). Being must be understood here as the individual in relation to the Whole, which is also the *en* vis-à-vis the *onta*, the singularity of the individual in relation to the community, and the singularity of time in relation to its predicates (past, present, future). It is essential at this stage to quote Agamben's crucial passage on singularity in its entirety:

> The Whatever ("il Qualunque") in question here relates to singularity ("singolarità") not in its indifference with respect to a common property (to a concept, for example: being red, being French, being Muslim), but only in its being *such as it is* ("nel suo essere *tale qual è*"). Singularity is thus freed from the false dilemma that obliges knowledge to choose between the ineffability of the individual and the intelligibility of the universal. The intelligible, according to a beautiful expression of Levi ben Gershon (Gersonides), is neither a universal ("un universale") nor an individual ("l'individuo") included in a series, but rather "singularity insofar as it is whatever singularity." In this conception, such-and-such being ("l'esser-*quale*") is reclaimed ("è ripreso") from its having this or that property, which identifies it as belonging to this or that set, to this or that class (the reds, the French, the Muslims)—and it is reclaimed not for another class nor for the simple generic absence of any belonging, but for its being-*such* ("il suo essere-*tale*"), for belonging itself ("l'appartenenza stessa"). Thus being-*such*, which remains constantly hidden in the condition of belonging ("there is an *x such that* it belongs to *y*") and which is in no way a real predicate, comes to light itself: the singularity exposed as such is whatever you *want*, that is, lovable ("la singolarità esposta come tale è qual-si-*voglia,* cioè amabile"). (*The Coming Community* 4; *La comunità* 3-4)

The singularity of time, its Whatever (and the same can be said for subjectivity) is not so much the individual moment opposed to the whole as rather the individual moment as such. The "moments" in Benjamin's reminiscences do not belong just because they are present, past, or future, and they do not acquire a meaning just as individual segments of a sequential whole. They belong and mean because they are "as such," because they exist. Their necessity, and the pleasure that one experiences in their presence, is not related to their belonging to a particular period or being a shade of a particular time. These necessities and pleasures are simply due to their appearance. It is no accident that in Agamben, too, one finds references to reclaiming something that had been hidden away, buried under "false" pretences and artificial oppositions. In this instance the recovery of singularity takes place at the moment when "conditions of belonging" are traded for "belonging itself." But is not the shift from conditioned to unconditioned existence reminiscent of Benjamin's distinction between reminiscences and autobiography? Whereas in autobiography, a moment must be recounted within the parameters of a whole to which the moment belongs, if it fits within the picture of the whole (like a piece in a puzzle), in Benjamin's reminiscences, the moment exists and belongs not as part of a pre-constituted picture but "as such." It is in this sense that Agamben's claim that singularity "is freed [but also frees, one might add] from the false dilemma that obliges knowledge to choose between the ineffability of the individual and the intelligibility of the universal" can be contextualized within and brought to bear on Benjamin's *A Berlin Chronicle. A Berlin Chronicle* is ultimately interested not in the intelligibility of the universal or in the ineffability of the individual—or in pitting one against the other—but in presenting the existence of the individual. And yet there is something more to Benjamin's reminiscences besides the notion of singularity.

Exposure

Benjamin's reminiscences, his moments and discontinuities, are temporal singularities and therefore, as we have seen, they exist as such irrespective of their relation to "real life." They are because they belong to existence by virtue of the writing that has captured them as singular images on the page, and as singular edifices of a mnemonic city, whose design and continuity must be renounced in order to be. But what one presents in renunciation is the halo of the whole through the singularity of the fragments. What is there, singularity, does not belong because of the whole that it partakes of; it belongs, it exists, because it simply is. And yet, it is in its essence of singular existence that singularity gestures toward that which is next to it, presenting its dark pleasure. Memory in Benjamin is this "strange" ("seltsam") temporality that lives as such, without linearity or circularity. It lives outside of the being that thinks it, detached from his life, from his biography, as an object of observation, a floating singularity whose lightness and halo are nothing more than the darkness of what lies next to it. It is a memory that does not tell time or the being that belongs to time, but presents them and their relation. Only singularity can achieve this presentation. But true singularity, the singularity that belongs by defying conditions of belonging, must be *open* to what lies next to it and must be the potential link of a long chain of other potential singularities, whose existence can be surmised by their renunciation. *Openness* is the quintessential characteristic of singularity, in that singularity's existence, its belonging as such, is only possible by virtue of its being exposed—in its giving itself to exposure—to what lies invisible beside it. The invisible must be understood here again as that which is unsayable, unknowable, foreign, unpredictable; that, in other words, which lies outside, next to us and yet so far removed.

In Book X of *The Confessions*, St Augustine twice uses the verbs *confiteor* and *indico* in the meaning of opening, revealing, confessing. They occur at the beginning of the book, at that crucial point at which Augustine sets the tone and the theoretical as well as theological framework for his discussion of time. In Chapter III of Book X we read: "My lord, to whom every day my conscience makes confession" (*The Confessions* 180; translation slightly modified; "quo itaque fructu, domine meus, cui cotidie *confitetur* conscientia mea"; *Le confessioni* 446; emphasis added); and in Chapter IV: "I will reveal myself" (*The Confessions* 181; "*indicabo* me talibus"; *Le confessioni* 446; emphasis added). *Confiteor* and *indico* (which in this instance are synonymous with "to open") are also accompanied by the verb *audire*, meaning to learn, make apparent, available, open. In Chapter III of Book X we in fact read: "Therefore they wish to learn about my inner self" (*The Confessions* 181; "volunt ergo *audire* confitente me, quid ipse intus sim"; *Le confessioni* 446; emphasis added).

The movement at work here is that from a closed subjectivity—Augustine's before *The Confessions*—to an open subjectivity—Augustine's as he writes *The Confessions*. The passage from "closedness" to "openness" is again arrived at through writing, in Augustine's case through "scattering" his internal and intimate dialogue with God by way of writing it down for others. *The Confessions* become singularity as such, and by throwing themselves open as that which exists by simply being they also present what is not yet there. They expose themselves on the stage of presentation and in doing so set in motion their potential relations with the others who are outside them; the halo of their openness shining already over their own unknowability.

The open confession

It is clear throughout *The Confessions*, including Book X, that Augustine writes a confession of himself not so much to let God know about his sins or achievements as to bring himself closer to God: "Indeed, Lord, to your eyes, the abyss of human consciousness is naked. What could be hidden within me, even if I were unwilling to confess it to you? I would be hiding you from myself, not myself from you" (*The Confessions* 179; "Et tibi quidem, domine, cuius oculis nuda est abyssus humanae conscientiae, quid occultum esset in me, etiamsi nollem confiteri tibi? te enim mihi absconderem, non me tibi"; *Le confessioni* 442).

God does not need to be told to know, he needs to be told in order to be known by the subject of telling. Augustine's confession is not to inform God, but to acknowledge his faith in Him, and show his willingness to meet Him. Absolution and redemption are attained by "opening" the self to God. It is the self's availability to God that affords the confession its real function and purpose. What is interesting is that this intimate interlocution between the subject Augustine and God must also take a public form: the subject's confession must also be witnessed by others, and these others must partake of this confession. It is in making public a private dialogue with God that the subject, Augustine, "scatters" his words. This also means that the subject must translate the intimate dialogues conducted in his "heart" through "the words of the soul and the cry of the mind" into a written dialogue, whose real audience is no longer God and the self but other people. To achieve this, Augustine must represent his very confession, he must literally sever the confession from himself by writing it down. It is in this sense that writing and "scattering" are one and the same. To write means to dissolve and diffuse, to depart from the self toward the other. But it is also precisely in departing from the self, and in the abandonment of the private, intimate sphere of subjectivity that the self can return to itself more knowledgeable and enlightened. Writing and its departure from the self, the scattering of the self in writing, also enacts and foreshadows a return to the self, the purpose of which is to know better. The process of dispersion and disorientation becomes, in this sense, a process toward knowledge. Those who lose themselves will find themselves. In writing, the subject turns itself into an object of analysis and observation. This is the primary function of writing as well as the primary function of Augustine's *The Confessions*. To understand himself before God, Augustine must leave himself. The same goes for time and memory. In order to know time one must wrest it away from the self and project it outside. The outside in question is narrative, and the objectification of inner time is narrative time.

Augustine wrote *The Confessions* between 397 and 398. He was forty-four years old. One year before he started *The Confessions*, in 396, he had become archbishop of Ippona, now Annaba, in Algeria. Augustine had returned to his birthplace, Africa, in 387, one year after his conversion and only three years after his meeting with Saint Ambrose, which was to have a lasting impact on his thought. *The Confessions* was Augustine's most loved book, the one that he continued to talk about with fondness and respect until his death in 430. In *The Confessions*, Augustine felt that he had not only brought himself closer to God but that, in the process, he had also brought out the best in others; their charity shining and streaming out through his self-exposure on the page. Augustine, as his own writer and biographer, sacrificed his being to his community and shared with it his singularity in the act of writing. *The Confessions* is therefore not only a book but also, and most importantly, a symbolic offering to a community. This offering, the self-sacrifice of Augustine's singularity, coincides with his appointment as archbishop of Ippona, and must be seen and understood as a result of the historical context in which it was conceived.

As Heidegger argues throughout his work on poetry and language, language is the most dangerous of gifts because it simultaneously exposes the individual to the sphere of being and not-being, and, in doing so threatens the very existence of being. In writing his biography, in writing himself into language, Augustine exposes his singularity to the threat of annihilation and disappearance, of insignificance and rejection. In other words, in writing the "I" into the temporal domain of the community, into history, Augustine enters the insidious territory of "being in language" and of "being in time and history" where his belonging as such is suddenly crossed and tested by a series of conditions of belonging. The decision to write the "I" into the world can either decree the disappearance of the "I" or its celebration, but less as an "I" than a symbol of belonging as such, that is recognized as such through the love and the charity of others. *Quodlibet*, the Whatever, as Agamben says, is "lovable." Love, true love, can only be bestowed on those who give themselves to it entirely by opening their singularity to the risk of losing their singularity. There would have been no better offering and gift the new archbishop could make to his community than to write *The Confessions*.

If this is true, language is then the necessary passage to true love and also to true singularity. By true love and true singularity we mean that love and that singularity which exist in their state of exposure, in their openness, which is also the risk of exposure and the risk of openness. Singularity can only have meaning if it is exposed to the menace of its destruction and if it coexists with a lack of singularity. Language is the vehicle of this exposure and the route through which singularity accesses its own being in community and history, its openness. Without language there can be no risk but only rest, in an indefinite a-temporal state of sterile eternity. Eternity, which does not know risk, for which risk has no meaning, does not need the language that exposes, does not need language at all—it ultimately does not need being. Eternity is an all-encompassing blur in which being is not at home. To be means to be exposed in language and to say simultaneously our being and our non-being, what we are and what we are not, and what we know and what we do not know.

The not knowing

In Chapter V of Book X of *The Confessions* we find an extraordinarily potent yet ambiguous statement: "Accordingly," writes Augustine, "let me confess what I know of myself. Let me confess too what I do not know of myself. For what I know of myself I know because you grant me light, and what I do not know of myself, I do not know until such time as my darkness becomes 'like noonday' before your face" (183; "Confitear ergo quid de me sciam, confitear et quid de me nesciam, quoniam et quod de me scio, te mihi lucente scio, et quod de me nescio, tamdiu nescio, donec fiant tenebrae meae sicut meridies in vultu tuo"; *Le confessioni* 450).

Augustine claims that he will write what he knows of himself and also what he does not know, and that what he knows depends on the grace of God, and what he does not know must remain in the dark until the light of God shines upon it. There could be no more significant and illuminating statement about the power of language to show and also to conceal things. Language says it all, indistinctly: what is known and also what is unknown. Everything resides in language because everything is good and just in the eyes of God. Language cannot not speak of everything because it encompasses all. As one speaks, the world speaks with one, and as one exposes oneself in language everything comes closer to the self, embracing and enveloping the self.

Language means openness and openness means belonging to all, indiscriminately. But of this whole, of this embracing entirety, only a small fraction is known and visible, the rest must be renounced in order to be. It is there but must be ignored. What does it mean "to renounce"? It means to learn to accept the thing in its potential presence. It literally equates with Stefan George's renunciation, as discussed by Heidegger. Augustine, as George will do centuries later, renounces saying what is actually there in order to see. But in great contrast to George, Augustine renounces not because words are lacking, but because the light of God has not yet illuminated their meaning. In Augustine language does not fail, it rather consigns to invisibility and darkness what is there not to be seen and known. The presence in language is total and yet partial to our eye, and the visibility of that which exists hides the presence of the whole. Similarly, memory in language contains "all" but must renounce it through contemplating its halo and celebrating the lovable singularity of that which is exposed among the invisibility of the whole. But if this is Benjamin's memory, is it also Augustine's memory?

The vast space of memory

What does memory mean for Augustine? Toward the end of Book X of *The Confessions*, more precisely in Chapter XL, we find a significant statement that reads almost like a summary, or better still, a *summa* of the previous chapters: "To the best of my powers of sense-perception, I travelled through the external world. Starting from myself I gave attention to the life of my own body, and examined my own senses. *From there I moved into the recesses of my memory, manifold vastnesses full of innumerable riches in wonderful ways*, and 'I considered and was afraid.' Without you I could discern none of these things, and I found that none of these things was you" (*The Confessions* 217; emphasis added; "lustravi mundum foris sensu, quo potui, et adtendi vitam corporis mei de me sensusque ipsos meos. *inde ingressus sum in recessus memoriae meae, multiplices amplitudines plenas miris modis copiarum innumerabilium*, et consideravi et expavi et nihil eorum discernere potui sine te et nihil eorum esse te inveni"; *Le confessioni* 526; emphasis added). Clearly, memory in Augustine is a vast space in which "inestimable riches" lie. Augustine goes there to look for things, to search for those clues, episodes, facts, truths, and lies that can tell him about what it is that he wants to know *now*, or why it is that he feels like this *now*, or how it is that he knows this way *now*. Memory in Augustine is the place where the self deposits itself over the years, in layer after layer, precipitating and lying down, settling. It is an unquantifiable, fascinating place where the actual self can see how, why, and what he is like in the present through images, feelings, and words. Memory is deep and, not unlike Benjamin's memory, one needs to dig deep to find some of the things that one looks for. It is this depth and the attendant notion of darkness that, in both Augustine and Benjamin, connect memory to time, in that memory grows vertically as time passes. Like the time of the body, memory grows taller and more complex and more intricate. To find oneself in the heap of time past, the self must dig and move layer upon layer of time, turning over this time to dig even further, discarding and ignoring many other selves in the process.

But why is it that one digs in the first place? What is it that one wishes to find? And how does one know that that something is somewhere, somehow, under there? The digging commences because the self has the capacity to remember, which also means the capacity to lose what it is that one wishes to remember. The memory of something is not necessarily linked to its immediate accessibility. On the contrary, the digging can only start when we become aware of having lost the thing of our remembrance and of having forgotten what it was like. It is the absence of what we remember that initiates the process of reminiscence. Memory is not presence, it is not the visibility of the past in the present. Memory is rather what might have existed, what might have been there but is there no longer. Memory is nothing other than the potentiality of existence and the presence of a lost, and therefore invisible, entity. Augustine, not without analogies to Benjamin, says that: "These objects [the concrete things of reality, the *res*] have no entry to the memory" (*The Confessions* 188; "istae quippe res non intromittuntur ad eam"; *Le confessioni* 462). What we entrust to memory are images ("imagines"), sensations, feelings. We do not store things and people in memory, we store their images, and these images deposit themselves in memory by transmuting into a world of potential existences.

Again, we remember only what we have lost, and what we remember is not the thing, or the person, or the idea itself, but an image of it, a remnant, a *torso*: in a word—a memory. The memory is, as such, only a halo of the thing itself, and its presence can only be predicated on its absence, that is, on the renunciation of the *realia*, of the real things. We only remember what has been lost and forgotten as reality. It is in this sense that memory is the *res amissa*, it is the existence of the *res amissa* in its present halo. The thing is here yet we do not see it, we only know that it is here because we remember that we have lost it and because we remember that we have forgotten what it is.

Not-being-there

We can now begin to interpret, and perhaps understand, the very significant yet obscure statement by Augustine quoted above. Indeed, we can start to appreciate the meaning of the words: "Without you I could discern none of these things, and I found that none of these things was you" ("nihil eorum discernere potui sine te et nihil eorum esse te inveni"). If it is true (and this is yet to be proved) that Augustine is here talking about memory, and if it is true, as we have suggested, that memory is the presence of that which exists in its invisibility, then the irreparable "absence" of God is an emblematic and emphatic definition of human knowledge in memory. Like Benjamin's reminiscences, Augustine's memory is the locus of fragments whose haloes are simultaneously their incompleteness and their essence, the cipher of an invisibility that shines in its not-being-there. But is it really true that Augustine refers to memory in the passage in which he writes, "et consideravi et expavi et nihil eorum discernere potui sine te et nihil eorum esse te inveni"? Or is he perhaps bringing together the totality of his experience—including his phenomenological searches ("mundum foris sensu"; "the external world"), his very physiological life, his inner senses and his memory—to bear on his exploration of the world and the soul in order to seek the presence and the face of God?

There is no doubt that the colon introducing "et consideravi et expavi" is in direct connection to memory, as if what follows were a further explanation of Augustine's experiences within memory: "From there I moved into the recesses of my memory, manifold vastnesses full of innumerable riches in wonderful ways, and 'I considered and was afraid.' Without you I could discern none of these things, and I found that none of these things was you" ("Inde ingressus sum in recessus memoriae meae, multiplices amplitudines plenas miris modis copiarum innumerabilium: et consideravi et expavi et nihil eorum discernere potui sine te et nihil eorum esse te inveni"). But even granting that Augustine's sifting encompasses all the experiences listed in the paragraph before the one on memory, their study cannot but take place in memory. Even present experiences invariably pass into memory as they happen, turning into past experiences as they deposit their images in memory. We must remember that for Augustine, human time is quintessentially transient and dynamic, and that subjectivity can only be in time and with time through memory and "waiting" (in expectation of the future). In Book XI of *The Confessions* we read: "Therefore let us not say 'The time past was long.' For we shall not discover anything to have been long when, after it has become past, it has ceased to be. But let us say 'That time once present was long' because it was long at the time when it was present. For it had not yet passed away into non-existence. It existed so as to be able to be long. But after it had passed away, it simultaneously ceased to be long because it ceased to be" (*The*

Confessions 231; translation modified; "non ergo dicamus: longum fuit praeteritum tempus: neque enim inveniemus, quid fuerit longum, quando, ex quo praeteritum est, non est, sed dicamus: 'longum fuit illud praesens tempus,' quia cum praesens esset, longum erat. nondum enim praeterierat, ut non esset, et ideo erat, quod longum esse posset; postea vero quam praeteriit, simul et longum esse destitit, quod esse destitit"; *Le confessioni* 560). The past no longer exists, the present passes into non-existence as it takes place, and the future does not exist as yet. And yet, we live in time and we know in time by experiencing our being in the world. The paradox, as Augustine appears to suggest, is that this knowing takes place in the "non-existence" of time. But this, as we have seen, is not a real non-existence; it is rather a renunciation of a real existence whose result is to bring its apparent invisibility into relief through its halo. The driving force of this knowledge that knows by renouncing its object of knowledge is memory.

Augustine's articulation of time is based on recurring images of absence and uncertainty; on fluctuation and on "becoming negative," on a continuous approach to non-existence. And our knowledge is based on remembering what no longer exists. Therefore, what we remember is the non-existence, or the not-being-there of time, subjectivity, and the world. It is much more than a commonplace to say that "memory is about that which no longer exists." In this apparently banal platitude rests the essence of memory as that which brings the non-existent to presence, and the essence of our mode of knowing as that which studies only what is no longer there. It is in this sense that one can better approach the notion of memory as the renunciation of the "real." In the act and the process of remembering the "real," connection with the past is renounced for a vision of its "death mask." Whenever we remember the past we remember that which is no longer present. "When a true narrative of the past is related," writes Augustine in Book XI, Chapter XVIII, "the memory produces not the actual events which have passed away but words conceived from images ["verba concepta ex imaginibus"] of them, which they fixed in the mind like imprints ["vestigia"] as they passed through the senses" (*The Confessions,* 234; "Quamquam praeterita cum vera narrantur, ex memoria proferuntur non res ipsae, quae praeterierunt, sed verba concepta ex imaginibus earum, quae in animo velut vestigia per sensus praetereundo fixerunt"; *Le confessioni* 564).

Is this the reason for the inherent nostalgia of our being? Nostalgia is the result of an apparently irreparable loss; a loss, however, whose object we live as if it were still present, still existent yet removed from us. Our pain, our nostalgia, is not so much the result of a simple loss as the feeling of a full presence whose enjoyment we have lost. If we were to rethink remembering as that which reconnects us to what no longer exists, to an absence whose images are not the ciphers of its presence but the ciphers of its total unavailability, we might also re-experience our dealings with the past, and indeed our relationship with nostalgia. If it is in fact true that we are nostalgic for what is not, for what does not exist, then we are nostalgic for "nothing."

A passage from Heidegger's *Being and Time* comes to mind, in which "anxiety" and "nothingness" are poignantly linked. In Section 62 of Division Two we read: "But this primordial anxiety ("Diese ursprüngliche Angst") strives to exact resoluteness upon itself ("trachtet die Entschlossenheit sich zuzumuten"). It moves out of the way everything which conceals the fact that *Dasein* has been abandoned to itself ("Sie räumt jede Verdeckung von der Überlassenheit des Daseins an es selbst weg"). The 'nothing' ('Das Nichts') with which anxiety brings us face to face, unveils the nullity ("enthüllt die Nichtigkeit") by which *Dasein*, in its very *basis* ("in seinem *Grunde*"), is defined" (*Being and Time* 356; *Sein und Zeit* 308). Memory might have more to do with forgetting than remembering.

The non-being of time

Time, according to Augustine, exists only if we can measure it. And since we measure only the present, the present is the only possible temporality or, to be precise, the only possible temporalizing temporality. In other words, it is the only experience of time that we can actually see unfolding before our eye as we measure time. But Augustine also tells us that this measuring is ephemeral because the present lacks extension. As we measure the present, the present disappears into non-existence. It becomes non-measurable past, and as such it is no longer present.

It is clear that for Augustine time can only be in relation to being, and that its existence is predicated upon something other than itself. There is no substance to time but only relatedness to that world which measures its progression, be it in a linear, circularly, or whatever other movement one wishes. Time beyond the human and created world is God's eternity; it is (and here language becomes incongruous), a "world" devoid of time. For Augustine time exists because we exist and vice-versa. But time exists only in our memory of time, and the locus of memory itself is the soul: "I am measuring," writes Augustine in Book XI, Chapter XXVII of *The Confessions*, "something in my memory which stays fixed there. So it is in you, my soul ("anime") that I measure time...In you, I affirm, I measure time. The impression that things ("res") make upon you abides when they are gone. That impression I measure as present, not the things that caused it. When I measure time, that is what I am actually measuring. Therefore, either this is what time is, or time is not what I am measuring" (*The Confessions* 242; translation modified; "sed aliquid in memoria mea metior, quod infixum manet. In te, anime meus, tempora metior...in te, inquam, tempora metior. affectionem, quam res praetereuntes in te faciunt et, cum illae praeterierint, manet, ipsam metior praesentem, non ea quae praeterierunt, ut fieret; ipsam metior, cum tempora metior. ergo aut ipsa sunt tempora, aut non tempora metior"; *Le confessioni* 582). Here Augustine lays a foundation for the subsequent Western understanding of time and links time and being in a manner that has conditioned all other interpretations of time since *The Confessions*. Not only does Augustine contradict the understanding of time based upon natural events, as expounded in ancient Greek philosophy, he also fuses unavoidably the destiny of time and the destiny of being. After Augustine, time and being are in a sense one and the same. Their separation would signify the end of being as we know it.

Time is memory and memory is the soul. Time in Augustine is that which takes place, that which happens within our very essence as an image of its own reality, of its own separateness and singularity. And yet, this singularity (the very thing that would separate time from being) is forever negative; it continuously negates itself into non-existence. The subjectivity of time ceases as it happens, as time translates its reality into subjectivity, into being. What is left of time is its non-being in being, it is its image in memory. Humans are the locus of time's negativity, sponges that absorb the non-being of time and release it into memory, into a narrative of non-existence. Memory is not time, it is rather the absence of time inhabiting us. It follows that the inextricable link between time and being announced by Augustine is really a false link, or rather a potential link where time moves into being as a translation of its singularity, as a halo that illuminates the non-being of time. It is therefore imprecise to say that time and being are one and the same. It would be more correct to say that memory and being are the same. Time disappears into the self as memory, and reappears as a death mask through its translation into memory. It is no accident that Benjamin, as we saw earlier, makes a strong link between language and memory, emphasizing that writing is an exceedingly effective tool of mnemonic excavation.

Waiting to become

Memory is not the only portal through which time passes into being and, accordingly, into non-existence. The other portal is what Augustine calls "expectatio" (expectation, which in Augustine is synonymous with "waiting to become"). Many years later Heidegger will rename "expectatio" as "Vorlaufen" ("anticipation, running ahead, catching up") or "anticipatory resoluteness" ("vorlaufenden Entschlossenheit"; see Being and Time 349ff; Sein und Zeit 301ff).

In Book XI, Chapter XX of *The Confessions*, Augustine defines "expectatio" as "the present of the future" ("praesens de futuris"; *Le confessioni* 568). In contrast to what we ordinarily think of "waiting," Augustine's *expectatio* is an active projection of the self into the future. The self goes ahead of itself toward its potential being in the future by relying on knowledge and experience already acquired. Through basing our assumptions on memorized knowledge we can predict the likely future occurrence of an event—that the sun will rise again at a certain hour, for instance, or that we can trust in our ability to recite unerringly an entire poem we have learned and practiced reciting. It is not that by doing this we measure the future or bring it into existence, it is rather the case that we project ourselves into a potential being-ahead. In other words, we take our life and the world, our being-there, into the domain of admissible possibilities. *Expectatio*, like memory, is a form of subjective experience of time, and a narrative that unfolds in the absence of its concrete referents. The "I" who speaks its own "waiting to become" in the expectation of the taking place of "waiting" is a doubly negative "I" because both subjectivity and time are suspended as they are placed in potentiality. The similarities between memory and "waiting to become" are strikingly obvious in that they both enact a narrative of suspension and potentiality. What differentiates memory from "waiting to become" in Augustine's thought is the relatively scant space he devotes to writing about *expectatio*, and his silence about the connection between "waiting to become" and the soul.

Augustine positions in this way the present of the past (memory) on a higher epistemological and ontological scale than the present of the future ("waiting to become"). *Memoria*, unlike *expectatio*, is characterized not only in relation to experience and phenomenological knowledge but also in relation to a primordial feeling for God. This becomes clear when Augustine draws the connection between memory and happiness, the latter being the primordial feeling to which humans are naturally predisposed. The origin and source of happiness is God. How could we in fact know that we experience happiness, Augustine argues, had we not a natural predisposition to happiness? "Waiting to become," in contrast, is exclusively characterized by phenomenological experience. Although Augustine does not say so explicitly, one is led to believe that for the Archbishop of Hippo memory, and therefore the past, has an ontological precedence over *expectatio* and the future. It is this Augustinian prioritization that Heidegger overturns in *Being and Time.*

Having-been-there

In Heidegger the Augustinian *expectatio* is rearticulated as "anticipation" and defined as the primordial resoluteness of *Dasein* toward the future. It is this primordial potentiality for being-ahead-of-itself that, according to Heidegger, grants *Dasein* its authenticity. It is *Dasein*'s innate knowledge of finitude, its knowing of "being-toward-death" that enables *Dasein* to be thrown into existence, and to become "being-there" (see also Young). *Dasein*'s facticity, its being phenomenologically there as part of the "they," is inscribed and predicated upon this primordial temporality. It is precisely *Dasein*'s temporal finitude that places it face-to-face with temporal infinitude. In Heidegger's words: "The authentic future ("Die eigentliche Zukunft") is temporalized primarily by that temporality which makes up the meaning of anticipatory resoluteness ("vorlaufenden Entschlossenheit"); it thus reveals itself as *finite* (*Being and Time* 378; "endlich"; *Sein und Zeit* 329-30). Heidegger continues: "The ecstatical character ("Der ekstatische Charakter") of the primordial future lies precisely in the fact that the future closes one's potentiality-for-Being ("daß sie das Seinkönnen schließt"); that is to say, the future itself is closed to one, and as such it makes possible the resolute existential understanding of nullity. Primordial and authentic coming-towards-oneself is the meaning of existing in one's ownmost nullity" (*Being and Time* 379; "Das ursprüngliche und eigentliche Auf-sich-zukommen ist der Sinn des Existierens in der eigensten Nichtigkeit"; *Sein und Zeit* 330).

We are now in a position to understand better the remark on anxiety and nothingness quoted earlier in relation to our discussion of Augustine ("But this primordial anxiety strives to exact resoluteness on itself. It moves out of the way everything which conceals the fact that *Dasein* has been abandoned to itself. The 'nothing' with which anxiety brings us face to face, unveils the nullity by which *Dasein*, in its very *basis*, is defined; and this basis itself is a thrownness into death"; *Being and Time* 356). We can also begin to explore and contextualize Heidegger's nothingness in relation to Augustine's memory.

The primordial temporality that temporalizes itself in "anticipation" is based on bringing *Dasein* face to face with its finitude and the nullity embracing this finitude. It follows that Heidegger's "anticipation" is the passage into existence across the threshold of nothingness. *Dasein* exists only after having-been face-to-face with "nothing." For Heidegger, the past and the present are necessarily preceded and anticipated by the future which is, however, not so much a "waiting to become" as a "having-been-there." *Dasein* lives its authentic being first and foremost through the anticipatory and primordial experience of having-been-towards death: "The future makes ontologically possible an entity ("Zukunft ermöglicht ontologisch ein Seiendes") which is in such a way that it exists understandingly in its potentiality-for-being" (*Being and Time* 385; "es verstehend in seinem Seinkönnen existiert"; *Sein und Zeit* 336). What is this if not a narrative of existence that inscribes itself into existence through non-existence? *Dasein* can exist only in the presence of its death mask, and only in the knowledge of its own having-been. It is this "futural" having-been and the anxiety before nothingness that *Dasein* must remember in order to be authentic.

It is here that remembering and memory enter Heidegger's thinking on temporality and subjectivity. But, interestingly enough, Heidegger's remembering is in actual fact a forgetting: "*remembering* ("Erinnerung") is possible only on the basis of forgetting ("auf dem Grunde des Vergessens"), *and not vice versa*; for in the mode of having-forgotten ("im Modus der Vergessenheit"), one's having been 'discloses' ('erschließt') primarily the horizon into which a *Dasein* lost in the 'superficiality' ('Äußerlichkeit') of its object of concern, can bring itself by remembering" (*Being and Time* 389; "das verlorene *Dasein* sich erinnern kann"; *Sein und Zeit* 339). And again: "This forgetting is not nothing ("Dies Vergessen ist nicht nichts"), nor is it just a failure to remember ("oder nur das Fehlen von Erinnerung"); it is rather a 'positive' ecstatic mode of one's having been' ('positiver' ekstatischer Modus der Gewesenheit')—a mode with a character of its own" (*Being and Time* 388; *Sein und Zeit* 339).

In Heidegger, as opposed to Augustine, we remember the future but, as in Augustine, this remembering is made possible by forgetting the real object of remembering, and by facing the nothing through which our remembering shines. As Kafka suggested in one of his aphorisms, forgetfulness may at times be more effective than remembering well: "I can swim just like the others. Only I have a better memory than the others ("nur habe ich ein besseres Gedächtnis als die andern"). I have not forgotten the former inability to swim ("ich habe das einstige Nicht-schwimmen-können nicht vergessen"). But since I have not forgotten it, being able to swim is of no help to me; and so, after all, I cannot swim" (*Zur Frage der Gesetze* 155; "Da ich es aber nicht vergessen habe, hilft mir das Schwimmenkönnen nichts und ich kann doch nicht schwimmen"; *Heller-Roazen* 146).

We are confronting two rather different notions of nothingness. In Augustine the nothing is the real past, which also includes the real-self-in-the-past; in Heidegger the nothing is the necessary passage to the authentic knowledge of *Dasein*; that is, *Dasein*'s nullity. The difference is also that between a linear understanding of time based on the self (Augustine), and an ecstatic understanding of time in which before, now, and after have lost their prescriptive attributes (Heidegger).

The presence of the forgotten

Heidegger's discussion of "anticipation"—and the centrality that "anticipation" acquires in Heidegger's thinking of *Dasein*, including *Dasein*'s authenticity—is the most direct route that one can take to enter one of the hypothetical journeys that we proposed at the beginning of this chapter. It is a journey that the preceding discussion has only prepared and made possible. This is the journey in which a reflection of being without time and vice-versa can take place and where the metaphorical bridge linking time and being can momentarily be broken. In other words, this is the thinking of a being without temporal origin and a time without human reference. Heidegger's *Dasein* brings us face-to-face with nullity, and with the absence of individual time. It also brings time face-to-face with the absence of the singular being. Can we say more about this facing nullity, apart from its anxious authenticity and its act of forgetting based on recollection? We remember that we will die because we have been there through others. Our memory of being finite and invariably toward-death is the memory of a necessarily forgotten experience, of something that we have lost as part of our singular specificity and which nonetheless accompanies us continuously. We live in the presence of our nullity, and the only way we can do so is to forget (and therefore to remember) that we face nullity. Our very existence is the *res amissa*; in other words, that thing which we have lost and yet remember with such care. We know that somewhere, somehow it will reappear out of our own disappearance.

For Heidegger, subjectivity, singularity, the very presence of the "I" (the Cartesian *cogito*) becomes authentic as it gradually takes itself into the void and into negativity. This negativity is primarily predicated upon the broken link between being and time. Being, the singular being, disappears as it recuperates its own *res amissa*. It is the entrance into ecstatic time that determines the end of the *cogito*. But against and in opposition to Heidegger, the authenticity of being is not its solipsistic fall into the contemplation of negativity. Authenticity is instead inscribed in being's belonging to a community. While the philosophical and literary journey in the space of disconnection between being and time can only be taken within the framework of singularity, the community is our only hope of temporal infinitude, the locus where memory is really the fusion between remembering and forgetting.

Heidegger's philosophy comes close but fails to think a place where an ontology of the "I" approaches an ontology of the "we." This is a thinking in which what counts is not the origin—nor, for that matter, the end—but an experience of time where being neither starts nor ends. What does the shift from the "I" to the "we" mean? Furthermore, what exactly is the philosophical result of turning away from the origin to face the ecstatic experience of time?

Giving language to the existent

The journey into a discourse in which the relation between being and time is broken leads us inevitably to a philosophical space where the equation being=time is reconstituted through the paradigm of plurality. The being facing nullity is also the being facing the community of others in which, perhaps, its own face may be reflected. This is not the locus of a generalized and abstract plural subjectivity, a nominal "us" or a generic "collective memory"; it is rather the place in which the language of the "I" encounters the language of the "we." In this instance, as throughout this chapter, the language of the "I" also implies its memory and its temporality; in other words, the ways in which the singular being inscribes itself in life by giving language to its existence. *To give* language to the existent is the way in which we partake of life, emphasize our singularity, and become part of a community, but it is also the manner in which we foretell our disappearance and our nullity. In speaking our life, in speaking ourselves, we simultaneously come to be and also come to "have been." Our speaking is at the same time the celebration of our singularity and the mourning of this very singularity. It is precisely this being and non-being and the attendant indistinction between presence and absence that characterize modernity and the contemporary condition—a condition that much literature and philosophy of the twentieth century has enacted. Yet this is far from being only and exclusively a modern and contemporary experience.

Some of the most powerful visual representations of the simultaneity of being and non-being are found in the Baroque period and especially in depictions of saints in the act of reading and meditating—which is extremely significant in itself. There are countless Baroque canvases whose central theme is that of the solitary saint, enclosed in a cave or cell, in the presence of, or holding, a skull (see for instance Jusepe de Ribera's *St Paul the Hermit*, c1640, Koelliker Collection, Milano; Georges de La Tour's *St Mary Magdalene with the Smoking Flame*, 1635/40, Los Angeles County Museum of Art; Orazio Gentileschi's *St Jerome*, c1610/11, Koelliker Collection, Milano; Trophime Bigot's *St Mary Magdalene Reading*, c1625, Koelliker Collection, Milano; Caravaggio's *St Francis in Meditation*, Galleria Nazionale d'Arte Antica, Palazzo Barberini, Rome).

In the manner of Caravaggio, the focus is entirely placed on a central figure and the few objects around it. The scene is dimly lit by an invisible source of light (Caravaggio's technique) or by a candle; the rest is obscured by a deep darkness. Solitude and darkness (the pure and unadulterated singularity of the self) are essential to these representations. But the self is not entirely alone; it is in the company of its own mortality (the skull) which is simultaneously, and this is important, both the self's own "having-been" and also its "will-be." The acts of reading and meditation, which, as we have seen earlier, are strictly connected with the act of remembering, are significantly conjoined in a temporality which is simultaneously singular and plural, individual and communal. While it is true that meditation and knowledge are represented here as a ritual of separation and solitude, it is also true that separation and solitude are only apparent. In the end they are reinscribed within the presence of not only the "will-be," and therefore the transience of human life, but also of the "having-been"; that is, the experience of death enacted upon the knowledge of "having-been-there."

Baroque visual art is deeply concerned with temporality. Time occurs again and again in pictures of the first half of the seventeenth century, and not only in religious works but also in more profane ones—for instance, in the stunning *Vanità* ("*Vanity*") by Trophime Bigot (Galleria Nazionale d'Arte Antica, Palazzo Barberini, Rome). The Baroque penchant for juxtaposing temporal levels through the use of clothing is well known. One can think of Caravaggio's *The Calling of St Matthew* (Contarelli Chapel, San Luigi dei Francesi, Rome), *The Taking of Christ* (National Gallery of Ireland, Dublin), and *The Crowning with Thorns* (Kunsthistorisches Museum, Vienna). The division of the canvas into two distinct temporalities is not only a strategy that enables Caravaggio to separate (but also bring together) the secular and the spiritual. It also allows him to bring forward the action, to make history present by retaining, at the same time, the historic and mnemonic "having-been." In *The Calling of St Matthew*, for instance, the left side of the painting is dominated by the figures of Christ and St Peter dressed in tunics. The right side of the canvas shows, by contrast, the party of players, including St Matthew, dressed in typical late-sixteenth-century clothes. The symbolism is strong and obvious, and it draws attention more to the intersection of two distinct temporal axes than to their strangeness or to the prosaic distinction between an eternal and a finite time.

The other Baroque theme in which time and being appears to considerable effect is that of the fortune-teller (see, for instance Caravaggio's *The Fortune Teller*, c 1594, Pinacoteca Capitolina, Rome; Simon Vouet's *The Fortune Teller*, 1617, Galleria Nazionale d'Arte Antica, Palazzo Barberini, Rome; Valentine de Boulogne's *A Fortune Teller, Bravo, Lute Player, Drinking Figure, and Pickpocket*, c 1618/20, Matthiesen Gallery, London; Nicolas Régnier's *Cardsharps with a Fortune Teller*, c 1620, Musée d'Art et Histoire, Ville de Genève, Geneva; Pietro Paolini's (1603-1681) *The Fortune Teller*, Auckland Art Gallery Toi o Tamaki, Auckland).

Paolini's painting (Figure 1) is a rich, witty, and multilayered narrative in which four figures enact an intricate and ironic play of deceit, hope, vanity, and lust. It is a painting that speaks not only through facial expressions but also through a hyper-emphasized gesturing in which fingers move in every direction: right, left, and center. The most striking aspect of this painting is, however, the mirror held by the fortune-teller's assistant. The image reflected by a mirroring surface is not only a symbol of vanity but, as the myth of Narcissus reminds us constantly, of decadence. Paolini's canvas is clearly cognizant of this and plays with notions of vanity and decadence as well as those of trickery and ephemeral satisfaction. The young suitor,

Figure 1. Pietro Paolini, *The Fortune Teller*

who has convinced his lover-to-be to listen to the words of a fortune-teller—who eulogizes the sincerity of the man's love—will obtain what he wishes. And yet, he is also reminded, by the assistant inviting him to look into the mirror, that this wish is destined to be temporary.

The interest of this playful work is heightened by the temporal collapsing of future, present, and past, represented on the one hand by the fortune-teller and on the other by the mirror. If the fortune-teller is predicting the future, the future is also available in the mirror, which is simultaneously the present but also, if not more importantly, the memory of the past. In Paolini's work this memory becomes the exact replica of the future, the expectation of a time already past.

Speaking as having-been

The claim that the "I" comes to life by disappearing into nothingness can only be accepted and understood from the perspective of a metaphysics of singularity. It is the void, the Heideggerian nullity facing the being towards-death, its "having-been," that must be rethought and problematized.

The language of singularity speaks through ruins, death masks, and torsos, it brings to life remnants or, in Benjamin's language, a rhapsody of images whose incompleteness shines forward, casting light on and drawing our attention to what is missing. We sing, in the sense in which Heidegger speaks of singing, our life, and the pauses (the white spaces in between and within the song's lines) assume an importance that is both dazzling and baffling. Our presence, our "visible" language, is always interspersed with that which is invisible in it. We live in this constant flux between being and non-being, and in the space of the potential, in order to say that which remains without language. It is in this sense that our language enacts a singularity that is always declined in the language of memory. We always speak as having-been. In other words, we always speak in the "ecstatical" mode of language. From this we infer that our temporality, our very essence as singular beings, is also our language, and that our singularity is made as much of presence as of absence and potentiality. What we say makes us as much as what we do not say and what we could or might say. But it is precisely this making of the self through language that necessarily enacts a performability demanding an audience, a "we" from whom an interpretation is required. As singularity, we must "consent" (*con-sentire*, literally to "feel with")—a verb that Agamben uses to great effect in an essay on friendship, "Amicizia" (2004)—to be with the other, and to share with the other our being. We must consent to *donate* the *mise en scene* of our being as singularity in the world to the interaction between ourselves and others. But this interpretation must be offered not to traditional and conventional language, to that language that only hears what is said, but to that feeling for language in which the shining of the invisible and the potential may become apparent. The *rhapsodus* requires a listener who can enter deep into language and see through it the interstices connecting the said and the unsaid. It is from this meeting between the "I" and the "you," this coming together of singularities as "we," that a philosophy and a literature of plurality commence, and that the nullity of the individual is reconfigured in the presence of a multisingular community.

I am with you, and you are me as I speak. You are the other who can shine upon the gaps of my language by feeling it and by living with (con-vivere) my language. If it is true that language encompasses everything—what is said, what is unsaid, and what might be said—it is also true that the mode of potentiality is the mode that brings together the said and the unsaid in the linguistic locus of indistinction. It is here that the "ruin" of the said meets the invisibility of the unsaid and they together give rise to the halo, to a language in the making or, as Benjamin would have it, to a language of becoming. And it is here that the "we" intervenes to perform its function, which is principally that of keeping alive and bringing to the front of attention and interpretability the space of potentiality. This purpose is not so much that of turning the invisible into the visible—or the unsaid into the said—as to draw our attention to what lies in between, to what might be; in other words, to that mode of being where singularity concretely encounters the community in a potentially powerful and empowering dialogue. In the language of potentiality resides the whole in its many facets and possibility—happiness, anger, joy, nostalgia, hope, anxiety, sadness, bliss—and it is here that our singularity as being can become dialogical and choral.

Our memory (our "having-been") will thus appear not necessarily as mourning for something lost; or as relief for having sidestepped danger, as hope for a reunion or a definite closure, as anxiety and apprehension for our limitations or the limitations of others. Memory will be the site where all this is able to intermingle and converse. To consent to share our singularity means to rewrite our nullity which, ultimately, means to rewrite our temporality and our language. The ecstatical mode of being announced by Heidegger can, in this way, be wrested from the inherent stasis of Heidegger's philosophy and cast into a philosophy of becoming.

Chapter Three

Exile

"One alone into one"

In "Politica dell'esilio" ("Politics of Exile") Agamben states that: "Only now that exile is no longer the banning of an individual from the community, but 'of one alone into one,' the condition of negativity and exclusion that exile enunciates appears to turn instead into a state of 'bliss' and lightness" (my translation; "Solo ora che l'esilio non è più il bando di un singolo dalla comunità, ma 'di un solo presso uno' e la condizione di negatività ed esclusione che esso esprime sembra, invece, rovesciarsi in uno stato di 'felicità' ["eudaimonion bios"] e di leggerezza ["kouphisthesetai"]"; "Politica" 25). Agamben introduces here a radical shift which may have significant implications for the understanding of exile. The *solo ora* ("only now") in Agamben's remark must, however, be correctly understood in its original context. Agamben is reflecting on the articulation of exile found in Plotinus's *Enneads* (Plotinus's pupil, Porphyry, published the works of his master in 301). The adverbial indicator, "now," refers to the time of Plotinus (204-70), and yet the statement is not without analogy to our contemporary situation. According to Agamben, the significance of Plotinus's reading of exile rests on the adaptation of a juridical and political term to describe the life of the philosopher.

At the end of the *Enneads* Plotinus introduces the image of "one alone into one" to characterize the life proper to gods and to "divine and blissful men," using the formula: "phygé monou pros monon," which is usually translated as "the flight of one alone into one" (see Plotinus VI 9, 11, 50). This is the chosen departure of the philosopher from the life of the polis; a separation that in antiquity was conceived as a necessary step toward a proper contemplative life. For Plotinus, and for a long and important tradition of thinkers who followed in his footsteps, including the Neoplatonists, a life dedicated to thought could only be achieved through self-imposed exclusion from the community. This is the mental enclosure in which writers and philosophers accept they must immerse themselves to achieve an experience of heightened sensitivity and concentration. It is in this sense that the separation from the community described by Plotinus becomes self-enforced isolation and exile.

The literary and philosophical isolation, the exile of which Plotinus speaks, is incompatible with exile's other meaning, which has its origin in the juridical structure of human society. In this latter case, exile is not liberation but a punishment imposed on the individual guilty of a crime against the state. Isolation is here the physical removal of the individual from its "proper dwelling," and the deprivation of the rights which gave that individual its place as a citizen of the community. Through the passage from citizenship to exile, the individual is also deprived of political life and forced to re-enter the original state of a life without community, acceptance, or recognition.

In exile, the lone individual confronts its "naked self." It is an event that can only be predicated upon a self reduced to one, reduced to its own voice and language. The individual in exile is utterly alone in the company of itself, grappling with a set of values that are neither recognizable nor comprehensible to anyone but the exile. Thus, the exile becomes its own world, its own community, the cipher and parameter, the "other" of any comparison. This state of being with oneself equates with the image of the imprisoned self and the gnawing wretchedness that goes hand in hand with the feeling of being unavoidably apart from the familiar voices of usual life. This state of exile is not even a case of the unusual confronting the usual in a dynamic marked by nostalgia and longing. It is simply life in the company of a presence which has been lost. It is in this sense that the usual is always "there," before the eye of the exile and yet removed from it, unreachable. This dynamic generates melancholia to the extent that the presence of the usual is not counterbalanced by that of the unusual in a constant renegotiation of the proper dwelling in the face of the improper dwelling. It is rather the experience of living with a phantasm, and in a world that only lives in the fever of memory and imagination. At the origin of the anguish experienced by the exile, there is a simulacrum.

But it is precisely the appearance of this simulacrum that enables the philosophical and literary imperatives of solitude to meet and match the isolation of political exile. In the former, solitude and isolation are sought after as prizes; in the latter, they are regarded as unspeakable and demeaning punishment. But why is it that the self potentially tends toward yet is also repulsed by isolation and exile? In other words, why is it that the ascetic and monastic life is poetically and philosophically inspiring, while exile is so feared and loathed?

Nakedness

There is at least one other form of exile separate from its political and poetic counterparts. This is the voluntary exile of those who, for many different reasons and motives, decide to leave their home and start anew as citizens of another place. The act of choosing implies the desire to reconstruct the unusual as usual and to discover and subsequently adopt as true and proper a series of previously "foreign" conditions of belonging that may replace altogether or else intersect and cohabit with the old conditions of belonging. This is, for instance, the experience of migrants who constantly hesitate between the preservation of the usual and the full acceptance of the unusual. It is the condition of lingering in between nostalgia and the denial of the previous self. But this condition can also bring about the sublimation of nostalgia and denial into a state of passive or active suspension between two communities.

Poetic isolation and political exile are two drastically different modes of existence, in spite of the identical spatial and temporal zones they invoke. In the first instance, the solitude of the self is merely mental. It becomes an imaginative domain or state in which the senses roam at ease in a world devoid of others. In the second instance, the solitude is physical as well as mental. This is a real world where the senses can actually roam in a given temporal and spatial domain without the "usual others." And yet in enforced exile, all the senses, and the language employed to articulate them, appear to be capable of nothing other than a continuous struggle to reclaim possession of the senses and languages of others; in a word, to reconnect and be subsumed again by the language and the senses of the individual's lost community.

In the experience of enforced exile the subject demonstrates that what matters above all else is communion with similar individuals and the sharing of a set of conditions of belonging, including language, without which the subject feels bereft of significance and, ultimately, of life. This basic principle appears to teach the contemporary individual that a life worth living is only possible in the context of a set of conditions of belonging which throw the subject into contact with instances of otherness, where individuality and life acquire significance not as "life as such" but as "life as part of a group." Life outside the group, life as such, is debasing and unworthy. It is by reflecting on this basic tenet that one can understand why the sovereign insists on instituting, preserving, and maintaining a set of conditions of belonging which are used not only to take care of and include the subject but also to judge, sentence, and exclude the subject.

If poetic isolation is a rarefied attempt to achieve sublime authenticity by removing oneself from an existence deemed inauthentic, political exile is the struggle to regain an inauthentic existence from within the framework of a potentially authentic existence. Poetic isolation is the mental flight of the individual determined to gain or regain an originality and purity predicated upon the exclusion of others. This search is paradoxically entangled with the necessity to reconnect the ultimate experience to the stage of others, as if authenticity by itself were not enough unless reduced once again to inauthenticity. This is why poetic language is interested, even at its highest degree of opaqueness, in performability and communicability. On the other hand, a language that is finally alone, unshared, devoid of a communicable and signifying context, a language that is finally as such in the experience of exile, constantly works toward regaining its anonimity through a desperate wish to shed its authenticity.

The juxtaposition of poetic and political exile demonstrates at least one thing: that exile is not negative *a priori*: isolation is not necessarily punishment. What could the contemporary subject and community learn from a reflection hinging upon the problematization of exile and exilic experience?

Potentiality

The characterization of exile as either a cleansing process toward authenticity (as in the poetic experience), or as a traumatic loss of the community and an attendant loss of significance and recognition (as in the experience of political exile), is based on the firm opposition between authenticity and inauthenticity, where the second term of the equation is commonly considered negatively. Inauthenticity has usually been thought of as synonymous with inferiority, impurity, bastardization, hybridity. The irreconcilable split between authenticity and inauthenticity marks the entire history of Western thought, from Aristotle's division between *zoe* and *bios* to Heidegger's juxtaposition between "eigentlich" and "uneigentlich" ("proper" and "improper"). This split has propelled the dialectical paradigm informing Western thought and has also given rise to its inevitably aporetic tone, which in turn has determined the privileging of an actual encounter with authenticity, as in Plato's idea, the Neoplatonist's poetic *stantia* ("room"), or the infinite circumnavigation of a tantalizing authenticity described in Heidegger's thought. If it is true that authenticity and inauthenticity are irreconcilable opposites, it is also true that they have something in common. This something is potentiality, out of which authenticity and inauthenticity are both in fact born. The potentiality of inauthenticity is that of becoming authenticity; the potentiality of authenticity is to pass into inauthenticity. As Agamben argues, drawing on Aristotle, potentiality is the capacity to be and the capacity not-to-be. It is the simultaneous taking place of two opposite modes of existence within the context of a further mode of existence which is neither actuality nor negativity. Potentiality is the threshold at which authenticity and inauthenticity become indistinguishable and ultimately irrelevant as an ontological paradigm of subjectivity.

Potentiality, or the possibility of going beyond the fracture of the self, is a central theme in Heidegger's work too. It is perhaps in Heidegger that one finds the first attempt to rethink inauthenticity as not necessarily negative, but rather as an unavoidable aspect of authenticity. The analysis of factuality conducted by Heidegger goes some way toward articulating a being in which authenticity and inauthenticity are not merely irreducible opposites. By contrast, they co-exist and fuse as the characteristic and original principle of being. It is in this sense that the notion of "Ereignis" ("the event") found in the later works of Heidegger can be understood. But is it possible to articulate the mode of potentiality, to give it, in other words, a visibility and tangibility that will rescue it from the intractable sense of remoteness and opaqueness so characteristic of Heidegger's thought? More importantly, is it possible to describe a new ontology based on potentiality as the new habitus of the coming subject? Can we, as humans, inhabit a space in which the founding structure of our society—the opposition between authenticity and inauthenticity—is removed? Are we ready to think of a social and political community whose principles are so radically new? The political aporia that confronts the world today invites us, indeed demands that we think differently and that we challenge the ways in which people come together to form a nation, a community, a state; ways which we have until now assumed to be inalienably human and natural.

The availability of potentiality depends on whether or not being accepts the simple fact of being-as-such. Being-as-such, Agamben argues, opens the way for a reappraisal of, for instance, subjectivity as singularity. In contrast to the subject divided and caught in a constant conflict between its irreconcilable authenticity and inauthenticity, singularity deactivates this opposition. To live in singularity also means to rethink space and time, not in their actuality as constantly dynamic and restless vectors intent on reaching a destination, but as anamnesic events: "The movement Plato describes as erotic anamnesis ("l'anamnesi erotica")," writes Agamben in *The Coming Community*, "is the movement that transports the object not toward another thing or another place, but toward its own taking-place" (*The Coming Community* 2; "è quello che trasporta l'oggetto non verso un'altra cosa o un altro luogo, ma verso il suo stesso aver-luogo"; *La comunità* 4). It is in this "own taking-place" that, according to Agamben, "humankind's original home" can be found.

In "The Carcass of Time," Brian Dillon reads this "original home" not as "a process ["génesis"] or a movement ["kinesis"]." He adds that this zone is not correlated with a measurable space of time. "The time of pleasurable plenitude," continues Dillon, "which Agamben discovers in Aristotle is decidedly not, however, that extra-temporal realm which enables Augustine, in *The Confessions*, to step outside of the abstract flow of time: it is not, in other words, the eternal" (Dillon 142). This time is rather the pure "now," the *interim*, the atemporal *cairos* Aristotle speaks of. It is ultimately pleasure. Pleasure, as Aristotle defines it in Book X of the *Ethics* (all manuscripts by Aristotle were arranged by editors after Aristotle's death in 322 BC), is not a process, "that is, it does not acquire meaning or value in terms of its completeness, but is a certain experience of the present: it is not dependent upon a projected future point at which it will become *whole*" (Dillon 142). Aristotle writes: "The act of seeing is regarded as complete at any moment of its duration, because it does not lack anything that, realized later, will perfect its specific quality. Now pleasure also seems to be of this nature, because it is a sort of whole, i.e., at no moment in time can one fasten upon a pleasure the prolongation of which will enable its specific quality to be perfected. For this reason pleasure is not a process because every process is in time, and has an end (i.e., the process of building), and is complete when it has accomplished its object. Thus it is complete either in the whole of the time that it takes or at the instant of reaching its end" (Aristotle 318). We might be tempted to say that singularity is that subjectivity which finds the pleasure of its own being, and that individuality which finds it possible to break free from the constraints of authenticity and inauthenticity in the experience of potentiality. Clearly this is a subjectivity that has discarded any conditions of integration as the foundational principles of the individual's belonging to the community. In the singular subjectivity, or in singularity, the notion of belonging itself becomes the new ontology of the self and regulates the interaction between the self and the community. In a community made up of singularities, singularity experiences itself as such and not as a series of superimposed categories such as language, race, religion, politics, and social class. What we come to meet is a subject that redefines its ontological status through the tangible experience of a life in which authenticity and inauthenticity have disappeared by way of melting into one another. Potentiality is finally able to exist as a mode of living, as a workable ontology at the intense moment of the encounter between authenticity and inauthenticity. But for this to happen, the encounter between authenticity and inauthenticity must be predicated upon their absolute con-fusion, and upon a process of sedimentation and pollination that, instead of decreeing the triumph of one or the other, is simply able to articulate its state of suchness. Thus, in singularity, it no longer makes sense to talk about the potentiality of authenticity and the potentiality of inauthenticity. It can only make sense to talk about potentiality itself. Potentiality is the cause of singularity, and singularity is the concrete, visible, and speakable existence of potentiality.

Singularity, or life as such, is informed by immanence and its primacy over transcendence. Following Deleuze, and departing from Augustine and Christian theology, Agamben has articulated an ontological space in which life as such is contrasted to the aporetic dynamic of subjectivity. Agamben's singularity, like Deleuze's singularity, questions the centrality of the *cogito* and attempts to replace it with life. It is in this way that the subject is able to disentangle itself from the need to assert its individual belonging and happiness by conforming to the community's conditions. In doing so, the subject can exist as a singularity among other singularities under the principle of life. The shift from "I and the others" to "I in life with the others" is also the shift from a temporality directed outward—be it toward a re-union with God or the more secular aspiration toward authenticity and acceptance—to an inward temporality where the search for and the epiphany of being is conducted by "one alone into one." Thus we return to exile, which is now "sweet," "light," and "blissful" because it is the recognition, indeed the habitus, of life as such, of singularity and potentiality. But exactly what kind of community can this be? Can we really conceive of a multisingular community based on and regulated by the original and simple fact of belonging to life?

Returning

The flight of one into one, the Plotinian steering of subjectivity toward a purity uncontaminated by other living presences, is also the ultimate attempt to reconnect with the Platonic idea of subjectivity (as if in philosophical exile the subject could be—*essere*—its own idea). For Plotinus, the production of philosophical thought is also the cipher of the conjunction of "to be" and "being," and the moment at which "being" gives way to "to be," to the experience of the "idea" of subjectivity as life. The Plotinian exile is, therefore, a going home, a return journey from "being with others" to "being with oneself." It is a process that rewinds the disclosure of subjectivity and places subjectivity back in the space of concealment. Seen through the lens of Heidegger's philosophy, the experience of Plotinian exile equates with the experience of closure, and with a subjectivity that turns its back on the will to risk exposure and thrownness. Plotinus's exile is a retreat; but is it a retreat enacted in wisdom and enlightenment (as described in the *Enneads*), or a retreat enacted by fear and escapism?

A return to the place of origin is never simply a return. On his return to Ithaca, Odysseus was recognized only by his faithful dog and his old nurse. Everyone else, including his wife, saw him as a stranger, as a person that had never been "there." Going back means continuing the journey forward, and going back home is always a journey abroad (as myriads of migrants have experienced on their return). The foreignness of those who return is compounded by those traits they still share with the category of "home," including people, food, light, language. And yet their language is different, the people have changed. Being the same and yet different is a mark unlikely to be forgotten and forgiven, not only by others but also, and more importantly, by the very individuals who return. There is no going home, simply because there is no home. Even the Platonic idea and the utopian notion of purity and origin are false, and yet they remain powerful, determining human behavior and existence in the world.

Traveling languages

"Origin," "purity," and "home" are models and ideas that are cherished and nourished because they offer guidance and orientation. They are thought of as the usual, the familiar. As a consequence, they not only provide a sense of comfort, but also of security—the security of an identity. They are treasured because they often come to rescue us in our routine struggle against impurity, inauthenticity, and strangeness. They offer orientation and an anchorage, providing the very sense of being. Yet they are mere fabrications, useful tools to fight a battle that perhaps should not be fought at all. Are we ever really at home? The experience of philosophical and literary exile appears to be a convincing example of home's inherent absence, or, at least, home's inherent ambiguity. Blanchot once wrote that "existence is an exile in the fullest sense: we are not there, we are elsewhere, and we will never stop being there" (*The Work of Fire* 9; "existence est un exil au sens le plus fort: nous n'y sommes pas, nous y sommes ailleurs et jamais nous ne cesserons d'y être"; *La Part du feu* 17).

If one believes Plotinus, poets and philosophers are simultaneously at home and abroad; physically at home and mentally abroad. They crave a mental reunion with a zone which is foreign to their familiar day-to-day-life, as if body and mind were two separate and distinct things. It is in this sense that their flight is also a flight from the body and from the physicality of their being in the world. In approaching the ideal world of the mind they also suspend their existence as living beings, and their bodies gradually retreat into oblivion, into the uncertain space of liminality. But oblivion, as we shall see when discussing Blanchot's and Caproni's work in chapter 4, might well be invisibility and liminality, but it is certainly not inexistence. It is indeed in oblivion that the traits and the characteristics of that which has been banned attain a higher degree of intensity and presence.

What is language like in philosophical and literary exile? We would be mistaken to think that the language of solitude, the language of those who take flight into their singularity, equates with the idea of language, with pure language. It is rather a language that attempts a return to pure language (home) by retracing the footsteps of its departure from home. It does not matter which trajectories it follows on its return journey. Indeed, these routes might be different from those taken in the past, and yet memories of departure, of leaving, will invariably inform the return. This is a strange journey which changes everything and yet simultaneously preserves everything.

The journey I am writing about now must be understood as the sum of the journey forward, from pure language to language, and the journey backward, from language to pure language, and must be seen as the result of a lengthy process of relation, of exchanges, and of borrowing. The most obvious relations are those between pure language and language and among pure language, language, and the product generated by this relation; that is, potential language. A language that travels is always made of many languages since a language that *really* travels is always an open language, porous, inclusive, and willing to disappear into another language, from within which its very own singularity will resurface more fully. This is the case of translation, but also of the philosophical and literary language of exile. This traveling, as well as the process of translation, can be understood better if one keeps in mind Heidegger's understanding of translation as not so much a substitution of a word for another word (a replacement), as a transferral of a word, and a language, into another language. Transferring—from the Latin *transferre*—means to take something from one place to another place. This has commonly been thought of as a mere act of substitution, in the process of which one language disappears to give place to another language (the latter replacing the former, literally annulling the former). Transferring, in contrast, is a process that brings about the simultaneous coexistence of two languages. One language enters another, is transferred into it, and, in doing so, replenishes both itself and the host language. What is less clear, though, is why this process of fusion—some might term it *confusion*—ought to be replenishing and empowering. Would not the superimposition of two languages ultimately result in unintelligibility?

One thinks immediately of certain poetic experimentations of the avant-garde movements, in which different texts are superimposed on one another, and where a potentially readable text (written in a familiar language) is rendered illegible by scrawl (a potentially readable text written in a foreign, strange idiom). I am thinking here of the visual poetry of the 1970s, especially of Vincenzo Accame's "Nuova scrittura" (c 1975; "New Writing"; Figure 2). Today we are apt to treat these poetic experimentations as significant yet ephemeral provocations. We interpret them as necessary challenges mounted against the cultural establishment in order to open up new avenues, new ways of thinking and writing, alternative poetic modes. They are all this and perhaps no more; clever specimens of protest against a whole society and its canons. And yet—perhaps in spite of themselves—they also make us think of something else, of the clarity that might arise from opacity or, even more simply, of an ontological condition which is inextricably linked with potentiality.

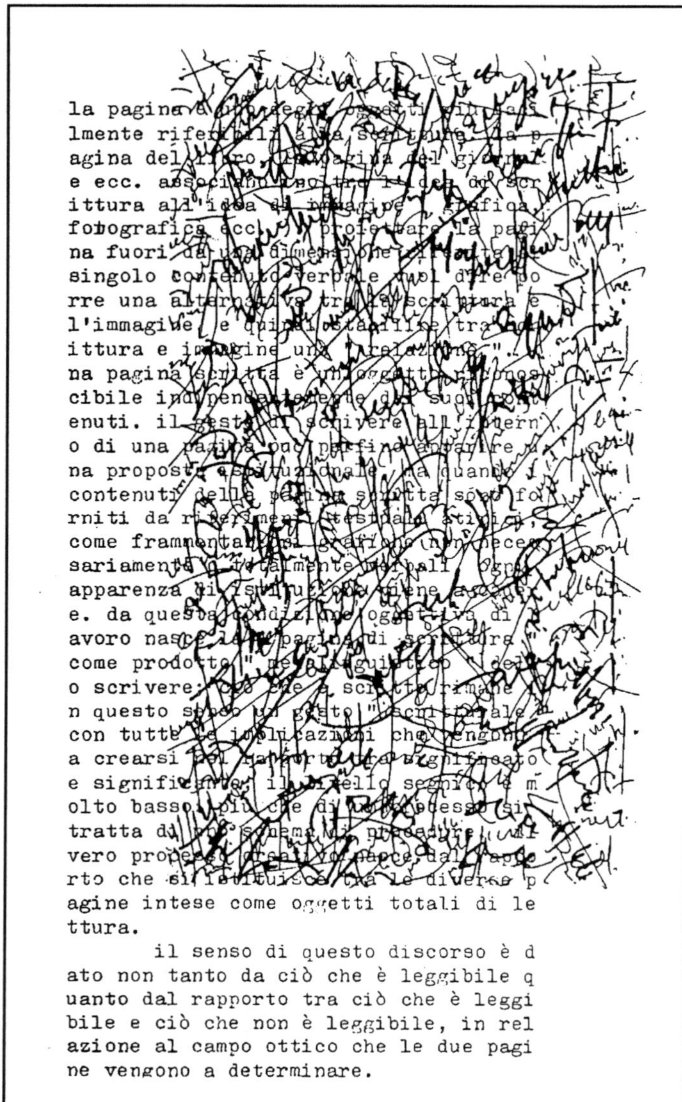

Figure 2. Vincenzo Accame, "Nuova scrittura"

They are clearly jumbled-up texts, gratuitous games apparently intent on acts of pure vandalism and sabotage against the known (usual) language upon which mindless and undecipherable scribbles (a potential foreign tongue) are inscribed. Though they might appear to be innocent tricks, or perverse exercises, or even useless maps, they may also more perfidiously be conceived to disorient, distract, and frustrate the reader who is looking for points of orientation. What they principally lack is precision, order, clarity, identity; all of those categories so essential to our sense of security and comfort. These texts are certainly not closed or finished. They are suspended instead in an uncertain, ambiguous space which demands a resolution, an act of faith and courage, a productive leap that will turn them once and for all into clear, precise, and orderly texts.

Disorder and chaos are here the products of a conscious collage of two potentially clear and orderly idioms, and unintelligibility is the result of a peculiar combination of the intelligible. It is the superimposition of sayability that gives rise to the potential and to its very power to restore orientation and familiarity, but also to further suspend sayability in the zone of waiting and oblivion. The scribble can be removed, erased from the face of the familiar, but the familiar can also be removed to focus more clearly on the unknown. We must be mindful of the fact that the act of superimposition does not only occlude what is already known; it also precludes the full and unimpeded visibility of the unknown. The scribble defaces what lies underneath it (making it unreadable) but, by the same token, the writing underneath alters the perception of the scribble. The act of superimposition, because of its very nature of uncategorical and non-normative inclusion, introduces another language that speaks the unspeakable and that communicates the very negativity of language. It is not that translation and exile leave us without language, or identity, or clarity, or orientation. Rather, they leave us with a further language that can say what the other two cannot, that can expose and communicate their limitations.

In contrast to the poetic experiments of twentieth-century avant-garde movements, the relational language of exile and translation is the result of an uncategorical and non-normative process of combination. It might begin with the conscious desire to suspend or even to blur an existing textuality by writing on it a foreign language (mere scribble, or nonsensical sentences), and yet it ends up not as a programmatic manifesto or spectacular gesture of non-conformity and defiance but as a murmur of self-reflective disorientation, ambivalence, and uncertainty through which intense shaft of lights might appear from time to time. This language is uncategorical because it has no premeditated purpose apart from that of moving deep inside the relation that sustains it. The results of such non-normative movement vary greatly and can never be predicted, either polemically or programmatically. It is because of this that exile might be conceived of as the very *stuff* of productivity and the very core of thinking.

The exile (the translator among them) is first of all one who transfers. The task of transferring is not that of substituting one language with another language, one culture with another culture or one identity with another identity, but that of transferring one language into another language, one culture into another culture, and one identity into another identity. There is no sense in replacing because nothing can be replaced. Everything will remain, yet will be changed in its relation with the other. But how is it possible to write over a given language and subjectivity, a given identity, with a language that is not yet known? Is it enough to scribble at will and to cover the known with seemingly inane signs? Here the difference between the translator and the exile begins to emerge more vividly. While the translator moves from the foreign to the known, the exile moves from the known to the foreign. They engage with exactly opposite transferal vectors. Yet the process is similar; they both expose, open, break, and reduce to rubble what appeared to be complete and finished, and from the rubble they start rebuilding something which will nonetheless never again be complete. Translators inscribe their language on another language. In doing so, they make language "catch fire" at the instant in which language exposes its limitations but also its great power as absolute guardian of the non-linguistic. In the process of exile, by contrast, it is language that gradually undoes itself by softening its norms, those great pretensions of grandeur and omnipotence, as it abandons the clamors of the familiar. Language's securities gradually dissipate in the presence of the unknown. Now, let us remain for a moment in the space of poetic and philosophical exile.

Astonishment

The language of poetic exile does to itself exactly what it did as it departed from the origin. In order to be *language*, language had to write itself over "pure language." As the subject embarks on the process of self-exile from the world, language must retrace its trajectory backward, first by rewinding itself, by unlearning itself. There is no other way, since the other option, the writing of pure language over language, is impossible. Language's going back to its alleged purity can never be completed (see chapter 1), and its movement is always destined to remain underway, firmly located in the space of reverberating echoes. It is in this sense that the Plotinian flight of one into one is simultaneously erroneous and correct. One never flies into oneself but always into the memory of oneself, and always into the translation of oneself. The wholeness of the self is irredeemably broken by the opposition between a before and an after, but also rehabilitated as potential in the space of indistinction. The flight of the one is inevitably a flight into the relational and reciprocal zone of potentiality. If language constructs, it also deconstructs. Language constructs and deconstructs subjectivities, identities, and communities just as subjectivities, identities, and communities construct and deconstruct language. What is less clear, but potentially more significant, is how language speaks at the threshold of indistinguishability where construction and deconstruction cannot be told apart, and how subjectivities, identities, and communities operate as they come to this threshold.

The thresholds of translation and exile may appear identical but they are marked by something significantly different. Let us imagine two building sites. The first, the site of translation, will strike us as a ruin that needs restoration. The second site, exile, appears to be a new building, not quite finished, perhaps only temporarily left by the workers on a lunch-break or at the end of a working day. Work will presumably recommence on both buildings soon. Yet the opposite may also be true. Both could well be aborted projects, unfinished business. We observe them, and nothing moves; there is no sign of activity. But it is precisely because of their unfinished status, their ambiguity, that we are prompted to continue building them, imagining how they could be finished: the colour of a façade, the angle of a roof, the size of a window, every ornament and detail. Poets go into exile (in the Plotinian sense of the word) and into translation to enter more deeply, and to see more clearly, the productive processes of both subjectivity and language. This imagining, which is also the beginning of creativity, correlates with, and in fact is complemented by, a sense of astonishment in the face of what is taking place before one's eyes and in the language that lends tangibility to production.

In *What is Philosophy?*, Heidegger defines astonishment thus: "In astonishment ("im Erstaunen") we restrain ourselves ("être en arrêt"). We step back, as it were, from being ("Wir treten gleichsam zurück vor dem Seienden"), from the fact that it is as it is and not otherwise" (85). It is at once philosophically significant and poetic that Heidegger chose to define astonishment as an act of self-restraint, where restraint is the active refusal to accept that which is pre-arranged and pre-ordained, pre-packaged, arbitrarily complete. Heidegger invites us instead to break this artificial, un-philosophical, and un-poetical reading of life, to destroy it in order to pave the way, the path, to seeing and to saying it "otherwise" ("anders"). It is in this sense that "suspension" as we have articulated it so far must be understood (on this, see also Vattimo, *Essere* 121).

Suspension is not, therefore, an idle temporality devoid of *energeia* (intended here in the Aristotelian sense of actuality), but rather the opposite; the will, that is, to suspend our unproblematic acceptance of life, indeed to destroy it. It is no accident that in the same book, Heidegger speaks of destruction ("Destruktion") in a way that leaves no doubt about his understanding of the meaning of philosophizing, and which clarifies even further our current discussion. "Destruction," writes Heidegger, "does not mean destroying but dismantling, demolishing, putting to one side the merely historical assertions about the history of philosophy ("Destruktion bedeutet nicht Zerstören, sondern Abbauen, Abtragen und Auf-die-Seite-stellen"). Destruction means—to open our ears, to make ourselves free for what speaks to us in tradition as the Being of being ("Sein des Seienden"). By listening to this interpellation ("Indem wir auf diesen Zuspruch hören") we attain the correspondence" (*What is Philosophy?* 73; "die Entsprechung"; translation modified).

Most of modern production (the language of modernity) is predicated upon the notions of suspension and destruction, and upon the creative power of ambiguity and antinomy. Modernity is, in other words, concerned with and indeed informed by the notion of exile. Examples abound. Discussing the work of Charles Baudelaire in *Infancy and History*, Agamben claimed that: "In Baudelaire, a man expropriated from experience ("espropriato dell'esperienza") exposes himself to the force of shock. Poetry responds to the expropriation of experience by converting this expropriation into a reason for surviving and making the inexperiencible its normal condition ("facendo dell'inesperibile la sua condizione normale"). In this perspective, the search for the 'new' ('nuovo') does not appear as the search for a new object of experience; instead, it implies an eclipse and a suspension of experience" (*Infancy and History* 41; "implica al contrario, un'eclisse e una sospensione dell'esperienza"; *Infanzia e storia* 38). But what exactly does "a suspension of experience" mean, and more importantly, what kind of language and literature are "a language and a literature of suspension"?

It is worth reflecting further on Agamben's emphasis on the suspension of experience. In chapter 3 of *Infancy and History*, under the subheading "La poesia moderna e l'esperienza" ("Modern Poetry and Experience"), we read: "modern poetry from Baudelaire onwards is seen to be founded not on new experience, but on an unprecedented lack of experience ("una mancanza di esperienza senza precedenti"). Hence the boldness ("disinvoltura") with which Baudelaire can place shock at the centre of his artistic work. It is experience that best affords us protection from surprises ("protezione dalle sorprese"), and the production of shock always implies a gap ("falla") in experience. To experience something means divesting it of novelty ("novità"), neutralizing its shock potential" (41; "neutralizzare il suo potenziale di choc"; *Infanzia e storia* 37). The word "shock" occupies a central and commanding position in this important passage. It appears to be in close relation to "surprise," and opposed to experience. "Shock" is the "surprise" that upsets experience and relegates experience to the background, puts it out of sight, renders it useless and impracticable. It is not that experience disappears because of exposure to "shock." Rather, experience becomes devoid of meaning, empty, voiceless. It speaks no more, and with its silence comes the *nakedness* of the subject and, at least for Kafka (as Blanchot reminds us, quoting him), the beginning of writing: "Intrépide, *nu*, puissant, surprenant comme je ne le suis d'habitude que lorsque j'écris" (*La Part du feu* 24; "brave, *naked*, powerful, surprising as I am usually only when I write"; *The Work of Fire* 17; emphasis added). By nakedness I mean here the simple event of being devoid of experience, which in turn means being in that moment devoid of historiography, that abyss so vital to the thinking of Heidegger and Blanchot, the present-now (*Jetzt-Zeit*) to which Benjamin devotes so many pages and so much thought. In other words, by nakedness I mean a suspension of existence by virtue of which existence manifests itself as existence as such.

In his study entitled *On Nietzsche*, Bataille defines nakedness as the space of inaction or the suspension of action. He writes: "If I give up the viewpoint of action, my perfect nakedness is revealed to me" (xxvii). Two pages later he adds: "Art constitutes a minor free zone outside action, paying for its freedom by giving up the real world" (xxix). In Benjamin's *Arcades Project*, in the chapter on the *flâneur*, we read: "Truth becomes something living; it lives solely in the rhythm by which statement and counterstatement displace each other in order to think each other" (418). Living truth is nothing other, then, than naked truth; the truth that exists as it confronts the shock of its own existence. What is extraordinary about Benjamin's thought is its emphasis on life beyond the ordinary conception of life, and of existence beyond the common understanding of existence.

"Speaking more gently to things"

How does this relate to our discussion of poetic exile and its language? In a short essay discussing his translation of Céline's *Mort à credit*, first published in the literary journal *Il Verri* in the January-February issue of 1968, and re-published almost thirty years later in the collection of essays *La scatola nera* (*The Black Box*; 1996), Giorgio Caproni writes that translation has taught him to "to speak more gently to things" (my translation; "parler...plus doucement aux choses"; Caproni, *La scatola nera* 58). The significance of this statement is considerable, especially in the light of the central position given to the preposition *aux* ("to"), around which the meaning of the sentence revolves. Caproni claims that translation has enabled him to talk *to* things, and not *about* things. This form of speech, of writing, is not indirect, is not descriptive, or representational. It is rather an encounter and an intersection in language. Translation leads Caproni to a territory where "thingness," that is, both the subject of speech and its interlocutor and listener, are united by that language-event that does not speak *about*. In other words, the experience of being exposed to the presence of the non-linguistic does not happen *through* language but *in* language. Language is therefore no longer a means but more precisely, and certainly more poignantly, the end and the very locus of shared life. The "gentle speaking to things" is that climactic moment at which the subject arrives at its maximal unconcealment and openness, pouring itself out in language, simultaneously uttering its whole vulnerability by willingly sharing it with the life around it. And life responds to these bouts of utter exposure (of destruction) through its consent to listen and its devoted attention. This is the language of Ponge and Pascoli and of those poets and writers for whom language becomes life.

It is a paradox and also an irony that the recognition of language as life is confined to poetry and madness, to those "anarchic" experiences which are treated either with suspicion, indifference, and disdain or, in a contrary manner, with unconsidered and often incongruous enthusiasm. It is doubly puzzling that life must renounce its juridical status to regain its fullness. But this is precisely what Caproni claims as a result of his reflections on translation. He can speak "more gently to things" because he has exposed himself to the experience of linguistic exile. And translation is the door to linguistic exile. The mistake that is often made when speaking about translation—and to a certain extent about the notion of exile, too—is that translating consigns the translator to another language and culture. In translating, the translator, who already knows well—or reasonably well—the language and the culture that he translates from, will gain an even better and deeper knowledge of the other language and culture. What is less often discussed is that in translating, which means continually exiting and re-entering one's own language and culture, the translator gains a deeper understanding of his own language and culture and of his own life. The translator, can, as in the case of Caproni, experience language as life.

In taking itself beyond its known boundaries, the self comes to know itself better. It is in this sense that departing, as we shall see, never implies a return to the same but rather a discovery of new and unfamiliar territories which are nonetheless already inside the self. This also means that *leaving* can be the best way to stay in one's own company, and the most precious gift that one can make to oneself. If it is true, as Adriana Cavarero argues in *Tu che mi guardi, tu che mi racconti* (1997; *Relating Narratives*, 2000), that auto/biographical stories catch the essence of the unique identity of a person through the necessary process of relation with another who tells or listens to the stories, then it is also true that translation, the relational narrative *par excellence*, is another essential path to discovery. It was in translating René Char that Caproni realized that: "The literature and the poetry-one-already-knew no longer offer any help to the reader, who, caught up from head to toe in those *bouts d'existence incorruptible* that are the *poèmes*, is left entirely alone to feel himself invested with a power—an inner freedom: a vital energy and moral courage—that for a moment he thinks he receives femininely from the outside, until he realizes that this richness was already in him, slumbering but present, as if the poet had done nothing other than to *reawaken* it, not *inventing*, but *discovering*; and so exciting an impulse, more than of admiration, of gratitude" (trans. Joseph Falsone; "La letteratura e la poesia-che-si-sapeva-già non porgono più alcun soccorso al lettore, e questi, coinvolto da capo a piedi in quei *bouts d'existence incorruptible* che sono i *poèmes*, rimane perfettamente solo a sentirsi investito d'un potere—d'un interiore libertà: d'uno slancio vitale e d'un coraggio morale—che per un istante egli crede di ricevere femminilmente dall'esterno, mentre poi s'accorge che tale ricchezza era già in lui, sonnecchiante ma presente, come se il poeta altro non avesse fatto che *risvegliarla*, non *inventando*, ma *scoprendo*; e quindi suscitando un moto, più che d'ammirazione, di gratitudine"; *La scatola nera* 61)

We find in this passage many of the things discussed so far. And yet, these "things" are illuminated by a clarity and precision that demand attention. Translation is not only an exile from the usual (from "the literature and the poetry-one-already-knew"), it is also an exile into the self where the consent to listen, indeed the consent to receive the other as part of the self, awakens an ethical courage and a passion living dormant, neglected, and uncertain. The richness of the self can be found in the dialectic relation with the other, and this richness is not an invention, a creation from nothing. It is rather a discovery which is nothing other than the result of a process of disorientation and defamiliarization. Caproni could not be more explicit when, quoting from Char, he stresses that "Those who invent, by contrast to those who discover, do not add to things, they only endow beings with masks" (my translation; "Celui qui invente, au contraire de celui qui découvre, n'ajoute aux choses, n'apporte aux êtres que des masques"; *La scatola nera*). The central argument is that the poet comes to understand what he believes is the real essence of art through translation. The notion that nothing is actually created, and that artistic creation is a process of discovery, casts new light on the idea of originality and purity, and also on the relation between the original and the translation. A redefinition of artistic exile, but also of migration, must commence from this premise.

"Hermit in Paris"

In 1964 Italo Calvino married Esther Judith Singer and took up residence in Paris. From that year until 1980, Calvino commuted more or less regularly between France and Italy, and yet for about sixteen years his home was Paris; a home that for Calvino also signified poetic exile. In one of the few autobiographical pieces about those years, the essay "Eremita a Parigi" (1974; *Hermit in Paris*, 2003), Calvino writes: "I often say, and I have said it so often that I have now become a bit bored with it, that in Paris I have my country home ("la mia casa di campagna"), in the sense that as a writer I can conduct part of my activity in solitude, it does not matter where, in a house isolated in the midst of the country-side, or on an island, and this country house of mine is right in the middle of Paris. In this way, while the part of my life that is connected with my work ("la vita di relazione connessa col mio lavoro") takes place entirely in Italy, I come here when I can or have to be on my own ("quando posso o devo stare da solo"), something that is easier for me to do in Paris" (*Hermit in Paris* 169; *Eremita a Parigi* 9). A clear analogy would be James Joyce's self-exile from Ireland in order to create the bold experimental prose of *Ulysses* and *Finnegans Wake*. This is the poetic and philosophical exile that, as we saw when discussing Plotinus, writers and philosophers impose on themselves to escape the distraction of day-to-day life in order to concentrate on a search whose ultimate goal is to present them with an image, a form, or just a glimpse or a feeling of what they know exists but remains invisible, missing, out of reach. The author must abandon life in the community, those distractions such as business, marriage, family, and daily chores, to prepare, facilitate, and arrange an encounter with the ever present unknown and unfamiliar, whatever this might be: God, the unconscious, the Platonic ideas, love, imagination, death, or pure and unfettered nothingness. But why is it that in the Western literary and philosophical tradition the search for the ultimate truth, or even for the ultimate negation of universal truths, must take place in isolation, in the flight of one into oneself?

As Calvino reflects on the reason why he has not written about Paris, he muses that: "Maybe to write about Paris I ought to leave, to distance myself from it ("dovrei staccarmene, esserne lontano"), if it is true that all writing starts out from a lack or an absence" (*Hermit in Paris* 167; "se è vero che si scrive sempre partendo da una mancanza, da un'assenza"; *Eremita a Parigi* 5). What is of interest in this passage, especially for the present discussion, is Calvino's final hypothesis that all writing "starts out from a lack or an absence." If we now combine the first and the second quotation from "Hermit in Paris" we find that Calvino says two things. He says that the desire, the will, and the impulse to write is generated from a sense of loss and that this writing about the loss must be attended by the imposition of a further loss. The latter is the abandonment of the quotidian self. It literally means closing the door to life with others in order to enter the rooms of a life where the only relations are those played out within the isolated self.

Calvino closes the door. And yet, this door (which Kafka allegorized so powerfully in "Before the Law"), ought to be left open at all times, regardless of whether we are on this or that side of it, and whether we are invited or forbidden to pass through it. And yet, the Western tradition has kept on closing and opening the door. Only from time to time, as this book attempts to argue, has the door been left open. It is indeed possible that the Western literary and philosophical tradition, starting from Plato, is based on a fundamental mistake, or perhaps on a simple and yet damaging misunderstanding. The loss upon which the production of language and thought is predicated is both the cause and the result of this very production and its inherent exclusiveness and closure. It is by closing the door of existence that the loss is inevitably and artificially created. By assuming that what is lost must be looked for in exile, the principle that there would not be an absence without exile must also be accepted. As a matter of fact, exile is not a means to an end, it is rather the inevitable and inescapable condition of historical and cultural existence. By artificially producing loss, we merely reproduce what we already are and as such we do not "add" anything, in the sense that Char gives to the notion of adding; we only mask what is already there. If it is true that creation is not invention but discovery, the door of existence must be left open. This is the great challenge for contemporary thought. The writing and language on and of the threshold may initiate an alternative articulation of experience as well as ontology.

But there is something else in Calvino's autobiographical essay that is worth noting. As a caveat to his hypothesis that "all writing starts out from a lack" and that to write about Paris he would need to leave it, Calvino adds what seems to be the opposite course of action: "Or else be more inside it ("Oppure esserci più dentro"), but for that I would need to have lived there from when I was young, if it is true that it is the first years of our existence ("gli scenari dei primi anni della nostra vita"), not the places of our maturity, that shape the world of our imagination ("che danno forma al nostro mondo immaginario"). Or rather: a place has to become an inner landscape ("bisogna che un luogo diventi un paesaggio interiore") for the imagination to start to inhabit that place, to turn it into its theatre" (*Hermit in Paris* 167; *Eremita a Parigi* 5). Once again Calvino articulates his thought on the premise of an exclusion, and of a life enclosed in what appear to be sealed compartments. So it is infancy that informs the imagination, as opposed, let us say, to a dialectic and relational process between the past and the present. The door of existence remains shut. And yet, what is interesting is that Calvino, just a few lines later, refers to a theater, that is, a performative place in which imagination commences its own staging.

The image and the notion of a performative act are of considerable significance in the process of making memory. Indeed, memory is a performance, a theater where subjectivity—but also the collective—is allowed to combine and configure its own disjointed temporalities and identities, and where a readable and meaningful shape might be distinguished among the many, often unrelated lines of life. Autobiography and biography are obvious examples of the theatralization of memory. However, it is not only the acting that is relevant in this context. The reception is also essential. For Calvino the spectator is first and foremost the same as the subject on stage. This means that the performance is enacted for the benefit of the solitary figure who observes the theater of the imagination inside the private "home" of exile. By closing the door, the subject will not be able to see the effects that the theatralization of memory has on other potential spectators and, in turn, will not be exposed to their return gaze. By contrast, it is the reflection of our own story in the eyes of the other, this vital confrontation, that enables our story to go forward on its path towards discovery. In fact, it is not really the theatralization of memory that makes memory, and autobiography is not the making of memories. Autobiography is simply reminiscence, remembering. The making of memory, its production, takes place when reminiscence moves out of its past to meet its own image in the becoming present.

Remembering forward

In *Material Thinking* (2004), Paul Carter asks an important question: "What would it be like, not to remember *backwards*, towards the recovery of a lost object, but *forwards* toward its transformation and re-invention?" (126). The context in which the question is asked, that of migrant memories, makes Carter's ensuing reflection of considerable significance for the present discussion on exile. Paul Carter is an artist and theorist based in Melbourne, Australia. A significant part of his work is devoted to discussing migratory experiences and the ways in which they shape the psychology of exile. Carter portrays "the migrant as a philosophical skeptic, painfully making himself anew at that place" (126).

Carter's "anti-fictional" (his own definition) novel, *Baroque Memories* (1994), presents two emblematic examples of migratory experiences: one is personified by Doctor Duende, who is "always looking forwards" (127) and the other by his daughter Nostalgia, who looks backward. The doctor believes that living in a new country means to remove signs of nostalgia from the present, which in his case means to accept that the present hides or, perhaps better, *guards* nothing—so that the white façade opposite his house "was not a breast. It was not his white-haired grandfather. It was not a photograph. There was nothing behind its luminous presence" (128). Nostalgia, however, remarks to her father that the pattern of her life is "always to be out of step with my surroundings. Always to be gathering fragments of the past and putting them in order in another country. Always to be constructing memories as if I had no past, as if memory was always another country" (127). While Nostalgia believes that the past must be re-assembled in the absence of the past (in the present of the past), Duende defines the present as a luminous presence without depth, that is, as present as such. What Nostalgia means, of course, is that the past must be recreated, reconstructed from scratch, filling its irreparable absence with bits and pieces which have remained, scattered and yet jealously guarded by an overwhelming sense of longing and loss. Nostalgia knows that the past is gone and cannot come back. It can only be, as Carter sums up elegantly, "re-membered." To "re-member" must be understood here in its literal sense of re-constituting but not so much, as Carter appears to believe, through invention as through addition. The distinction between invention and addition is an essential one, and needs to be discussed further.

Invention and addition

It is Duende who provides, perhaps implicitly, the first key to unlocking the difference between invention and addition. He believes that the present glows, that it is luminous. And yet this luminosity is a luminosity as such; it does not conceal and, consequently, does not reveal. The present is just the present, nothing else. This belief, according to Duende, is the only cure for a migrant's anxieties and nostalgia. To accept this would not only imply resigning oneself to the fact that the past is irretrievable, but also discarding those fragments of the past through which memory remembers. In other words, it would mean the end of narration and experience. Clearly, this is not what Duende (and Carter) means. The luminous façade becomes a kind of *tabula rasa* onto which what is inscribed is not so much the past as the productive relation between the splintered past, through memory, and the luminous presence of the present. It is this relation that makes memory. It is clear that Carter's solution to the opposition between forwardness and backwardness is in the end to combine them when, in *Material Thinking*, he writes that: "She [Nostalgia], too, has faith that the Baroque aesthetic can endow the façade with a new meaning, evolving at that place" (128) and, quoting Husserl, that "'the active recollection of what is past'—with the emphasis on *active*—involves an activity of concurrent actual production" (136).

According to Carter, the Baroque is that which "grows more superficial, more irrational, more mimetic. Its winding tendrils—of dogma as well as design—show themselves capable of incorporating the most heterogeneous forms and beliefs. Promiscuous cross-fertilisation and miscegenation replace tradition and influence as the means of generating new forms" (*Material Thinking* 127). It is on this Baroque surface, so supple and porous, so inclusive and "inviting," that the migratory experience engraves its reminiscence. But while we have seen what this reminiscence is made of (that is: memory and the present, a Baroque present), we have not reflected enough on how it comes to take on form and language, and whether it is, in fact, a process of invention or addition. It might, of course, be either invention or addition. But while invention prefigures the solitary and exclusive labor of the subject enclosed in its protective exilic space, addition presumes a process of relation and openness, whose results and outcomes are the combinations of a comparison between the presence of the present (the Baroque façade to which Carter refers) and the absence of the present (the memories of the past). Invention ends, in other words, by masking; by covering the surface of the present with a set of superimposed narratives that have nothing or little in common with the present. It is no surprise, then, that Calvino says of Paris that "it was an already known image that I recognized ("era un'immagine già nota che riconoscevo"), an image to which I could add nothing (*Hermit in Paris* 167; "un'immagine a cui io non potevo aggiungere nulla"; *Eremita a Parigi* 6). The Paris Calvino saw was the Paris that he already knew through books, and that had already left a strong and almost ineradicable mark on his imagination. The present Paris washed away in the Paris of Calvino's imagination and reminiscences, as if his eyes could only see the absence of the present but not the presence of the present. Calvino could only write about Paris by transforming it, by changing and reinventing it. Addition, on the other hand, keeps the presence of the present in full view, and adds to it the fragments and the rubble that memory has transported to the present from the past. The presence of the present becomes, in this way, a surface to write on and yet, as the surface of writing, it enters and belongs to the text.

Once again, translation offers an instructive metaphor for and a useful example of this form of textuality. Imagine the surface, the presence of the present, as the language and the culture into which one translates—the known and the familiar, the accepted, the surface without depth—and the language and culture that one translates from as fragments that are added to that surface. All of a sudden, we are looking at something new and unknown, and because of this we start learning again, and start discovering and exploring again. It is perhaps in this sense that true creation is not really invention but addition.

Choices?

Exile is a complex experience because of its inherent multifariousness. It takes many different forms. For example, as Sophia McClennen writes in *The Dialectics of Exile* (2004), exile can be differentiated by choice: "'Exile,' 'diaspora,' and 'refugee' are generally considered to be terms related to forced dislocations, whereas *immigrant* and *emigrant* describe a person who *migrates*, *immigrates*, or *emigrates* by choice" (15). But what exactly do we mean by *choice*? Is it a political, ethical, or economic choice?

My discussion thus far has focused on creative and poetic choices, but also on the implications that these choices might have for a broader understanding and reevaluation of exile in some of its other forms. A person or a group of people decide to leave their country of origin because they are disaffected with the politics and the economy of their situation or because they believe that their country is ethically and morally corrupt. But their decision to leave and their actual departure demonstrate, first, that they have the means to turn their will into practical action, and second that they have the freedom to do so. The ability to translate choice into practice depends not only on the individual or communal will but also on a series of circumstantial determinants. It is indeed possible that a person might wish to leave but cannot because of lack of means or because permission to leave is denied. Exile can be sought, can be intensely and profoundly desired and yet may remain impossible, unachievable. If it is true that exile is characterized by the impossibility of returning, it might be correct to say that it could also be marked by the impossibility of departing. There are many examples of people exiled in their own country, perhaps away from their villages or towns or cities yet still within the borders of their nation, unable to escape the tyranny of their jailers. Is this more or less an exile than other forms of exile? Is the loss of freedom compounded by the presence of the familiar? This is not only imprisonment but also, as it was known in Italy during the Fascist period, *il confino*. It is, in other words, marginalization, living at the borders of one's own life, time, and space. Here the present is also the past and vice-versa. Its presence is before the eye, and yet it remains out of reach, painfully potential. The impossibility of leaving may be more disabling than the impossibility of returning, in that loss, in the former instance, is a double loss: not only is the past missing, the present too is void. Is this the *destiempo* ("being outside of time") that McClennen speaks of when, articulating Józef Wittlin's thoughts on exile, she argues that: "In Spanish, there exists a word for describing an exile, the word *destierro*, a man deprived of his land. I take the liberty to forge one more definition, *destiempo*, a man who has been deprived of his time. That means deprived of the time which now passes in his country. The time of his exile is different. Or rather, the exile lives in two different times simultaneously, in the present and in the past. Wittlin suggests that the exile lives in the present of his country of exile and in the past of his native land. The exile is *exiled* from the present time of his native land. Such a condition heightens the exile's remembrance of the past and creates a great nostalgia. But living in the past of your native land and in the present of your adoptive residence is not quite the same as living *destiempo*, which would literally mean outside of time" (58). What is of interest for the present discussion is not so much the simultaneity of different temporalities in relation to the experience of exile—something that we have already discussed at length—as the notion of being outside time. Forced relegation to the extreme borders and peripheries of one's own land, *il confino*, plunges the subject not so much into an experience devoid of time as into an experience in which time is suspended. What happens here is not temporal simultaneity, but waiting for that which is already there yet forbidden.

There is another kind of exile whose processes are rather different from those described above. This is the physical and spatial exile of those who decide to leave their country of birth. They may leave for different reasons and under different circumstances: to look for a better future, for intellectual or cultural motives, out of pure boredom, propelled by a sense of adventure, for work-related purposes or to follow a loved one. What unites these very disparate forms of exile is the free choice to leave; what separates them from the mental poetic exile is the actual physical journey. Whereas the poetic exile implies the necessary unlearning of one's language and one's subjectivity—this unlearning is indeed the unavoidable condition through which another language and another subjectivity can be produced—the self-chosen exile is unconditional. It might originate from the desire to shed a given skin, and yet this divestment is not required, and it is definitely not an obligatory threshold that must be crossed. The ritualistic passage from one place to another is provided instead by the actual journey in time and space. The longer the journey, both in time and space, the more tangible and extraordinarily vivid is the experience of exile. It is not by accident that in today's globalized society, in which mobility, space, and time have been radically transformed, the notion of self-imposed exile is more porous and considerably less perceptible. Indeed, it is interesting to reflect that in the Western world the notion of self-imposed exile equates increasingly with the notion of poetic exile, including various forms of spiritual flight of "one alone into one." It is also true that when talking about the experience of self-imposed exile, the twentieth century made use of other analytical categories such as migration. But is not migration an experience of exile? Is not migration an experience of separation, banishment, spatial, and temporal barriers? If exile implies the suspension of return, either as a self-imposed desire to cut oneself off from the usual, or as the practical impossibility of going back, then migration is exile.

There is no doubt that exile is informed by social and class determinants. A migrant peasant and worker will live migration much more as a form of exile than, let us say, a professional for whom the return home—the going back in space—is not an insurmountable financial barrier. While the principle stating that the further one travels the more one is in exile provides a clearer understanding of the exilic feelings experienced by migrant workers in the 1950s, it has lost currency in the contemporary Western world, which perceives itself to be globalized and barrier-free. But if it is true, as we have argued so far, that returning to the same is impossible and that any form of departure from the origin is also and inevitably a form of exile—a condition that, by its very nature, defies the notion of homecoming—any movement in space and time, regardless of its duration, is then an entrance into exile. Every form of leaving—be it the daily routine of the worker (catching the bus or the train, driving the car to work); that of the busy professional hopping on airplanes to attend meetings or conduct business in other cities; the pleasure of going to the movies and theaters or the necessary trips to the supermarket and the corner shop; even indeed minimal movements within the house, from room to room—all automatically imply a return, the backward repetition of that very movement. It is precisely the extent and the degree of automatism connected with the expectation of return, of repetition, that distinguishes the many forms that an act of leaving may take. Furthermore, it is not the origin, the point of departure, that engenders repetition—that is, the desire to return—but rather the destination. Our desire is always that of returning to the origin. But, precisely because the origin has increasingly become porous and blurred, our sense of repetition and return has also weakened. Is the origin home or the office, home or the shopping mall, the family or business, the comfort of a hotel room welcoming us after an extended plunge into unfamiliarity and anonymity, or the comfort of our own home whose walls may extend to the neighbourhood, to the office, and to the security of the familiar? The indeterminacy of origin and arrival is so entrenched in our daily routines that we rarely entertain the notion of return. We take return and repetition for granted, and as such we glide on the presupposition that our daily journeys are not really journeys, and that we never leave and therefore never return. We move but without the sense of moving, of traveling, and we walk the streets distractedly. Calvino articulated something similar when in his autobiographical essay "Hermit in Paris" he wrote: "international journeys as much as short journeys in the city are no longer an exploration of a series of different places ("un'esplorazione attraverso una serie di luoghi diversi"): they are simply movements from one point to another between which there is an empty interval ("un intervallo vuoto"), a discontinuity ("una discontinuità"), a parenthesis above the clouds if it is an air trip, and a parenthesis beneath the earth if it is a city journey" (*Hermit in Paris* 169; *Eremita a Parigi* 10-11).

Turning back

The feeling of returning, of going back, and of being inescapably caught in exile, occurs when nostalgia, not so much for the origin as for the soon-to be-left destination, catches us. We stand at the door of a hotel room, at the door of a rented apartment—suitcases packed and ready at our feet—but we cannot leave before turning back to take one last look at the room that hosted us. We have rehearsed on many occasions, with a feeling of sweet expectation and sometimes even with impatience and frustration, our departure and return to the familiar. Never in those rehearsals did we turn back to look with nostalgia upon exilic, foreign walls. We imagined rushing through the door, elated, ready to catch a taxi and speed as quickly as possible to the airport, to the station. But now that we are on the threshold, now that we are about to leave, now that we are no longer imagining but living the return, we turn back and pause. We wait for a moment.

We see rooms already empty of our presence, already abandoned by us, already unavailable to us, and at that precise moment what was unusual and foreign becomes usual, ours. It becomes a fragment of our life. It is only an instant, but what we do in those few seconds at the door, just before leaving and shutting the door behind us forever, is to fill those rooms again with our presence and our possessions, to see ourselves there again as if we had always been there, and as if we will always continue to be there. Our impulse is to fill time and space with our presence and to put a spell on our natural being in exile. It is then that we realize, if only for a moment, that our living is always a leaving, that our origin is always a myriad of origins and that our returning is always ephemeral. True nostalgia is not for a distant home, unreachable and unavailable, but for the memories that we have of our filling the space and time of that distant home. It is not the return to a present, actual home without us that we crave, but the return to a home that *already contains us* and in which we are already present. Return, therefore, is possible, but only as a condition and as a product of memory. As such it is only the potential production of language and thought. Return is never an action. By contrast, action always and invariably moves ahead, even when we might wish to go backward. That is why the language and thinking of exile, of life in exile, is inextricably linked with production. And that is why artists and thinkers are always considered to be in exile and always seek forms of exile and of errancy.

If it is true that the feeling of being exiled, and the pain and nostalgia that arise as a result of exile, find their origin in our mnemonic filling of space and time, in our forceful imposition of a temporal and spatial capsule, then it is also true that memory is inextricably linked with, indeed essential to, the experience of exile. In fact, we can shed even more light on memory by reflecting on exile. As we have noted, exile is connected to time and space and, more specifically, to duration in time and space. The longer a journey and the longer the sojourn in another place become, the more acute is the feeling of nostalgia (that gnawing reminder that something essential to being and identity is missing, or rather that what completes the individual is in its presence but only as memory). What exacerbates nostalgia and the feeling of loss is not that there is something missing, but that there is something present yet shut up in the past.

This qualification is essential to understand more clearly the condition of and processes of exile. We can be in the presence of our sense of loss, we can produce nostalgia, only if we are one and the same with the loss. We are, then, only in exile when we are intensely living, inhabiting the presence of our past. It is in this sense that exile cannot be and is not exclusively related to a place or to a psychological and emotional condition. Rather, exile is connected to many places and is the result of many psychological and emotional conditions. More importantly, exile is the place—but also a clear example—of our differentiated singularity and uniqueness. It follows that exile is not the topography of lands but the topography of individuals; a map that is drawn in the production of memories in the present, and of lives that weave their present stories declined in the past. It is when we are about to leave in order to return—at that moment when we turn around to cast a final glance at our fading present—that we have a first apprehension that what we are about to leave is nothing other than our origin, yet another of our many lost and gained origins and our lost and gained identities subsumed by and housed in our singular uniqueness. This moment at the threshold of a present about to turn past, and a past about to turn present, is also one of the most striking and formidable examples of the making of the self, that moment, that is, in which the narration of life takes an unexpected turn, adding to the biography of the self another branching path. We shut the door, but not before taking with us what we have left behind it. It is no accident that life has been so often compared to a seemingly mindless opening and closing of doors.

Making memories

But, for this to happen, we need memories through which to narrate our life, our being, our presence in the space of the non-present. It is here that we begin to comprehend that, in order to have memories, we need to produce them, we need to make them. But precisely how and when does one produce memories? Language and culture tell us that memory is "strong," "good," "exceptional" or, conversely, "weak," "loose," "unreliable," "fragmented"; that somebody has a visual memory while others have kinetic memory, and that strategies to retain what we wish to memorize vary according to individuals but also according to age, culture, and traditions. We are also told that we have, as contemporary humans, a much weaker memory than our predecessors simply because we rely on artificial and technical devices to retain and store information rather than on our natural capacity and predisposition to memorize. As we know, the Middle Ages were renowned for having implemented a series of mnemonic strategies that aided individuals to recall at ease all sorts of teachings. What is less known and discussed is that what was required to be retained and produced on request or choice was, for the most part, a set of established values and rules, especially of a religious kind. How different, then, were the Middle Ages from our own age, where icons, images, and visual stimulations are constant reminders of what it is that we need to remember? Other values and rules have replaced religious ones, but the significance of contemporary images is not dissimilar from the canvases and frescos decorating the walls of churches and palaces.

What mnemonic strategies do not tell us is why we memorize and when and why we are more likely to remember some things than others. This cognitive gap is mirrored by language, which does not seem to have commonly available sayings for the *farsi della memoria* ("the making of memory"), and *il quando della memoria* ("the when of memory"). One never says that: "I produced this memory last year when I was drinking coffee at my favourite café." One just says, "I remember," or many variations on the theme, including the very interesting synonyms of "remembering": "seeing" and "reliving." "I see myself reading this book; saying this to my children; walking on a street; thinking; loving; suffering." "I have relived this episode of my life, of our life, of our history." While "remembering" is semantically precise (too precise, to the extent of becoming virtually neutral and meaningless), "seeing" and "reliving" acquire more interesting and instructive connotations when placed in the context of reminiscence. They express the casting of the gaze on the past together with the attendant implications that the past is there to be watched and observed, and to be lived as we watch and observe a movie. We turn on the screen of our life, sit, and watch. And we do this, we can do this, because it is our life, it is our uniqueness irrespective of where we were and how we felt. We can rewind our life to the extent that we allow ourselves to turn around as we are about to leave and cast a last glance on our being in the past. It is in placing ourselves *in there* and in making that *there* another part of our origin that we can then remember, see, and live again. We now understand that memory exists as return in a journey without return and that "returning" is only possible if one never leaves. "Seeing" and "reliving" can help us come closer to the meaning of the "making of memory," to those moments, that is, when we feel the urge to pause and turn for a moment. Our body is already poised and committed to forward movement. We know that we are going and yet we stop to sow the seed of our memories, to *fare la memoria* ("to make memory"). Memory is the narration of the past in language. For this narration to happen, to be produced, a strong and vivid sense of the past is necessary. But this past cannot be abstract, a mere idea; it must instead be tangible, and when we look at it, as when we look at a sequence on a screen, we must see it precisely, so precisely that it becomes the living present of our life.

There is an instructive ambiguity at work in the process of generating memory which goes something like this: for memory to take place, the existence of a meaningful past is vital and yet, because of its very meaningfulness, the past turns into the present. In other words, the production of memories requires that something be left irretrievably and irreparably behind. A severance, a fracture must take place between the now and the then, and this gap must be insurmountable. The long, strenuous, sometimes dangerous journeys that were experienced in the past provided this rupture, which to the eyes of many migrants and exiled people must have appeared like an abyss. It still happens today, especially for those who cannot enjoy the comforts afforded by modern means of transport. And yet, I would argue that the general and widespread weakening of memory in contemporary society, particularly in Western industrialized societies, is related much more to the dramatic reduction in traveling time than to the appearance of technology.

Contemporary Western lives are characterized by a lack of temporal and spatial gaps to the extent that leaving is really never a leaving, just an apparently seamless and uninterrupted continuation. Traveling has become so widespread, so relatively cheap, efficient, and effective, that the very meaning of traveling has changed dramatically. It is in this sense that today many Westerners travel without traveling, at least in the traditional sense of the word. And they can happily return, precisely because they have never left. If returning implies never leaving, then the category of the journey in time and space can bring about a rearticulation of memory and temporal and spatial subjectivity. It can also aid our discussion of poetic language, but with a twist. The twist is found in the fact that literary language, the language of exile, is a language that proceeds by constantly turning back and keeping within its gaze the life of the past.

It is a past, however, that is constantly reconstituted as present through memory. The poetic "return" is in this sense never backward but always forward, and in poetry, "returning" does not mean going back to the same, to the origin. The opposite is in fact true. "Returning" simply means to be in the space of linguistic and subjective indistinction, to ride a temporal wave. It ultimately means to be in potentiality and to produce memories in language, images whose crisp visibility contains and preserves the presentness of the non-present. Caproni's poem, "Ritorno" ("Return"; 1971) is pertinent here: "I returned there / where I had never been. / Nothing, from how it was not, has changed. / On the table (the checkered / cloth), half filled / I found the glass / never filled. Everything / is still as / I have never left it" (*The Wall* 81; "Sono tornato là / dove non ero mai stato. / Nulla, da come non fu, è mutato. / Sul tavolo (sull'incerato / a quadretti) ammezzato / ho ritrovato il bicchiere / mai riempito. Tutto / è ancora rimasto quale / mai l'avevo lasciato"; *L'opera* 374).

The reflection on the "making of memory" is necessarily also a reflection on its opposite, which is not so much the "unmaking of memory" as the inability to produce memories. As we have seen, forgetfulness is as productive as remembrance and it partakes of all those characteristics typical of a *poietic* category. Forgetfulness creates the space for a re-semanticization of the past in the present, and as such is nothing other than a particular—we could perhaps call it a "special"—kind of memory in which, either deliberately or unconsciously, memory operates a selection from among the things that might be remembered. Furthermore, it would be an error to distinguish memory and forgetfulness by calling one positive (memory) and the other negative (forgetfulness), and by labelling one with the notion of visibility in opposition to the other's invisibility.

Both memory and forgetfulness are modes of production, enabling the creation of a poetic and intellectual space for the elaboration and *mise en scène* of stories. Through its ability to make and unmake memories, the self conjures up a formidable creative habitus, some examples of which have been discussed in the preceding chapters. Powerful reminders of this productive capacity can also be found in the streets, squares, and public spaces of those cities which to a greater or lesser degree have been home to scores of migrants.

When?

Before we descend further into the process of making memory, it is essential to pause and think about the inability to make memory; about those instances, that is, in which the urge to "turn around" is unfelt, irrelevant, and ultimately non-existent. Why do we turn around? We do it to take stock, to observe, and admire or commemorate what has been done or what might have been done; to look once again at life and its many possibilities. This question is relatively simple to answer. Yet there is another question, related to the "why" and perhaps even more important, whose answer is both more complex but also more instructive. The question is: "When is it that we turn around?"

One of the most enduring and enchanting narratives of the Western poetic tradition might help to answer this question. The gods allowed Orpheus to take Eurydice back to life as homage and tribute to his exquisite poetry. They imposed only one condition: that Orpheus should not turn around to look at Eurydice until he and his wife had completed the journey from the realm of the dead to that of the living. It might sound like a strange and unduly cruel condition, as strange and cruel as the imposition that the same journey must be undertaken separately—one of the lovers preceding the other. One has to remember that, as he travels in the world of the dead, Orpheus is a guest, the only mortal. His mortality must be retained, emphasized as a total and complete difference. For as long as he is "there," Orpheus cannot be confused with the dead and cannot partake of their presence. The union of death and life would dissolve the spell and separate Orpheus and Eurydice once and for all.

In the end this is precisely what happens. Orpheus turns around, and his turning precipitates him and Eurydice in opposite directions. As they travel separately, they are in fact traveling together; as Orpheus attempts to bring Eurydice within his view (and his journey) they separate forever. The question is not really: why did Orpheus turn around? It is rather: when did Orpheus decide to turn around? We know why. Because his desire to look back at his wife is overpowering, because he can no longer endure the pain of knowing whether she is really there, perhaps only a few paces away from him and yet so unreachable, present and yet invisible. Because he offends the gods as he turns to check if their promise has been maintained, because, in doubting them, he ultimately doubts himself and even, perhaps, the loyalty of

Eurydice. Orpheus turns back because he has to, because the memory of Eurydice is so strong, so present, so visible that it has replaced reality in the presence of reality. Memory has disfigured reality to the extent that reality has to be reclaimed. The present has to be forced upon and reinstated in the place of the narration of the present. In turning back, Orpheus trades his poetry for what he thinks is reality, and in doing so he loses both. But when does he do it?

He does it when his love for Eurydice fuses and becomes one with a sense of loss. This by no means unusual conjunction is heightened and becomes unbearable when the actual presence—nearly palpable, just a few paces removed—overcomes its narrative counterpart; that is, when the actual Eurydice replaces the phantasmal Eurydice. It is then that Orpheus has to turn around to fill the gap between him and his beloved with his gaze. It is to his gaze, and no longer to his poetry, that Orpheus delegates the task of fetching Eurydice in order to possess her once again. It is a matter of love, and more precisely of a love that is no longer satisfied with the production of images and with the making of mnemonic narratives. Orpheus turns around *when* he believes that his memory is insufficient and perhaps even unfaithful, when he doubts his art, and when the desire for physical repossession becomes overwhelming. This story, which has endured largely due to its openness to several interpretations, to the fascination of a journey that can be read from many different perspectives, can also tell us something about exile. Orpheus, the living, is exiled from Eurydice, the dead. She is present in his memory, whose language produces exceptional songs, the beauty of which moves even the gods. She is simultaneously unreachable and present only in her not-being-present. It is extremely instructive that the narrative of Orpheus and Eurydice favors Orpheus so markedly. Eurydice is merely the object of the quest, a presence which is simultaneously here and nowhere, alive and dead. The passivity of Eurydice is magisterially exemplified by the fact that she cannot *return*. The only one who can return her to life, indeed, who *can return to her*, is Orpheus. It is no accident that of the two, the only one who can go forward by turning back is Orpheus. Eurydice appears as if she has nothing and nobody to turn back to. Only the living can turn back, only the living have memories and only the living can experience exile. This is not so much a patriarchal account as a very subjective account of love, loss, desire, and exile; an account which nonetheless demands our attention. The life and the work of Orpheus are constantly and continually devoted to returning to Eurydice. Orpheus's entire life is a return but also, and perhaps more importantly, the impossibility of returning. And his story appears intent on alerting those in exile that the only possibility left is to return by not returning, and that any attempts to contravene this rule will be accompanied by disaster.

Is the story of Orpheus and Eurydice applicable to everybody, or only to poets and artists (after all, Orpheus is one of the most enduring personifications of poetry)? But before we attempt to deal with this question we must not forget that there is another that awaits our attention. While we have seen why and when we turn around—at least in relation to the quintessential poetic example of "returning"—we have left the "not-turning-around" unanswered.

flânerie

It is true that in answering in the positive one also alludes to the negative, which, in our case, equates with a movement forward; a life, that is, whose present reflects and narrates nothing. The story of Orpheus and Eurydice suggests that the life that reflects nothing is not really life; it is rather death. It is Eurydice who walks ahead without seeing. The example is fitting, and this apart from the fact that the most outstanding contemporary renditions of the Orpheus myth have reread the story from the perspective of Eurydice, giving back to Eurydice her presence and also her life. Let us think for instance of the poem "Eurydice" by the American poet H.D. But this is precisely the point: what these contemporary renditions of the myth do is to call Eurydice back to life, to reclaim her memory and her body, to offer Eurydice the language with which she can produce a narrative which is, as in the example of H.D., a mixture of past and present. They actually do what Orpheus failed to do, and their celebration is therefore more a celebration of poetry than of the feminine. What these narratives recognize, either implicitly or explicitly, is that for poetry to exist there must be a subject that makes memory: in short, there must be a life. But the question that concerns us here is whether it is possible to conceive of the existence of a life that proceeds without seeing. In other words, is it possible to live without making memories, and therefore without turning back as we narrate these memories to ourselves and to others? Let us again remind ourselves that "making memory" is not the same as "having memory." Everybody has memories but not everybody makes memories, makes them speak, gives them structure. The making of memories coincides with the *when* of turning around. For the *when* to take place a particular context is required. This context might be a person who invites the telling of somebody's life, a fortuitous accident (like those made famous by Proust), but also moments of utter boredom, of sadness, and the like; those states, that is, of suspension and detachment in which it is impossible to ascertain if one is on the brink of despair or experiencing life in its fullness. *Flânerie*, especially of the kind articulated by Benjamin, is one of these instances, and perhaps one of the most poignant examples, of a being that proceeds by constantly and continually turning back.

The haphazard, piecemeal, apparently purposeless movement of a person who walks to experience the pure feeling of walking (Carter would say to experience the thrill of exposing the vulnerability of one's very existence; *Repressed Spaces* 15ff); this unbearable, embarrassing, almost unnatural way of being is only attainable and blissful because, contrary to common belief, it is utterly purposeful. Through wandering, the *flâneur* follows a natural instinct, traversing temporality and perhaps even experiencing eternity as he embraces, with a seemingly vague gaze, the present, past, and the future in a movement that encompasses them all. The reason why it is so difficult to tell what one sees when the self is given to the pure movement of walking is because too much is seen. The mind and the eyes are filled with images, and it is this richness, this love, that stops the *flâneur* in his tracks, inviting the turning around and the comparing. The similarities between *flânerie* (exposure to movement) and exposure to the production of language are striking. The origin of these similarities rests in potentiality. The potential to use language as discourse is innate but, as we have seen, the production of discourse is also the moment at which being exposes itself, when being wills the desire to stage the vulnerability of its being in discourse. We have compared this moment to the opening of a door, and to the passage from the individual enclosure of the pure being in language to the community of discourse. It is in this second zone, this other house, that language and being change from the potential *to be* to the potential *to be with*. This passage is not dissimilar to a stroll testifying to the deliberate transition from a stationary to a mobile mode of being. In this case it is mobility in language.

As we speak, we also move in time and space, we cover a certain amount of ground with various degrees of intentionality and/or accidentality. On pausing after a long speech we feel exhausted, and we feel either elated or utterly despondent and disappointed. But the point at which *flânerie* becomes a virtual metaphor for the exposure of language is in the experience of poetic language. Poetry is nothing other than a seemingly pointless movement in the space of a language which is no longer stationary yet not fully mobile. This apparent hesitation, this lack of clearly defined directions—an almost chaotic negotiation of the white space of the page, these fragmented and asyntactic movements—tell the story of a great clarity of purpose that, in the course of this study, we have ascribed to the relational function of poetry and its being like a bridge between the purity (and immobility) of language on the one hand, and the dynamism of languages on the other. This indistinctive language is the same as the indistinctive movements of the *flâneur*, and the *flâneur*'s atemporality, suspension, and potentiality, the *flâneur*'s "oblivion," are the same as the atemporality, suspension, potentiality, and "oblivion" of poetic language (for a discussion of oblivion in poetic language see chapter 4). But when do we find the courage to will the experience of wandering? And is the "why" in this context as important as the "when"? We give ourselves to the pleasure of wandering, to this visceral sense of freedom and lightness, because we know that we do not have to go anywhere and that we can stroll nonchalantly, as if in a dream. The *flâneur* lives in a kind of oneiric state, blissful and ignorant of the chores, the business of the day-to-day life that passes around him without intruding. The *flâneur* is like the child in Kierkegaard's narrative, *Repetition* (1843), who observes life as if she is simultaneously inside and outside it, amused by its happenings and yet removed from it, saved from the dangers of a life intent on going somewhere, on doing something, on enacting its good and evil deeds: "I remember once seeing on the street a nursemaid pushing a perambulator in which there were two children. One of them was hardly a year old, had fallen asleep and showed no sign of life. The other was a little girl of about two years, stout and chubby and with short arms, quite like a diminutive Madame. She had shoved herself forward in the baby-carriage till she occupied by good measure two-thirds of the space, and the smaller child lay by her side as if it were a bag my lady had brought with her. With an egoism worthy of admiration she did not deign to be concerned about anybody but herself or about any human affairs, if only she could procure a good place. Then came a runaway cart, the baby-carriage was in evident danger, people came running up, by a quick movement the nurse steered the carriage into a safe harbor; everybody present was alarmed, including myself. Through all this the little madame sat perfectly tranquil, and without changing her expression continued to pick her nose. She thought, presumably, 'What has that to do with me? It's the nurse's affair.' Such heroism one seeks in vain among grown-up people" (Kierkegaard 73-74).

The *flâneur*, like Kierkegaard's child, inhabits the threshold between the actuality of life and its passive opposite. The *flâneur* is right in the middle of the open door of life, and can go either way, toward actuality or into negativity. And yet, the *flâneur* remains in the middle, in the potential zone of *flânerie*, "in" yet "out," moving, ambulating, living the life of indistinction and suspension. While the answer to *why* we summon the courage to will the exit from actuality is that we are already out of actuality, and our movements are movements predicated on and molded by indistinction, the moments at which (*when*) we will the acceptance of this experience (the "heroism" of which Kierkegaard speaks) are instructive and need to be investigated further. It is more correct, then, to speak of a will to accept our experience of potentiality than to speak of a will to exit actuality. We do not exit actuality, we simply find ourselves in potentiality (we do not embark on *flânerie*, we are in *flânerie*, we do not go into exile, we are in exile), and it is at that stage (when we are in potentiality) that the courage to summon the will to accept this state becomes significant, bearing considerable effects on our life, or better still on the ways in which we produce our life for ourselves and for others.

Turning ahead

In *The Interpretation of Dreams* (1900), Sigmund Freud finds some striking similarities between night-time oneiric activity and so-called daydreaming (530; see also the essay "Creative Writers and Day-dreaming" 139). In both instances, the images stored in the unconscious manage to establish a connection with the conscious, thus producing meaningful and narratable stories. What links daydreaming and dreams is, according to Freud, the resurfacing of old memories, often memories that date back to infancy. For Freud, *flânerie* is an instance of daydreaming. One may arrive at the conclusion that the *flâneur* is not only a dreamer but also a childlike dreamer. The *flâneur* is, in other words, a person who is able to bring into consciousness the memories of the past through an imaginative relation with the present. The similarity between the *flâneur* and the child, as expressed in Freud, appears to find some confirmation in Kierkegaard's episode of the little girl. The issue, however, is not really that of taking the meaning of infancy to the letter (as Freud and Freudian psychoanalysis seem to do) but that of reconnecting this experience to the state of suspension and indistinction, and to see if it can shed light on what we have called the making of memories or the lack thereof.

We are in suspension when we travel, or more simply when we are out of our ordinary routine, when we exile ourselves, and when we are exiled. Is turning around then the product of suspension? It is in the case of Orpheus, and it is in the case of the *flâneur*. But it also is in the case of the migrant and the exile. It is the power of a clearly visible image that stamps itself over the playable surface of the present, its extraordinary visibility and vividness, that suddenly demands that the gaze turn back to compare that image with manifest reality. Unlike Orpheus, however, the migrant and the exile do not turn to the reality of their origin, but instead to the reality of their exilic condition. Their turning back is a movement ahead into the present where the visionary memories of the past crumble and dissolve against the backdrop of incomparability. It is this impossibility of comparison that induces the migrant to build structures, real buildings that can actually sustain and absorb the turning gaze. The urban designs of migrant suburbs all around the world are testimonies to the urgency and necessity to erect these screens, these theatrical props which are there as tangible phantoms and simulacra, whose ultimate purpose is simply to reflect. These buildings are not reminders of a lost past, rather essential supports for a present whose existence depends entirely on their being there. But they cannot be the same. In fact, sameness will annul and destroy the memories, and will ultimately deny the present. They have to be different and yet similar; we might call these buildings bad translations. And yet their essence, their very purpose is predicated upon their being "bad."

Memory, like poetry, can only exist in the latency of its origin. It is in this sense that these buildings reflect, not as a mirror does, but rather as a window in which the form of the observer is faintly sketched. The perfection of the memories of the origin is vaguely imprinted on these buildings, and yet so removed that the gaze turning back must *perforce* resume its forward looking. This turning is therefore a "turning ahead," and as such it is not only the site of suspension but also the site of the making of memories. It is here, in the production of the setting for our memories, that we also make memory, and it is in the uncertainty of the comparison (which is also the necessary relation of production) that memory grows, incessantly. The perfect memory of the origin that we carry before us is nothing other than the result of this "turning ahead" to face the indefinite, the "bad," and the unfinished. There is no memory, and there is no remembering, without "turning ahead." The question that must be asked is whether the culture of contemporaneity, and experience in contemporaneity, are a culture and experiences of remembering. As early as 1978, Agamben could claim that: "The question of experience can be approached nowadays only with an acknowledgement ("constatazione") that it is no longer accessible to us ("che essa non è più qualcosa che ci sia ancora dato di fare"). For just as modern man has been deprived of his biography, his experience has likewise been expropriated. Indeed, his incapacity to have and communicate experiences ("l'incapacità di fare e trasmettere esperienze") is perhaps one of the few self-certainties to which he can lay claim" (*Infancy and History* 13; *Infanzia e storia* 5).

To be sure, Agamben's *Infancy and History*, from which this quotation is taken, is not a book intent on weaving a nostalgic account of a glorious past and an indictment of the shallow and vulgar present. It is rather a study of the ways in which experience and knowledge have developed over the years through a close reading of literary and philosophical texts. The fact that Agamben states that contemporaneity is the time of the destruction of experience must not be read as necessarily negative or critical of contemporary culture. It must instead be investigated in order to focus on what it is that we do in our daily commerce with life. Moreover, Agamben's articulation of experience demands to be reconnected to a more general analysis of remembering along the lines we have described so far. To this end, it is important to note that Agamben's choice of words in relation to contemporary experience is not without analogies to my discussion of memory. Agamben says, explicitly, that "experience...is no longer accessible to us" ("non è più qualcosa che ci sia ancora dato di fare"); and again that man's "incapacity to have and communicate experiences ("l'incapacità di fare e trasmettere esperienze") is perhaps one of the few self-certainties to which he can lay claim." The emphasis is on making (something that is not sufficiently conveyed in the English translation), and on the actual process of experience as a product requiring labor. This significant aspect of experience will become more apparent a page later when Agamben emphasizes that: "experience has its necessary correlative ("necessario correlato") not in knowledge but in authority—that is to say, the power of words and narration" (*Infancy and History* 14; "cioè nella parola e nel racconto"; *Infanzia e storia* 6). The considerable importance of the making of experience must now be fully contextualized within Agamben's general thesis, whose main argument is that modern and contemporary being has lost the capacity to tell stories: "It is this non-translatability into experience that now makes everyday existence intolerable—as never before—rather than an alleged poor quality ("una pretesa cattiva qualità") of life or its meaninglessness ("insignificanza") compared with the past [....While] each event, however commonplace and insignificant ("comune e insignificante"), thus became the speck ("particella") of impurity around which experience accrued ("addensava") its authority, like a pearl...no one now seems to wield ("disporre") sufficient authority to guarantee the truth of experience, and if they do, it does not in the least occur to them ("non è nemmeno sfiorato dall'idea") that their own authority has its roots ("il fondamento") in an experience" (*Infancy and History* 14; *Infanzia e storia* 6). Here, Agamben makes essential remarks but also commits a series of oversimplifications. He connects experience to quotidianity, and emphasizes that the stories of experience originate from the narration of the translatability of quotidian impurities. Agamben also argues, rather problematically, for the presence of non-specified authorities to whom the narration of experience might be delegated (who are these authorities, for whom and to whom do they speak?); and then passes a quick verdict on the contemporary as the locus of "intolerable life." Life today may or may not be intolerable. Or rather, it may be tolerable for some and intolerable for others. Is it possible, and even desirable, to legislate tolerability, as if tolerability were a universally valid and recognized principle? This is not the point. The point is to dig deep not so much to pass moral judgement as to think and understand how life, and its tale, is lived today.

Unfolding

Memory and experience are inextricably linked through the paradigm of narration. A story tells what took place, what was, and what remains in the experience of telling. It unfolds, to use a Deleuzian image (see *The Fold,* 1988), over its own folds, and over a time and a space that can never be completely smoothed out, no matter how beautiful and pleasing the story might be. The unfolding will preserve the irregular and the jagged contours of the many temporal and spatial pleats that made it in the first place. The telling of an experience can never be rectilinear, orderly, and precise, simply because if it were, it would no longer be a story. A story, to use another Deleuzian metaphor, is like origami, or even perhaps a spring that in order to unwind must first be wound tight. In other words, in order to be, a story must possess the energy to leap out of itself by exposing its own "impurities." And these "impurities" (the folds and creases appearing on the surface of a story) are precisely what gives rise to the story's energy and force. They propel the story forward in uncoiling, and in doing so they allow the unpredictable, imprecise, and disorderly face of the present to toss about in the weaving folds of the past. This is the destiny of Orpheus's myth, whose ending is predicated upon the telling of a tale that is also and inevitably the translation of a seemingly perfect and pure construction into imperfect, yet present, narratives (e.g., Vergil's, Rilke's, H.D.'s). And this is also the case of exilic and migrant productions in which the purity of the untold memory turns into the "bad translation" of the told. Telling, narrating, producing, remembering are not acts and processes of folding but of unfolding, and the story is found not in what we wanted to say but in what we say as we undertake to unfold the origin into the actual. Because of this, however, the actual is (as discussed in chapter 1), the "death mask" of that which can never be said. In it lie the echoes, folds, and latent presence of the origin. And yet, it is precisely because of this innate incompleteness and openness that the actual is also, and invariably, the potential and the forever unfinished and interminable. But is there a life that does not narrate, that does not tell stories?

As we have seen, Agamben finds this life in modernity. Yet modernity is so vast a concept that it would mean nothing simply to say that life in modernity does not narrate. Of course, Agamben's modernity is related to a poetic (but also ontological) experience in which the incommensurability of language acquires significant epistemological values. It is no accident that Agamben's main example of modern experience is Baudelaire. Let us quote Agamben again: "on close scrutiny, modern poetry from Baudelaire onwards is seen to be founded not on new experience, but on an unprecedented lack of experience. Hence the boldness with which Baudelaire can place shock at the centre of his artistic work. It is experience that best affords us protection from surprises, and the production of shock always implies a gap in experience. To experience something means divesting it of novelty, neutralizing its shock potential" (*Infancy and History* 41; *Infanzia e storia* 37).

Agamben is not actually claiming that Baudelaire's poetry says nothing. He states instead that Baudelaire's poetry exposes the unknown. In other words, Baudelaire's poetry sings that which is new, unfamiliar, and, because of this, non-narratable. What Baudelaire's poetry—and, according to Agamben, all poetry after Baudelaire—says is an alternative mode of being which emerges from the destruction of accepted experience. It is not surprising, then, if in *Infancy and History* Agamben draws a parallel between the poetry of Baudelaire and the language of infancy and mysticism, defining them as modes of being and language that expose the non-linguistic for what it actually is; a language beyond experience, a language that arises with the very destruction of experience. This position is taken up again in *Il linguaggio e la morte* (1982; *Language and Death*, 1991) when Agamben discusses Hegel's reflection on language as that which preserves and guards the non-sayable and the non-linguistic (see also chapter 4 of the present book). But it is precisely in preserving and guarding the non-linguistic that language says it, by remembering its status as language. Language remembers "not to be the language of experience" and in remembering this it says something else. In order to be other than oneself one must will the desire to remember to forget oneself. This is also the Heideggerian passage from concealment to unconcealment and the literary and philosophical ambiguity on which human production and life are founded (see my discussion of Blanchot's and Caproni's work in chapter 4).

Modern sameness

Agamben's remarks on modernity are of considerable importance and, for this reason, they require further analysis. If it is true, as we have argued, that the production of memories is predicated upon the relation between an ideal construction of the past and its traces in the present, it is also true that this production takes place at the moment in which being wills the desire to turn away from memory and from remembering. It is by forgetting, even momentarily, the narration of a known experience and being shocked by the exposure to the unfamiliar, to the "bad translation" of the present, that being continues to make memories.

The life of memory, its existence, is based on the incessant suspension of the ideal memory (that is, the constructed and familiar narration of the self for the self) through the appearance of a disquieting otherness in its often banal garb. Contrary to Agamben's position, the argument this book proposes is that modernity does narrate, and yet this narration hinges, by necessity, on the taking place of a relational exchange between two distinct levels of experience. It is therefore in the absence of this relation that the remark "there is no narration" attains its true meaning. The scarcity of meaningful stories that appears to characterize contemporaneity might be considered from the point of view of the weak, if not altogether absent, process of relation described above. This condition could simultaneously explain the seemingly opposite, but in fact related, phenomenon of the overabundance of pre-packaged stories that spill out on a daily basis from television, the Internet, magazines, billboards, and so on. The alleged incapacity to narrate meaningful stories is counterbalanced by an amazing inflation of narratives that originate from the anonymous and homogenizing zone of an experience without memory, without history. This zone is in fact nothing other than a more or less sophisticated representation of substantial sameness (mostly consumerist sameness) in which the need to think, to produce language, and to make memory is irrelevant and unnecessary.

If this is true, contemporary life is a life that proceeds without "turning ahead," a life blissfully content in its sense of groundedness, purposefulness, and productivity devoid of language, thinking, and memory. This is a life that, in fact, has no sense of exile and of the experiential shock that results from the experience of exile. Exile must be understood here as that psychological habitus that determines a process of wandering, in the course of which the collision between past and present, familiar and unfamiliar, generates a productive desire and, as consequence of this desire, a story. It is in the zone of the active suspension of time and space, in those interstices between ideal and real that narration takes place. Could we then postulate that contemporaneity is a time increasingly devoid of interstices, of zones where the self might let itself wander? Would it be possible to think of life in a contemporary Western metropolis, from Rome to New York, Paris to Sydney, as a great conglomerate of concealed singularities that go about their individual business impelled by needs that transcend them and at the same time are them? It is perhaps these needs, simultaneously in and out, above and beneath, that keep on spinning the multitude of singularities as if they were part of a larger community. But the idea of a community is only a pretence, it cannot be other than a pretence, especially if one considers that concrete and workable communities are built up upon story-telling, and upon the narration of experience.

The polis demands an agora where people can speak the language of experience and where things that cannot be said otherwise can finally be uttered in public (see also Carter, *Material Thinking*). Contemporary cities have virtually abolished the agora, replacing it with the media where narrations are reified accounts of the same homogenizing and therefore concealing story. Explicitly or implicitly, contemporaneity is on the way to building around the self an uncannily sophisticated idea of sameness that invites being to remain cozily inside itself, in a world where the challenges of language and thinking and the labor of unconcealment are removed.

Chapter Four

Writing

The written and the spoken

Writing simultaneously celebrates and questions the metaphysical foundations of Western thought. It asserts the tangibility of the subject that performs the act of writing but it also exposes the limitations of this very subjectivity. When we talk about writing we speak of a corporality mediated through ideas and inscribed in language. We do not see the author who writes, we only hear and listen to the language resonating on the page. The concrete meeting we experience as readers is with the author's language. It is indeed instructive that recent critical trends in literary study—in particular in the study of biography and autobiography—are poised to negotiate, and perhaps overcome, the severance between body and language in an attempt to gain control of the writing subject's physicality and, in doing so, to close the gap between body and language. This critical move is living proof of how ingrained the metaphysics of subjectivity is in Western culture. Western thought is inextricably linked to and informed by metaphysics. It is so now more than ever—thanks in part to the work of supposed masters of antimetaphysics such as Heidegger and Derrida, whose thought, ironically, has reinforced our sense of subjectivity and its centrality within Western literature and philosophy (for a discussion of Heidegger and metaphysics, see Vattimo, *Essere* 13ff).

What biography and autobiography attempt is a direct response to the ancient separation between corporeal and intellectual subjectivity, and the corresponding separation between a flesh-and-blood presence on the one hand, and a presence in language on the other. Recent critical studies on the voice (not only Derrida's seminal work, but also works of the Italian philosophers Adriana Cavarero, Giorgio Agamben, and Paolo Virno) are further examples of how this separation and philosophical and literary preoccupation are still current. Writing is distinct from the voice. This means not only that the presence of subjectivity in the voice is different from the presence of subjectivity in writing, but also that the metaphysics of voice is different from the metaphysics of writing. The same is true if we shift the metaphysical perspective from a metaphysics of presence to a metaphysics of absence. In this case, we might say that the absence of subjectivity in the voice is different from the absence of subjectivity in writing, and that the metaphysics of "absent voices" is different from the metaphysics of "absent writing." What is of interest to the present study is not, however, an argument in favor of one or the other of these metaphysics, but rather the presentation of a further mode of being which, latent in the two metaphysics of absence and presence, might prove helpful for a discussion of contemporary subjectivity and writing. This mode of being is potentiality. In order to do justice to the subtlety and complexity of potentiality, it will be necessary to discuss presence and absence further. The mode of potentiality, being at the interstices of presence and absence, is after all informed by them and made of them.

It is well known that Western metaphysics begins with the object. At the centre of Plato's philosophical thought is the *idea*, an archetype around which everything appears to revolve. The subject, for instance, attempts to reconnect with the idea of itself through intellectual as well as political and ethical acts, which are usually carried out through or in language. The idea becomes, therefore, the object of knowledge continuously sought by the subject. It is this directedness toward the object that characterizes the beginning of Western metaphysics and that continues to inform Western thought until Descartes. Descartes initiated a remarkable shift which, in time, replaced the object with the subject as the pivotal preoccupation of Western metaphysics. Attention gradually moved from the Platonic idea, lying beyond the subject, to the conscience/consciousness located within the subject. In other words, the presence of the "I" replaced the presence of the idea as the driving force of Western metaphysics.

What did not change was the belief in a presence toward which cognitive, philosophical, and literary efforts must be directed in order, allegedly, to know and to possess the essence of subjectivity. This search, whether it be external or internal to the self, has taken many forms and has been conducted under many different banners, including those of music, painting, sculpture, architecture, and photography, up to the most recent textual experiments available on the Internet. What interests us here, though, are the types of engagement performed by language, especially written language. The written has never enjoyed great favor, especially among those who practice it: writers and philosophers. Classical philosophers such as Plato and his followers, most notably Plotinus, subordinated the written to the spoken. This subordination has continued, albeit subtly, to mark Western thought over time. Clear signs can be found in the philosophy of Husserl and, less directly, in that of Heidegger, Benjamin, and Derrida.

The object and the subject of knowledge exist in their essence. All attempts to know them will inevitably pass through a form of representation—visual or linguistic. As one speaks of the object or the subject, these are replaced by a series of verbal categories which, although faithful, are destined never to be anything but copies of the originals. For Plato, words are simulacra of the idea which they aspire to say.

Plato would argue, moreover, that the written is a simulacrum of a simulacrum since writing implies a further passage, a further distancing from the origin. If the spoken is in direct contact with, yet never identical to, the idea, the written is a step further away still. A hierarchy is here established: the idea exists at the apex of a pyramid, followed by the spoken and, finally, by the written, as if the written were a subsequent manifestation of the spoken. This philosophical position seems to declare that we speak first and write later, and that the written must always follow the spoken. Thinking, the Descartian "I," is clearly still to come and its appearance will have a considerable effect on the relation between the spoken and the written, but not as great an effect as it will have in relation to the equation object/subject.

In Husserl, the voice is directly linked with the thinking "I." This is the silence but also the solitary voice of a subjectivity that knows itself in a perfect, if utterly exclusive, enclosure. When the voice is uttered or written it becomes something else, it is transformed into spoken and written language. As the voice leaves the solitary confinement of the subject, it enters a community of many other singularities. It is this passage from the inside to the outside that Heidegger, Husserl's pupil, read as the simultaneous celebration of singularity but also as its inevitable oblivion. Language, be it spoken or written, risks betraying the intellectual but also, in a sense, the physical proximity of pure thought and voice. It is in fact the enclosure of an unconcealed singularity that safeguards the specificity of singularity itself, and that ensures a visceral, carnal contact of voice and thought. The silent and solitary voice adheres to and softly caresses thought. The voice speaks for itself only, and it speaks entirely within itself. It just exists, simultaneously corporeal and incorporeal; corporeal in its promiscuous being with thought, and incorporeal in its defiance of a common space, the locus of that which can be shared. The phonocentrism of Western metaphysics after Descartes is based on this privileged and exclusive relationship between the solitary voice of the self and thought, between the idea of being and its silent language. It is this asphyxiating space that Heidegger and, after him, Derrida question and challenge. If, however, by forcing out the voice they on the one hand rupture the metaphysical enclosure constructed by Husserl's philosophy, on the other hand they continue to emphasize the privileged link between subjectivity and voice/language. As we have seen, in Heidegger's analysis of poetry (see chapter 2), language departs the inner sanctum of subjectivity by becoming sonorous. It retains its essence precisely by defying all compromise with the language of communicability; by resisting, in other words, the cage of language—as Wittgenstein would call it ("This running against the walls of our cage [language] is perfectly, absolutely hopeless"; 44). Language flows freely, unencumbered, it floats in the air as language as such. And yet, it is this buoyancy, this potential to encounter others (language's ability to be shared) that Heidegger fails to explore and articulate. For whom does language float? For itself? For the subject who sings it? For an audience? Or for all simultaneously?

Derrida's answer is that poetic language, *l'ecriture*, does not answer to anyone other than itself, and that it does not approach anything other than itself. In a sense, what one finds in Derrida's analysis of language is a confirmation of language's unreliability as well as a celebration of its great power of dissemination. Language takes us nowhere and everywhere, and by continuously opening doors and adding to our knowledge it leads us to nothing. But this antimetaphysical knowledge, this knowledge that—like language itself—floats in the air, vivid yet ambiguous, falls again into metaphysics by way of its privileged relationship with the "I" who utters it. What is missing in Derrida's reflection on language and the voice is the dialogical element, the interaction of the "I" with the "we" of language that I have referred to in chapters 2 and 3. In this sense Derrida's work corroborates Bakhtin's understanding of Western philosophy as profoundly monological. What is at stake is the relationship between language and subjectivity and the assumption (that I have made in the preceding chapters) that language is subjectivity and that subjectivity is language. What has not yet been fully illustrated is the experience of a language simultaneously present to its epistemological function in relation to either an object or a subject, and absent from this very task; a language, in other words, that is simultaneously metaphysical and antimetaphysical; a language simultaneously "through" and "in."

Praxis and poiesis

Derrida's essay "L'Aphorisme à contretemps" (1987; "Aphorism Countertime"; 1992) provides the necessary point of departure for our analysis of language and subjectivity, and of the potentiality of language. This essay was originally written in 1986 for a production of Shakespeare's *Romeo and Juliet* by Daniel Mesguich. "L'Aphorisme à contretemps" focuses on the voice and the spoken language. In the first instance, the subject listens to itself as it speaks, while in the second, the subject listens to somebody else calling it by name. Two categories of particular significance arise, which we might call, following Adriana Cavarero, *sentirsi parlare* ("to listen to oneself speaking"), a category that in the play is enacted by the aside, and *sentirsi chiamare* ("to listen to somebody addressing us"; see Cavarero, *A più voci* 233-63).

In Derrida's essay, the subject in question is Romeo, who listens to himself talking as well as listening to Juliet, who calls him by name. In the first instance there is a physical union between the subject and the language that it speaks: "Shall I hear more, or shall I speak at this?" It is as if the language uttered aloud by the subject compounds its singularity, its unique existence: "I speak therefore I am." Through *sentirsi parlare* the subject experiences its concrete existence in the world. But, for this existence to take place, the *sentirsi parlare* must remain within the enclosure of the self and cannot include anyone else. Even if the subject talks to someone else, only the subject's own listening can be included in the *sentirsi parlare*. By excluding the *condivisibilità* of language (language's capacity to be shared), the subject can experience pure singularity while keeping at bay its own disappearance in the community of others.

In the second instance, the *sentirsi chiamare*, the name uttered by Juliet (the other) points to Romeo's identity yet simultaneously defies that identity. When Juliet utters the name "Romeo," she is in actual fact attempting to remove from her lover the label "Romeo Montague." Her calling him, "O Romeo, Romeo, wherefore art thou Romeo?" is an attempt to rename him and, as Derrida points out, to obliterate Romeo's identity in order to gain Romeo's singularity. In the words of Derrida: "When she [Juliet] addresses Romeo in the night, when she asks him 'O Romeo, Romeo, wherefore art thou Romeo? / Deny thy father and refuse thy name,' she seems to be addressing *him, himself,* Romeo bearer of the name Romeo ("porteur du nom de Roméo"), the one who is not Romeo since he has been asked to disown his father and his name. She seems, then, to call him beyond his name" (*Acts* 425; "Elle semble donc l'appeler au-delà de son nom"). If this is correct, one might assume that for Derrida *sentirsi parlare* is equivalent to singularity while *sentirsi chiamare* equates with identity.

I would like to add a few things to Derrida's reflection. First, *sentirsi chiamare* and *sentirsi parlare* are categories that pertain not only to spoken language, but also to written language. Second, *sentirsi chiamare* may happen within the enclosure of the self which creates other selves in order to call itself (one thinks of Fernando Pessoa's famous heteronyms). Conversely, *sentirsi parlare* can include the other at the moment at which the subject monitors its own existence through the eyes of someone outside the self. From whatever angle we look at this equation, subjectivity is invariably *within* but also *without*, as is language. But what exactly do we mean by a subjectivity that "is in" as opposed to a subjectivity that "is out" and by a language that "is in" and a language that "is out"? To explain the opposition of "in" and "out" it will be necessary to return to the distinction between spoken and written language. The difference is not only between a language accompanied by a presence—the subject who speaks it—and a language deprived of this presence, as Plato has it (on this see Derrida's essay "Plato's Pharmacy," in *Dissémination* 65:156). It is also the difference between what the Italian philosopher Paolo Virno defines as *praxis* on the one hand, and *poiesis* on the other. In his book *Quando il verbo si fa carne* (*When the Word Becomes Flesh*; 2003), Virno locates the spoken language in the domain of action (*praxis*) and the written language in that of production (*poiesis*). This is not a new distinction. Aristotle in fact argues along similar lines in *Ethics*. What one finds in Virno, however, is a contemporary clarification and contextualization of the categories of *praxis* and *poiesis,* which are particularly useful for our present discussion.

According to Virno, while both modes of language assume a performative principle, the spoken mode corrresponds to a performance which does not include a work ("opera") whereas the written language is a performative act that demands, indeed requires, the production ("la produzione") of a work. This implies that the spoken language enacts its own happening, as well as the taking place of a given subjectivity in the presence of an audience. Speaking is first of all the taking place of language and the exposure of subjectivity. This notion not only comes closer to the Aristotelian understanding of language, it also confirms the view (shared by

Benveniste) that there is no separation between language and subjectivity. Spoken language is as natural to humans as the act of breathing (see Virno 18). As such there is not, nor can there be, a chronological relation between language and subjectivity. The self, the subject, is biologically predisposed to language as it is predisposed to breathing. Speaking is therefore nothing other than the continual enactment of a biological imprinting through which we simultaneously claim our belonging to humanity and share the fruit of this belonging. Language is, firstly, our ontological cipher, and, secondly, the potential mode *par excellence* that enables us to choose between being and non-being, between action and inaction. It is in this sense that language can *be* without being attached to any ends or outcomes since its being is strictly connected to the simple fact of existence. We might read this simple fact of existence as the very work of language, its essential purpose. Language exists in order to produce our existence. But that would in turn imply the pre-existence of language and also the pre-existence of a suprahistorical entity that produces language in order to produce humans. This would take us back to original language and to a theological framework from which we must depart if we wish to reconnect with the purpose of this chapter. My task here is to focus on the relation language/subjectivity and on the psychological, literary and ethical issues at work in our interaction with language, both as individuals in ourselves and as individuals in a community.

The work of language cannot be that of producing us since in speaking we not only express our being but also the being of language. The taking place of language is a production as well as an auto-production, but it is most importantly an action through which we *are*. The simple pleasure of being is inscribed in the pure act of speaking for the pleasure of speaking. We can be just by speaking. The purely ontological mode of being is inextricably linked to the category, or, better still, to the mode of property. In other words, the *action* of being is invariably connected to the *production* of a property that will define our contingent and historical position in the world. As we speak we are, but how we will be and what we will be are determined by the linguistic work we produce both for ourselves and for others. Thus, linguistic production, be it spoken or written, is marked by potentiality. While mere speaking is characterized by its natural taking place, production involves a process which might or might not arrive at completion. It is in this sense that, whereas our being is located in actuality, our being-in-the-world (our being with others as well as with ourselves) is housed in potentiality. Contrary to what Virno believes, and to what has hitherto been taken to be the logical progress of language, the potentiality of language resides not so much in the actual utterance (in its taking place) as in its process of production. In fact, if language exists as such, and as part and parcel of our essence, its potentiality is not its utterance (which is not potential but normal and natural), but rather its utterance in the context of a performance that must imply either the *sentirsi parlare* or the *sentirsi chiamare*. In other words, language is potential only in the space of a performance and in the presence of an audience, be it the self who speaks/writes or the other who listens/reads; and the potentiality of language is inscribed in the possibility of constructing a meaning. It is in its progressing that language is potential. We must look for the potentiality of language midway between origin and conclusion, between the action of its taking place and its silence.

"Before the world"

As we write or speak ourselves in the world, we also fashion our essential being, which equates with saying that we manipulate our essential language. We transform language from action into production and from *praxis* into *poiesis*. And it is precisely at this crucial juncture that we accept the greatest risk of all, which is nothing other than the abandonment of our original home and our essential being. As we speak ourselves into the world we lose our elemental singularity and gain our singular potentiality. This is the great risk Heidegger speaks of in his surprisingly emotional essay titled "Wozu Dichter?" (1946; "Why Poets?" in *Off the Beaten Track*, 2002). As Heidegger sees it, we are brought to accept this risk by the "will to will it" and by the desire to ground ourselves in the open, in the world. Let us enter more deeply into this writing, where Heidegger's very own language appears to shuffle continuously and so uneasily between action and production, as if Heidegger felt the extent to which he was putting himself personally at risk through his philosophical language.

As often happens in the work of Heidegger, the thinking in "Why Poets?" is stimulated by the close reading of a poem (on the relation between philosophy and poetry in the work of Heidegger, see Fynsk; Fóti; Bruns, *Heidegger's Estrangements*; and Vattimo, *Essere*). In this instance, the stimulus is a poem by Rilke found, as Heidegger himself tells us, "on page 118 of the *Gesammelte Gedichte* that was published in 1934 and on page 90 of the collection *Späte Gedichte* (published in 1935)" (*Off the Beaten Track* 206). "Why Poets?" is a deconstruction of Rilke's verses, from which the production of a complex and often obscure mass of ideas springs, at times in the most elemental state of articulation, locating itself, as it were, at the threshold of action and production. The key passage of this essay is found after nineteen pages of writing and reads:

Rilke's poem thinks man as the creature that is risked into a will that ("das in ein Wollen gewagt ist"), without yet experiencing it, is willed in the will to will ("im Willen zum Willen gewillt wird"). Willing in this way, man can go with the risk ("Wagnis") in such a way that he thereby sets himself forth in all that he does as the one who asserts himself. Therefore man risks ("Mensch wagender") more than plant or animal. Accordingly he is also differently in danger than they are. None of the creatures ("plant and animal") are particularly sheltered ("geschützt") even though they are admitted into the open ("Offene") and made secure in it. Man, in contrast, as the one who wills himself ("Sichwollende"), is not merely not particularly sheltered by the entirety of beings, but he is also outside of all defense ("sondern er ist schutzlos"). As the representer and the producer ("Vor-und Herstellende"), he stands before the obstructed ("verstellte") open. Thereby he himself and his things are exposed ("ausgesetzt") to the growing danger of becoming mere material, a mere function of objectification. The intention ("Der Vorsatz") itself of self-assertion ("Sichdurchsetzen") expands the realm of danger that man will lose his own self to absolute producing. The threat ("Die Bedrohung") which the human essence ("das Wesen des Menschen") incurs arises from this essence itself. However, this human essence is located in the attraction of being to it. Therefore, by his self-willing, man in an essential sense is threatened, i.e., in need of defense, but by nature of his essence, he is at the same time defenseless ("d.h. schutzbedürftig, aber durch dieselbe Wesensart zugleich schutz-los"). (Heidegger, *Off the Beaten Track* 219-20; *Holzwege* 293)

As Heidegger states a few pages earlier, "man" is "before the world" ("vor der Welt"; 214; *Holzwege* 286) rather than inside the world like animals or plants. Entry into the world, into the "open," must be brought about by a movement, which is essentially a movement of language ("The ones who risk more are the ones who risk saying" *Off the Beaten Track* 233; "Die Wagenderen wagen das Sagen"; *Holzwege* 312). And yet this movement implies a risk which is, as we have already hinted, the risk of trading the security of a state of pure being (the pure enclosure of the self) for the defenseless state of being in the world. Is there a choice to be made for being? In other words, can being decide to remain as being or must it accept the change to being-in-the-world and, in doing so, enter the open? According to Heidegger, there is no choice: the passage from being "before the world" to "being in the world" is at the very core of human essence, and determines being's will to will the risk of becoming a defenseless being. At the juncture between action and production, being, in accepting the will to risk its security, also accepts the entrance into the state of potentiality and being in potentiality. Being in potentiality is therefore being in the mode of production, being in the open, being located *with*-in a plurality of beings. This is also the moment at which potentiality is actualized as the potential to produce and the potential to be. It is the moment when the man from the country in Kafka's "Before the Law" could actually enter the door and be in the Law. But why, then, does the man in Kafka's story remain outside the door, before the Law, if his very essence, like that of every human being, is that of naturally willing the will to risk? Is it perhaps that he is already on the other side of the door, and therefore in the Law without realizing it? If this were right, what would it mean to be simultaneously defenseless and secure; or, in other words, to be simultaneously actual and potential?

An answer to this question can be found in poetry, although in a poetry of a particular kind. One soon realizes that Heidegger's essay "Why Poets?" is not only an essay on poetry; most importantly, it is an essay about life achieved through a discussion of poetry. Moreover, it is an essay which essentially equates poetry with life, albeit a unique experience of life. The main argument of the essay is that human life is determined by and inscribed in language. There is no human life without language and language is therefore, as Heidegger explicitly states in "Why Poets?," "the precinct ("templum"), i.e., the house of being" (*Off the Beaten Track* 232; *Holzwege* 310). The *templum*, the house that Heidegger speaks of, is, like all houses that protect and nourish, an enclosure that defines the essence and communality of humans, but also one that determines their inherent fracture and separation from the world.

Humans are before the world, facing it from the security of their enclosing temple, which is also a fortress, safe and comforting, but exclusive and stifling. In enacting, performing the pure taking place of language in the action of saying, humans come to exist as such, and simultaneously erect a house around them, constructing an ontological barrier between "in" and "out"; an ontological division which, furthermore, implies an inevitable movement between the "in" and the "out," and a crossing of or, better still, a passing through the threshold between the "in" and the "out." The mistake made by Western thought and metaphysics has been that of unjustly emphasizing the "in/out" opposition at the expense of the threshold, of that perhaps small, quasi-invisible fissure that separates but also connects the "in" and the "out." The threshold is the moment of transition and translation where oppositions and dichotomies become indistinguishable, and where being is perceived at the moment of its simultaneous state of "in" and "out." What takes place when we are at the threshold? Can we think this space ontologically? More importantly, can we experience it ontically?

The countryman in Kafka's story, "Before the Law," waits for the right moment to enter the Law, which means to pass through a door leading into the Law. He waits for years and years, until he dies. But does the door really belong to the Law? A door can be said to belong to two spaces simultaneously. In the case of Kafka's story, and continuing to assume that this is the door to/of the Law, one side of the door belongs to the Law and the other one to the world outside the Law. To complicate things further, the door in Kafka's story is open, inviting movement, and yet this movement does not take place. Despite being open, the door remains a powerful reminder that in order to move we must pass over a threshold, which also means to be, although briefly, in the locus of indistinction. But what if the door in Kafka's story was not the door of the Law but the door of the man's own house? In other words, what if the world outside the Law was indeed the essence of the individual and his natural place as singularity standing before the world?

If language is the house of being in general, it is also the house of singularity in particular. Language is at one and the same time *langue* and *parole*, *praxis* and *poiesis*, action and production. Language unites us as human beings but also separates us as individuals. Language is our original house, but it is also *my* original house. It is my individual potentiality to produce, shape, and use language that protects me but also excludes me, and that throws me into the will to will the loss of my singularity. In reality, we are, as individuals, alone in the house of our language, standing before the universal house of language. We wait in our house for the will to will the entrance into the universal world of language. We wait to risk production and to exist not only as singularities but as singularities among other singularities. It is no accident, then, that the door in Kafka's story is guarded by a doorkeeper.

Poetry is the most powerful reminder that the movement between the taking place of language as such and the taking place of language as production must pass over the threshold of language and over the threshold of being. It is not by chance that Heidegger chose to title his essay on life "Why Poets?" It is not only because his thought converses with poetry; it is also, and more importantly, because life, especially of the kind Heidegger writes about in this essay (a life in between being and being-in-the-world), is so reminiscent of poetry. The language of poetry, like Heidegger's language in "Why Poets?," is the ultimate cipher of the co-existence of the language of action and the language of production, and the locus where the taking place of language meets the production of language. Poetry is the emblematic experience of an entanglement in which the subject is simultaneously secure in its elemental essence as being "before the world" but also already moving into the defenseless state of being "in the world." Language is here at its most vulnerable but also potentially enriching state, and being is balanced on a narrow path between assertion and annihilation, staring simultaneously at the abyss of negativity and at the groundedness of presence. In the words of Heidegger, poets "who risk more are the ones who say more in the manner of the singer ("Die Wagenderen sind die Sagenderen von der Art der Sänger"). Their singing is stolen ("entwenden") from all deliberate self-assertion ("vorsätzlichen Sichdurchsetzen"). It is not a willing in the sense of coveting ("des Begehrens"). Their song ("Ihr Gesang") does not solicit ("bewirbt sich nicht") something to be produced. In song it is world inner space itself that grants space ("Im Gesang räumt sich der Weltinnenraum selbst ein"). The song of the singer is not an advertisement ("Werben") and not a business ("Gewerbe")" (*Off the Beaten Track* 237; *Holzwege* 316). Poetry is, as Agamben has remarked, the archetypical discourse in between the semantic and the semiotic. As such, poetry, if it is not humankind's original home, it is the closest neighborhood to that home.

Poetic madness

But is this true for all poetry? In other words, does the word poetry imply a homogeneity, a string of continuous and identical experiences in language? If we believe Plato, the answer must be an emphatic "no." But it is not so much the answer in itself that interests us here as the fashion in which Plato arrives at it.

It is well known that Plato discusses poetry in many of his dialogues, including the *Republic* (c 375 BC) and the *Symposium* (c 384-379 BC). However, the dialogue that resonates more than any other with the present discussion is the *Phaedrus* (c 370 BC). Here, too, one finds doors: "The third type of possession and madness is possession by the Muses. When this seizes upon a gentle and virgin soul it rouses it to inspired expression in lyric and other sorts of poetry, and glorifies countless deeds of the heroes of old for the instruction of posterity. But if a man comes to *the door of poetry* untouched by the madness of the Muses, believing that technique alone will make him a good poet, he and his sane compositions never reach perfection, but are utterly eclipsed by the performances of the inspired madman" (*Phaedrus* 48; emphasis added). This is a section of Socrates' recantation of a previous speech in which, encouraged by Phaedrus, he had spun an apology to celebrate the merits and virtues of choosing a lover who is not in love over a lover who is in love. After realizing his blasphemy and the affront he has caused to the god of love, Socrates proffers a counter-speech, the significance of which is paramount for a correct understanding of Plato's philosophy of poetry. In his usual ventriloquist style, Plato elects his master and mentor, Socrates, to articulate his thoughts on love, beauty, and the poetic art. Madness must be interpreted here—as in other dialogues by Plato, including the *Symposium* (3-5)—as a sublime rapture that enables the subject to transcend the strictures of the earthly body and earthly knowledge and claim a closer proximity to the essential archetypal forms and ideas. This is the madness of the philosopher, his utter singularity, and perhaps even his disdain for day-to-day-life as opposed to the richness of philosophical and intellectual pursuits. The "madness" of the poet is not on the same level as the "madness" of the philosopher, and yet it is as essential to enter the doors of the poetic art as philosophical madness is to enter the doors of philosophy. Technique alone is not sufficient to pass through. In order to possess, the poet must be possessed by the voice of the Muses; the poet must be inspired, which literally means being "inhabited by the spirit." The "breathing might" of the gods, as Phaedrus claims in the *Symposium*, is not without analogies to poetic inspiration: "When Homer speaks about a god 'breathing might' into some of his heroes, this is just the effect that love has on lovers" (*Symposium* 11).

Was Kafka aware of these Platonic doors? The classical education he received while at the Altstädter Deutsches Gymnasium in Prague would suggest that he may have been. Are Kafka's doors, the doors to the Law, similar to Plato's doors to poetry? If there is something beyond question in Kafka's "Before the Law," it must be the man's lack of inspiration which, looked at from another angle, can be interpreted as his dull, regimented sanity. Not once does he question the doorkeeper. He accepts everything he is told out of fear and resignation, but also out of meek acceptance. It seems he had foreseen some difficulties: he did, after all, prepare so well for the trip, bringing all sorts of things, including objects to barter with should he face obstacles during his journey to the Law. What the man did not arm himself with, what he does not possess and therefore cannot use, is precisely Platonic madness.

The man from the country sits before a door leading to the Law, patiently and in vain until his death. He never allows himself to be "breathed into," to be inspired. His listening to the doorkeeper is a mechanical listening that interprets the doorkeeper's words technically, unpacking (if we can call it that) only their literal meaning. It does not come as a surprise, then, that this first of a long chain of doorkeepers—each stronger than the one before—never motions him in. The doorkeeper may just be waiting for that moment of madness when, as in the inscription on the temple of Apollo at Delphi, the man from the country would "come to know himself" (see *Phaedrus* 25). At that moment, a moment that never eventuates, the doorkeeper in "Before the Law" might change from hinderer to helper. At that moment, all of Kafka's unhelpful helpers might also begin to assist, and K. might finally cross the threshold of the Castle. And yet, in Kafka's words, while there is hope, this hope is not for us (Brod 75). In Kafka's world and cosmogony there is no place for Platonic madness as the dialogue between humans and God has been interrupted. While God exists, He is unavailable, unreachable, unthinkable. But what about other doors? More specifically, what about the doors of poetry. What lies behind them?

Literature and philosophy

Maurice Blanchot wrote *L'Attente l'oubli* (*Awaiting Oblivion*) in 1962, seven years after *L'Espace littéraire* and twenty-one years after the first edition of *Thomas l'Obscur*. Giorgio Caproni wrote *Il muro della terra* (*The Wall of the Earth*) between 1964 and 1975. This collection of poems marked a poetic as well as literary watershed, splitting Caproni's work into two major and distinct sections. *L'Attente l'oubli* and *Il muro della terra* appeared twelve years and twenty-five years respectively after the publication of Heidegger's *Holzwege* (*Off the Beaten Track*), which includes the essay "Why Poets?"

The historical context in which *Il muro della terra* and *L'Attente l'oubli* were conceived is instructive, if only for the relation that literature and philosophy seemed to enjoy at that particular time in European writing. This relation is typified not only by the willingness of poets and novelists to engage with philosophical issues as part of the creative process, but also by the overt stylistic fusion of two discourses that had for many years been deemed separate. Blanchot's work is emblematic of this stylistic encounter in which literature and philosophy melt into each other with linguistic as well as poetic ease. And yet, this apparent happy meeting is the public visage of a more problematic review of language, knowledge, and subjectivity. It is in this sense that Blanchot's writing demonstrates the simultaneous occurrence of linguistic flow and inscrutability. Blanchot's is a language that speaks the impossibility of expression and, in doing so, exists in the space of its own negativity.

Blanchot's literary position and voice are not entirely the product of the sixties, since the preoccupations one finds in *L'Attente l'oubli* also characterize his earlier works. The same qualification must also be made for Caproni's poetry, although, in Caproni's instance, the sixties do indeed appear to define a radical change of approach to poetry, language, and subjectivity. And yet, it is at the end of the fifties and at the beginning of the sixties that, more than at any other time, a literary and philosophical discourse in which borrowing, linguistic osmosis, and the intermingling of fiction and theory prevail. These are the trademarks of a generation of literary and philosophical figures, converging into the neo-avant-garde, or Gruppo '63, in Italy, and the Nouveau Roman and OuLiPo in France. To a certain extent, the work of philosophers from Jacques Derrida to Gilles Deleuze can also be seen as the product of a cultural climate typified by a mixture of literature and philosophy, and of creativity and theory. This phenomenon extends well into the seventies, as evidenced in the work of Italo Calvino and Thomas Bernhard and in the philosophical work of Giorgio Agamben. My interest is not so much in detailing a historical and literary trend as in reflecting on a linguistic and poetic encounter which is the result of a profound reappraisal of literature, philosophy, and their respective functions. It is from this point on that literature and philosophy will begin to engage with the zone of indistinction. But first, it remains essential to ask what the function of literature is, as opposed to, or in conjunction with, the function of philosophy. Despite the many answers to this question, the definition of literature's uses—to borrow a phrase from Calvino—is the central task of literary theory, especially at a time when there are enormous doubts and a lack of clarity both in academia and among writers about the purpose of literature. The close relation that literature and philosophy have had over the years is matched by unremitting claims of difference and irreducibility. Plato was the first to delimit territories and boundaries, emphasizing that philosophy intrinsically knows its object of enquiry whereas literature possesses it, yet fails to know it.

According to Plato, literature's language is destined to produce simulacra which, although giving a glimpse or an image of the object, are no more than mere copies. The original can only be thought, but not in a representational manner. Philosophical discourse can know the object by thinking it. For Plato, the fact that philosophy cannot possess the object by conjuring up its image is, at one and the same time, the limit but also the greatness of philosophy. In other words, while literature, by representing the object, obliterates the very identity and essence of the object, philosophy, by refusing to speak a language that represents, retains the identity of the object. Philosophy cannot visualize the object, it cannot see an image because that seeing would turn philosophy into literature. Philosophy says "nothing," and its language depends on the unsayable. "The language of philosophy," writes Hans-Georg Gadamer, "is a language that sublates itself, saying nothing and turning towards the whole at one and the same time" (*The Relevance* 138; *Gesammelte Werke* 238). Literature, on the other hand, by being tied to the imperative of utterability and representation, ends up by providing copy after copy which—and here lies the paradox of literature—take the subject away from, not closer to, the object of inquiry. Plato made some remarkable claims that have continued to shape the understanding and interpretation of the dynamics at work between knowledge, subjectivity, and language. As a matter of fact, philosophers, much more than novelists, poets, or literary theorists, have continued to discuss the relationship between literature and philosophy, reinforcing the belief that the language of literature and the language of philosophy are two distinct modes of articulating human experience.

The language of literature is made to show images: concrete shapes that can be crystallized on the page for the benefit of the reader/viewer. The powerful iconographic character of literary language has been described with different metaphors and with varying degrees of sophistication: from the *stanza* of medieval poetry—of which the *dolce stil novo* is the major example—to the notion of *mimesis*, investigated first by Aristotle and closer to our time by Auerbach, and to the ekphrastic strategies so central to the work of such writers as Italo Calvino. The unifying element among these diverse renderings of literary language is the belief that thinking starts from the eye. It is the primacy of vision over language that has decreed the statutory function of language as garment. Language becomes a tool for clothing the vision of thought and for making that vision both effable and visible to others. Medieval literature and philosophy are packed with references to language as that which covers, drapes, encloses. It is obvious that the notion of clothing is quintessentially linked to the image of covering and cloaking an elementary purity and its inherent essence and specificity. What is covered, and therefore hidden behind language, is the imagistic thought, whose originality and identity disappears within the folds of literary language. It is in this sense that one can understand better the remarks made by Hofmannstahl and, after him, Calvino, that depth must be looked for on the surface (see Calvino, *Lezioni americane* 77; *Six Memos* 74). The surface they refer to is not what is visible to the eye, but rather what is hidden under layers of language. The paradox, but also the great challenge of literature, is therefore that it must negate itself in order to arrive at the surface. Philosophy, on the other hand, by employing a language that defies images, is by definition already on the surface itself. Philosophy is the "superficial" language, the language that connects with the essence by not saying it into the world of representation, by remaining on the surface.

The question that must now be asked is whether representation equates with communication and, ultimately, with knowledge. By projecting concrete images, literature represents, but it also communicates through representation. If one accepts the connection between visibility and possession, literature conjures up a visual world whose visibility allows it to be possessed. The powerful production of clear images, whose shapes and forms appear to defy the chaos of an otherwise unstructured universe, has led some contemporary thinkers and authors to assert the ordering and clarifying function of literature (see, for instance, Brooks; Ricoeur, *Time and Narrative*; White). And it is also within this ordering and clarifying framework that possession, with which literature has been coupled for so long, begins to transform itself into knowledge as well. To see the world better means to know it better.

While the argument that literature realizes a knowledge-making function is a modern and contemporary suggestion, it finds its origin in the medieval reflection on knowledge, rhetoric, and memory (see Colish). Religious thinkers such as Augustine believed that the source of thinking is vision and that knowledge can be acquired, maintained, and increased by storing information in a well-constructed architectural, mental edifice. Information was translated into icons that could then be recovered at ease by the scholar for the purposes of meditation and further investigation. Ordering information was the principal aim of the scholar, whose capacity to think effectively depended on whether or not the organization of information and, ultimately, of knowledge, had been performed proficiently. In medieval thought, knowledge was consonant with clear pictures that could be projected into a mental screen, there to be contemplated by the thinker. There could be no thinking without images. The proximity between medieval visual ordering and the clarifying and ordering purpose of literature articulated in the twentieth century is striking yet problematic.

The first problem is that the opposition drawn by Plato between possession and knowledge begins to crumble if one believes that the actual possession of a clearly organized visual gallery of images equates with knowledge. If it does, possession and knowledge are connected. This does not mean that they are identical, but it means that they must be related to the extent that knowledge without possession is severely hampered. It is in this sense that the philosophical opposition between possession and knowledge, as argued in Plato, appears increasingly unconvincing. On the other hand, assuming that Platonic idealism has some currency, what can one make of a knowledge built on mere copies; on simulacra whose resemblance to the original is only apparent and perhaps even misleading?

If it is true that knowledge is based on the capacity to see the object of inquiry, this knowledge is then partial and limited, as is a language that attempts to know by communicating through representation. Is it possible to say without representing? In other words, is it possible to speak just by naming? This would equate with speaking or writing a language whose sayability is not affected by its translatability into meaningful images; a language, therefore, that stays on the surface. Is it possible to understand the meaning of a "superficial" language? It is important to remember that a language that remains on the surface is a language that does not represent but only says. The question arises: is a language that says without communicating really a language?

The language of indistinction

Visibility and knowledge are closely connected in Western thought. The capacity to project, retrieve, and use mental images through language is an old rhetorical as well as mnemonic strategy. The invitation to construct mental edifices as a way of ordering and constructing thought is originally found in St. Paul. It subsequently informs medieval thought to the extent that the enclosed citadel of God, so lucidly argued for by Augustine, occurs time and time again in rhetorical as well as religious and philosophical texts. The capacity to see in order to know is based on the belief that creation—both rational and fictional—depends on the capacity to order and clarify an otherwise chaotic and inscrutable universe. And yet, this inscrutability is not an innate deficiency of the universe, but rather a limitation of human beings, whose thought and language are inadequate to describe eternity and the infinite attributes of the universe and, ultimately God. Human thought and language are always and inherently less than the wholeness from which they derive. This deficiency can be partially counterbalanced through a series of techniques whose main purpose is to bring into the sphere of humanity the essential more-than-human purity of the whole. Human language and thought are quintessentially temporal and spatial. It is in this sense that visibility is the vital cornerstone of knowledge, and that thought must be crystallized in a series of ordering spatial and temporal images through, among other means, language.

Belief in the derivative nature of humanity and its corresponding limitations has informed linguistic and other means of representation, including visual representation. It is a limitation that has compelled artists, theoreticians, and philosophers to think of ways to know and possess without representing, which means without seeing. This process has introduced the notion of a knowledge devoid of vision and, as a consequence, of a form of knowledge that defies the very principles of knowing. Philosophy itself must renounce the rhetorical techniques of ordering and clarifying by constructing complex architectural structures in which visibility and knowledge are intrinsically intertwined. Philosophy has to question the limitations of human language from within; first by accepting them and second by summoning into existence a language that, although human, is outside the community of humans. Literature must do the same. It is the realization of this necessity that has given rise to a series of literary and theoretical reflections on language, and that has also generated the first examples of literary and philosophical convergence in the zone of poetic and linguistic indistinction.

The language of indistinction is brought into existence through abandoning, leaving behind the language of representation and moving backward in the direction of the original beginning. As such, the language of indistinction is interstitial and only potential in that it moves in the zone in between representation and essence, in between humanity and suchness. Its intention is to reconnect with the origin and to be one with the origin. And yet, as it is the product of an abandonment, it carries within itself the remnant of what was left behind. The language of indistinction includes the language of representation by excluding it. This is necessary and inevitable in that the language of indistinction is primarily and above all the result of a departure from itself. It is a language that communicates by not communicating, and a language that exists by not being. It is potentially representational and "superficial" but, because of its very nature of potentiality, it is neither representational nor "superficial" but simply itself. The identity of the language of indistinction, and the poetic and literary domain that it generates, is potentiality.

The literary stanza

L'Attente l'oubli is set in a hotel room in an undefined location at an undefined time. Two characters, a man and a woman, speak to each other, or rather, they appear to speak to each other (on the notion of "speaking" in *L'Attente l'oubli*, see also Smock). Later in the narrative, the reader is made to realize that the woman went to the man's room after the two had exchanged glances through their respective windows. There are several things to be learned from this simple narrative structure. The hotel room is an enclosed space, containing and circumscribing the narrative. It is this small and compact space, somewhat reminiscent of a meditative monastic cell, into which the gaze and hearing are drawn.

The expectation is that of witnessing a series of *tableaux vivants* or actions frozen on the page for the benefit of the onlooker. Is this not in fact the function of literature, that of crystallizing mental as well as phenomenological events to possess them visually and to know them better? The narrative structure of Blanchot's *L'Attente l'oubli* appears to be crafted specifically for this purpose by providing a well-defined architectural space in which a series of existential and metaphysical events can be ordered, stored, and crystallized so as to be observed and heard. It is the idea of the meditative mental space so central to medieval thought; a space deemed necessary for recollection and invention. Further, this space is unobstructed and uncluttered with day-to-day events; it is empty and quiet, purified of the contamination of quotidianity. Blanchot's hotel room is the quintessential example of the literary and philosophical exilic zone: it is solitary and elemental. Nothing can be heard besides the voices of the two protagonists, and nothing can be perceived other than their floating thoughts searching for a language that would ground them in some sort of oral and aural existence.

And yet, Blanchot's mental picture lacks visual continuity to the extent that the viewer is confronted by intermittent images whose visibility invariably gives way to moments of darkness and invisibility. We see but we do not see. The visual segmentation so typical of *L'Attente l'oubli* generates a mental dizziness and an iconographic short circuit whereby vision soon loses its bearings, becoming engulfed by disorientation and confusion. What is not affected is hearing. But the language we hear is the cause of our visual collapse and the reason for our sense of loss, of being disoriented in a peculiar landscape from which representation and communication have vanished: "Il la regardait à la dérobée. Peut-être parlait-elle, mais sur son visage nulle bienveillance à l'égard de ce qu'elle disait, nul consentement à parler, une affirmation à peine vivante, une souffrance à peine parlante. Il aurait voulu avoir le droit de lui dire: 'Cesse de parler, si tu veux que je t'entende.' Mais elle ne pouvait plus se taire à présent, même ne disant rien" (Blanchot, *L'Attente l'oubli* 12; "He was looking at her furtively. Perhaps she was speaking, but on her face, no expression of good will with respect to what she was saying, no agreement to speak, a barely living affirmation, a scarcely speaking suffering. He would have liked to have the right to say to her: 'Stop speaking, if you want me to hear you.' But at present, even saying nothing, she could no longer keep silent"; *Awaiting Oblivion* 3-4).

The language spoken by the woman says nothing in its uninterrupted saying. It has lost all sense of communication and all representational images. It merely floats around the room as pure sounds that can be heard but not understood. (The English translation is only partially correct when translating *entendre* as "hear." The verb *entendre* implies understanding and the successful outcome of communication.) In Blanchot's narrative, the character hears but does not understand what he hears, to the extent that he questions whether the woman is actually speaking: "Peut-être parlait-elle." The problem is that words and expression, language and images, do not relate, do not match. As words flow from the woman, her facial expression does not change. In other words, she does not make visible through her body the language she uses. Image and language are separated. This is language that speaks *in* itself and not through something outside of itself. The idea that communication could arise from the suppression of this disorienting noise, in silence, comes to the man as he wishes for the woman to stop uttering sounds without meaning. This possibility is soon obliterated by a further explanation. Perhaps she has forgotten how language works: "Il se rendait bien compte qu'elle avait peut-être tout oublié. Cela ne le gênait pas. Il se demandait s'il ne désirait pas s'emparer de ce qu'elle savait, plus par l'oubli que par le souvenir. Mais l'oubli...Il lui fallait entrer, lui aussi, dans l'oubli" (Blanchot, *L'Attente l'oubli* 12; "He understood quite well that she had possibly forgotten everything. That did not bother him. He wondered if he did not want to take possession of what she knew, more by forgetting than by remembering. But forgetting...It was necessary that he, too, enter into forgetting"; *Awaiting Oblivion* 4). The extraordinary thing that takes place here is that, in the woman's apparent aphasia, the man perceives an unquantifiable form of knowledge that he wishes to possess. In this nothing of language the man glimpses something that his knowledge lacks and desires. The sentences that follow are instructive. Entrance into this knowledge clothed by nothingness (the surface of knowledge) might be achieved by two different routes which conventional semantics treats as opposites: remembering or forgetting. But in this instance, forgetting and remembering are close; they share a common trait. They both imply a journey, and the journey is in both instances a reversal, a journey of return. And yet, in the case of forgetting, the journey takes place by accessing a totally new dimension in which the recovery of the origin must start from nothing. Remembering is based on the visualization of and meditation on an acquired knowledge, of a recovery of known and stored principles and notions. Forgetting depends on the erasure of such principles and notions, on unlearning the foundations of epistemological conditions for the benefit of a new experience. Forgetting means obliterating. As such it is the entrance into the domain of oblivion and the acceptance of knowing nothing: "Mais l'oubli...Il lui fallait entrer, lui aussi, dans l'oubli."

Oblivion is the banishment of the known. It is ushered in by the will to forget and by a conscious determination to exclude the known. If remembering is a careful elaboration of images and notions, forgetting is the studious deleting of such images and notions by pouring onto these very images and notions a layer of contrivances, whose effect is to disorient and confuse the already known. In the case of language, the language *through* which we speak can be disoriented by piling upon it sentence after sentence, whose communicative and representational value is unclear. The result is still a language that speaks in sentences, whose grammar and syntax are clear and correct, but whose meanings have crossed the threshold of indistinction. The man in Blanchot's *L'Attente l'oubli* is determined to connect with the woman by "saying nothing": "But I will say nothing; be aware of this. What I say is nothing" (*Awaiting Oblivion* 4; "Mais je ne dirai rien, sachez-le. Ce que je dis n'est rien"; *L'Attente l'oubli* 13).

"I returned there / where I had never been"

In the section *Bisogno di guida* (*In Need of a Guide*) of *Il muro della terra* we find the short poem "Istanza del medesimo" ("Instance of the similar"; 1972): "What should I ask for. / Leave me to my darkness. / Only this. That I may see" (Caproni, *The Wall* 48; "Cosa volete ch'io chieda. / Lasciatemi nel mio buio. / Solo questo. Ch'io veda."; *L'opera* 324). In *Il muro della terra*, as in many of Caproni's other collections of poems, the journey is a central image. It is not by accident that one of the three short poems introducing *Il muro della terra* revolves around movement in space: "'Border,' the sign said. / I looked for the Customs. Not there. / I saw no trace / of a foreign land / behind the fence" ("False Directions" Caproni, *The Wall*

18; "'Confine,' diceva il cartello. / Cercai la dogana. Non c'era. / Non vidi, dietro il cancello, / ombra di terra straniera"; "Falsa indicazione" *L'opera* 281).

The "I" of Caproni's poetry embarks on a journey to what he expects to be a foreign land. He wishes to go beyond his known borders to new, unknown places where, at least according to a traditional understanding of literature, one can find precious gems of knowledge which are not readily available in day-to-day life. Traveling to the unknown, which is either deep inside, buried underneath or high up, into stratospheric distances, is a classical literary trope. What dramatically changes in Caproni's poetry is the intelligibility of the unknown, whose existence is tightly interwoven with the known. The borders are signposted and yet the lands which they separate appear identical. A guide is required to travel into this novel terrain which has all the semblance of the old, yet is new. It is precisely the acute awareness of this novelty clothed in the familiar, an apparent visibility which cannot however be correctly understood if read through the usual instrument of learning, that puzzles but also reinforces the subject's desire to be left in an illuminated darkness, where vision (*vedere*, to see) is paired with its own impossibility (*buio*, darkness). Watching nothing equates with speaking nothing, and both inhabit the area of indistinction where knowing is coupled with not knowing and being with not being. It is in this sense that poems like "Ritorno" ("Return"; 1971) and "Esperienza" ("Experience"; 1972) in the section *Feuilleton* must be read. Their apparent nonsensical discourse—a clear example of enantioseme—based on a set of antinomic oppositions which simultaneously say and refute what has been said, is determined by a language that has chosen an epistemological route on which visibility and intelligibility are traded for indistinguishability. This is a language that inhabits the space of indistinction and potentiality in which myriad possible meanings and images are intertwined and tightly connected, to the extent that no clear image or meaning can be disentangled. What can this language of disorientation and estrangement tell us? Further, what kind of episteme can it bequeath us?

Let us read "Ritorno" and "Esperienza": "I returned there / where I had never been. / Nothing, from how it was not, has changed. / On the table (the checkered / cloth), half filled / I found the glass / never filled. Everything / is still as / I have never left it" (*The Wall* 81; "Sono tornato là / dove non ero mai stato. / Nulla, da come non fu, è mutato. / Sul tavolo (sull'incerato / a quadretti) ammezzato / ho ritrovato il bicchiere / mai riempito. Tutto / è ancora rimasto quale / mai l'avevo lasciato"; *L'opera* 374); "All the places I have seen, / I have visited, / now I know—I am certain of it: / I have never been there" (*The Wall* 88; "Tutti i luoghi che ho visto, / che ho visitato, / ora so—ne son certo: / non ci sono mai stato"; *L'opera* 382). The mirroring assertions and refutations that mark the pace of the two poems, the careful fracturing of meaning through enjambments, are typical of a language that searches in vain for its own face. This is a poetry that dares to look into a mirror that does not reflect, in which not even the self of poetry can recover its own features. This negation of visibility and refraction is made even more compelling by the actual presence of poetry and the actual presence of the self, both of which are actually *there* where they have never been. As such, this is not a discourse that annihilates and negates presence or cognition. It is rather a discourse that locates presence and cognition in a space in which they must be rediscovered and relearned by regaining the language of origin, and discarding the language of referentiality. What I am stressing here is that the area of indistinction, realized by a language which speaks nothing, is a tangible and experiential zone; a potentiality which ceases to be hypothetical in order to be.

A further question thus arises, and it must be asked in conjunction with the two preceding ones: what kind of *habitus*—in Bourdieu's sense of the word, as a cultural and ethical mindset—can a potentiality as such be? An answer is found in this passage from *L'Attente l'oubli*: "Something happened to him, and he can say neither that it was true, nor the contrary. Later, he thought that the event consisted in this manner of being neither true nor false" (Blanchot, *Awaiting Oblivion* 4; "Quelque chose lui est arrivé, et il ne peut dire que ce soit vrai, ni le contraire. Plus tard, il pensa que l'événement consistait dans cette manière de n'être ni vrai ni faux"; *L'Attente l'oubli* 13). The word *événement* must be stressed here, for it emphasizes the taking place of something concrete, a liveable experience that can be investigated and articulated. But this experience belongs in the interstices between truth and falsehood, and consequently in a process of cognition in which the impossibility of evaluation is the fundamental trait of the process's existence and the only possible *habitus* of Blanchot's characters. The ineffability of a potential truth or its opposite decrees their indistinguishability and ultimately their irrelevance. What remains to be explored and lived is the only possible ontological space lying between truth and falsehood and between their respective effability and ineffability and their visibility and invisibility. This is the zone of indistinction. It is here that language can be itself without being forced to speak and where it can roam at ease without losing itself in mere wandering: "An utterance that must be repeated before it has been heard, a traceless murmur that he follows, wandering nowhere, residing everywhere, the necessity of letting it go. It is always the ancient word that wants to be here again without speaking" (*Awaiting Oblivion* 4; "Parole qu'il faut répéter avant de l'avoir entendue, rumeur sans trace qu'il suit, nulle part-errante, partout-séjournante, nécessité de la laisser aller. C'est toujours la vieille parole qui veut être là à nouveau sans parler"; *L'Attente l'oubli* 13).

The ancient word

The messianic project that one finds in Benjamin's reflection on language and his interest in thinking the original language, *die reine Sprache*, is also present in Blanchot's work as *la vieille parole*. Both Blanchot and Benjamin speak and retrace in their writing the linguistic split that has characterized the Western understanding of language throughout the centuries. Blanchot engages with this fracture and attempts to understand and articulate its meaning by inhabiting the only possible and available vantage point. This is the fracture itself, where *in language* and *through language* intermingle and disappear into each other. It is the will to be in indistinction that urges the characters in Blanchot's *L'Attente l'oubli* to look for the "pauvreté dans le langage" (*L'Attente l'oubli* 19; "poverty in language"; *Awaiting Oblivion* 8), and that encourages them to "ignorer ce qu'on sait, seulement cela" (*L'Attente l'oubli* 16; "remain ignorant of what one knows, only that"; *Awaiting Oblivion* 6).

In 1796 the young Hegel wrote a poem titled "Eleusis" and dedicated it to Hölderlin. This poem on the Eleusinian mystery speaks of the impossibility of stating the ineffable, of proffering the sacred: "and in vain," writes Hegel, "strive / the scholars, their curiosity greater than their love / of wisdom (the seekers possess this love and / they disdain you)—to master it they dig for words, ("graben sie nach Worten") / in which your lofty meaning might be engraved ("In die Dein hoher Sinn gepräget")!" (Hegel, *Werke* 231; English translation in Agamben, *Language and Death* 8). The only way to apprehend the secret of the "sacred initiations" is to remain silent or to "speak the language of angels" ("Spräch er mit Engelzungen"), "to experience the poverty of words" ("fühlt' der Worte Armut"). In this poem the young Hegel reiterates the Platonic idea of words as mere simulacra—"only dust and ashes do they seize"—and the primacy of pure thought, the silence residing in the poverty of words. But the poem does something even more interesting, especially in relation to our present discussion: it appears to offer Blanchot the original platform on which to found his own project of language. Between Blanchot's *pauvreté dans le langage* and Hegel's *fühlt' der Worte Armut* there is a striking proximity. Indeed, this is a proximity of thought on which a whole philosophical and poetic experience hinges. Blanchot's could well be a translation of Hegel's poem, but only if by translation we mean that process that rewinds the work, that breaks its death mask (see also chapter 1). In the case of Blanchot we are not confronted with the translation of a given text, Hegel's "Eleusis," but rather with the translation of a philosophical condition; in other words, with the "property" Hegel, whose *imago* reaches us through the unconcealment of this very "property" mediated by and in language. But is Blanchot's translation faithful? Does *L'Attente l'oubli* say the same thing as "Eleusis"?

About 150 years separate Hegel's and Blanchot's texts. But more significantly the space in between "Eleusis" and *L'Attente l'oubli* is occupied by Hegel's *Phenomenology of Spirit*. The philosophical position articulated by the young Hegel in "Eleusis" is dramatically reviewed and changed by the Hegel of the *Phenomenology*. For the latter, the truth arrived at through "silence" and "the poverty of language," the sense-certainty, is void ("most abstract and poorest truth"; Hegel, *Phenomenology* 58), unless it is mediated by language. It is language that provides truth with a universal meaning and a concrete anchoring which, although plunging the object of utterability into negativity, preserves this object as a property and a universal truth. According to Hegel, language crystallizes truth by bringing to the fore of cognition not so much the singularity of truth (its very thingness) as its universality in opposition to or comparison with other universalities. It is in this sense that Hegel's dialectic sacrifices the suchness of things in favour of their properties. In effect, Hegel's language is a language that says the object by negating it, by removing the tangibility of the object from view and from knowledge. What we know through Hegelian language is not the object as such, it is not its singularity, it is not its "who." If we follow this to the letter, it becomes clear that whenever we speak or write, we speak and write a negativity, an absence, clothing the object of inquiry, hiding its essence under layers of words. Language speaks the truth by removing it. It is this significant contradiction that characterizes Western thought and indeed generates it.

Aletheia

If the Hegel of the *Phenomenology* is the philosopher of the *logos* and the dialectic, Heidegger is the philosopher who lent the Hegelian *logos* a fuller and more definite ontology. One must recognize that for Heidegger the true meaning of *Dasein* is far more than the commonly assumed "being-there." In a letter to Jean Beaufret dated 23 November 1945, Heidegger writes: "For me *Da-sein* does not so much signify here I am, so much as, if I may express myself in what is perhaps impossible French, *être-le-là*. And *le-là* is precisely *Aletheia*: unveiling-disclosure" (Heidegger, *Lettre* 182; English translation in Agamben, *Language and Death* 4). *Aletheia* ("truth, unconcealment") is one of the foundational terms of Heideggerian philosophy, a word to which the German philosopher returns time and time again in order to question, problematize, and translate. He enters the word and attempts to live, use, and think it as the ancient Greek philosophers did. For Heidegger, translation is not just a mere transposition from one language to another, a simple exchange of words—of this for that—it is rather the integration of a whole language and culture, a whole mode of thinking (in this case ancient Greek thinking), into another language and culture (German). This is more than just offering hospitality to something foreign, it is more like allowing the foreign to penetrate the familiar, and perhaps to introduce violence to the familiar, to change it forcefully. This is nowhere more apparent than in the essay Heidegger devotes to Anaximander's saying (*Der Spruch des Anaximander*); an essay that Heidegger wrote in 1946, just one year after writing the letter to Beaufret.

Anaximander's saying is considered the oldest fragment of Western philosophy, indeed the basis of Western philosophy. It is assumed that it is from this saying that subsequent conceptualizations of being and language developed, first and foremost through the interpretations of Plato and Aristotle. It is not possible to provide a detailed discussion of Heidegger's analysis of Anaximander's saying here. What is of considerable importance for our discussion is to relate the notion of *aletheia* to Anaximander's saying, and to see how Heidegger's thinking of it connects with his overall philosophical project, as well as the links between this project and Hegel's reflection on language. The word *aletheia* is not actually used in Anaximander's saying. The central role that *aletheia* acquires in Heidegger's thinking on the saying, to the extent that it becomes the key to its understanding and translation, originates from Heidegger's unique take on translation. Heidegger is convinced that the saying, the actual words said by Anaximander, produces an aura that contains a broader meaning. The potential discovery of this apparently invisible trace can only be predicated upon a careful and rigorous analysis of the semantic and semiotic content of what is left of Anaximander's saying. Heidegger focuses on two words to attempt a recovery of the lost whole: *eon* and *eonta*. According to Heidegger, it is from these two original words that "the fundamental words of early thinking are said" (*Off the Beaten Track* 265; "sind die Grundworte des frühen Denkens gesagt"; *Holzwege* 352). Among these fundamental words are *logos* and *aletheia*. "Only by means of *En* [the one]," writes Heidegger, "which is to be thought back into the realm of the fundamental words, do *eon* and *einai* [to be] become the explicit words for what is present ("zum ausgesprochenen Grundwort für das Anwesende"). Only from out of the destiny of being ("Erst aus dem Geschick des Seins"), the destiny of the *En*, does the modern age, after essential upheavals, enter the epoch of the monadology of substance ("Epoche der Monadologie der Substanz"), which completes itself in the phenomenology of the Spirit" (*Off the Beaten Track* 265; "die in der Phänomenologie des Geistes sich vollendet"; *Holzwege* 352).

Here the connection is made between ancient Greek philosophy and Hegel, *qua* modern philosophy. By way of translation Heidegger achieves two things: firstly, he bestows on language the power of bringing forward the essence of what is thought in language; secondly, he exposes the essence of Anaximander by way of his very language. It follows that being is that which constitutes itself as the unconcealed through language. It is this *Dasein*, this "being-there-in-language" that Heidegger calls the authentic being, the truthful being, the *aletheia*. Language is at one and the same time that which conceals being by placing it before the world and also that which unconceals being by throwing it into the world (on Heidegger's articulation of language see also Clark, especially 28-33). But if the language of concealment is the language that names and that shows—the Hegelian "this" (*Dieses*)—the language of unconcealment is that which devours the very "this" by annulling it in the process of absorbing it. Humans enter the world and partake of it by articulating language and by turning it into grammar. If one follows this idea to the letter, participation means removing the very singularity of whatever we participate in and with. Participation, communality, and being in the world come from sacrificing the very thing that participates, that becomes part of a community, that is in and with the community. In saying "this," the natural language that is responsible for naming things also creates an impassable barrier between the subject and the object, which will continue to confront each other as two irreconcilable and invariable singularities. It is by removing the singularity of the object through speaking it that the other can be reached and experienced, no longer as singularity but as negativity.

The story

Let us return now to the Hegel of "Eleusis" and the Blanchot of *L'Attente l'oubli* and compare them not only to each other but also to the Hegel of the *Phenomenology* and the Heidegger who propounds this reading of *aletheia*. It should be clearer now that the apparent contradiction between the young Hegel and the mature Hegel is not a contradiction at all. It is rather an evolution of the same line of thought, an ideal continuation in which the consistent study of language and being is taken to its conclusion. For the mature Hegel, as for the young Hegel, the "sacred initiations"—the essence and singularity of truth—cannot be rescued by language, or be brought to light and visibility in language. What changes, though, in the passage from "Eleusis" to the *Phenomenology* is that the impossibility of speaking the essence is not circumvented through silence or through the "poverty of words" but is actually spoken by language itself. The difference between the young and the mature Hegel is, as Agamben has clearly seen, that while for the young Hegel the mystery is guarded by silence, for the Hegel of the *Phenomenology* it is language that guards the mystery: "The Eleusinian mystery of the *Phenomenology* is," writes Agamben in *Language and Death*, "thus the same mystery of the poem *Eleusis*; but now language has captured in itself the power of silence, and that which appeared earlier as unspeakable 'profundity' can be guarded (in its negative capacity) in the very heart of the word (13-14; "ma ora, il linguaggio ha catturato in sé il potere del silenzio e ciò che appariva come indicibile 'profondità,' può essere custodito—in quanto negativo—nel cuore stesso della parola"; *Il linguaggio e la morte* 21).

The simple fact that Blanchot writes is testimony to the fact that he too believed that the "unspeakable 'profundity' can be guarded in the very heart of the word." And yet, when Blanchot speaks of silence, his positioning silence so closely to the "poverty of language" demands attention and a certain degree of caution (on language and silence in Blanchot, see also Hill 206-26; and Bruns, *Maurice Blanchot* 50). Let us quote again Blanchot's passage, with the addition this time of a further section: "His desire to hear her well had long since given way to a need for silence whose indifferent background would have been formed by everything that she had said. But only hearing could nourish this silence. They both searched for poverty in language. On this point, they agreed. For her there were always too many words and one word too many, as well as overly rich words that spoke excessively. Although she was apparently not very learned, she always seemed to prefer abstract words, which evoked nothing. Wasn't she trying, and he along with her, to create for herself at the heart of this story a shelter so as to protect herself from something that the story also helped attract?" (*Awaiting Oblivion* 8; "Le désir qu'il avait de bien l'entendre avait depuis longtemps fait place à un besoin de silence dont tout ce qu'elle avait dit aurait formé le fond indifférent. Mais seule l'entente pouvait nourrir ce silence. Ils cherchaient l'un et l'autre la pauvreté dans le langage. Sur ce point, ils s'accordaient. Toujours, pour elle, il y avait trop de mots et un mot de trop, de plus des mots trop riches et qui parlaient avec excès. Bien qu'elle fût apparemment peu savante, elle semblait toujours préférer les mots abstraits, qui n'évoquaient rien. Est-ce qu'elle n'essayait pas, et lui avec elle, de se former au sein de cette histoire un abri pour se protéger de quelque chose que l'histoire aussi contribuait à attirer?"; *L'Attente l'oubli* 19).

It is true that Blanchot writes about silence, but this is a silence that resounds with words and their demands to be heard. In *La Part du feu* (1948; *The Work of Fire*, 1995), Blanchot wrote: "this endless resifting of words without content ("ce ressassement sans terme de mots sans contenu"), this continuousness of speech through an immense pillage of words ("cette continuité de la parole à travers un immense saccage de mots"), is precisely the profound nature of a silence that talks" (*The Work of Fire* 332; "telle est justement la nature profonde du silence qui parle"; *La Part du feu* 334). Blanchot's silence is not the mute silence of the Eleusinian mystery, the no-sound effected by closing one's mouth and stopping the flow of words. But neither is it the preservation of a "property." This indifferent, indistinct humming of words, whose interpenetration has rendered them expressionless, does not represent anything—neither the "property" nor the negativity of the object. Its preservation—if it is a preservation at all—is the preservation of its own becoming of language in between sense-certainty and universality. As such, this indifferent language guards more than the negativity of truth; it guards both the negativity and the presence of truth by simultaneously incorporating and con-fusing negativity and presence. The language of indistinction, being the becoming and the potential, is also an auratic fragment, whose surrender of representation and presentation carries their echoes, their haloes, within itself. This language is not silence and it is not expression—"For her there were always too many words and one word too many, as well as overly rich words that spoke excessively. Although she was apparently not very learned, she always seemed to prefer abstract words, which evoked nothing." It is obviously not representation, unless by representation one means the Hegelian guarding of negativity. Indeed, at times Blanchot's *L'Attente l'oubli* is nothing more than a Hegelian parable about language and death, about language and its commensurability with the void. And yet this tale about the nothingness of language tells another story: "Wasn't she trying, and he along with her, to create for herself at the heart of *this story* a shelter so as to protect herself from something that the *story* also helped attract?"

Is there somebody telling a story, and to whom, and for what purpose? Clearly, the woman tells a story that the man sets to transcribing. Yet the story that she tells is unrepresentable because, as in the Eleusinian mystery, its essence, its secrets, are unsayable: "He picked up the sheets of paper and wrote, 'It is her voice that is entrusted to you, not what she says. What she says, the secrets that you collect and transcribe so as to give them their due, you must lead them gently, in spite of their attempt to seduce, toward the silence that you first drew out of them'" (*Awaiting Oblivion* 3; "Il reprit les feuillets et écrivit: 'C'est la voix qui t'est confiée, et non pas ce qu'elle dit. Ce qu'elle dit, les secrets que tu recueilles et que tu transcris pour les faire valoir, tu dois les ramener doucement, malgré leur tentative de séduction, vers le silence que tu as d'abord puisé en eux'"; Blanchot, *L'Attente l'oubli* 11).

Let us set aside for a moment the reference to the voice and draw attention not only to the inherent silence of the "secret" but also, more importantly, to the fact that in listening—or perhaps merely hearing—the man weaves a story himself and that both stories, the woman's and the man's, are ultimately encapsulated within another story. This is why "the story" provides shelter from what "the story" attracts. If words empty the essence of things—"it is a hotel room no different from those he has always lived in, the kind he likes, in a modest hotel. But as soon as he wants to describe it, it is empty, and the words that he uses apply only to the emptiness" (*Awaiting Oblivion* 7; "c'est une chambre d'hôtel, comme il en a toujours habité, comme il les aime, un hôtel de moyenne catégorie. Mais, dès qu'il veut la décrire, elle est vide, et les mots dont il se sert ne recouvrent que le vide"; *L'Attente l'oubli* 17)—words also point at things: "Yet with what interest she watches him when he says to her: here is the bed, there a table, over where you are, an armchair" (*Awaiting Oblivion* 7; "Pourtant avec quel intérêt elle le surveille, quand il lui dit: ici le lit, là une table, là où vous êtes un fauteuil"; *L'Attente l'oubli* 18). But if the Hegelian negativity of language is so fundamental to Blanchot's story, more important is the way in which Blanchot eschews the negativity that embraces him and his language by letting it be. It is the act of saying the thing of language, its quiddity—which is also the transcription into written language of the voice—that allows Blanchot to produce a language that is both negative and positive, a language firmly ensconced in the instant. Temporally speaking, the instant is that which makes itself as it undoes itself. Like the language of indistinction, the instant is the temporal cipher of the abandonment of the self. It is no accident that Blanchot's language, the language of indistinction, is also the language of instantiation.

Partire da sé

I suggest that we approach the notion of abandoning the self through the Italian expression *partire da sé* ("to depart from oneself"). *Partire da sé* incorporates and includes two apparently opposite and irreconcilable ideas; it can mean constructing something from the self or leaving the self behind. In the first instance, there is a firm connection to and grasping of the self. The self is the grounding and supervising presence. In the second instance there is a leave-taking from the self, the casting off a shell. The link between these two diametrically opposed meanings is provided by the verb *partire* ("to depart"). In both instances we confront a departure and an abandonment, which is perhaps temporary on the one hand, and definite on the other. But what interests us here, irrespective of the outcome, is that the departure and the abandonment imply and subsume a disclosure. They imply an unveiling: the Heideggerian *aletheia*. And it is precisely in the Heideggerian notion of *aletheia* that the distinction between the two meanings of *partire da sé* collapses. Moreover, it is in *aletheia* that *partire da sé* draws language and being into an indissoluble knot. If, on the one hand, language is the original home of human beings, the shelter that protects and guarantees our communality, on the other hand language is the very tool through which we will the risk of exposure and unconcealment. In the words of Heidegger, *aletheia* is the sheltering which discloses. And in the words of Blanchot, language is the shelter that protects the woman "from something that the *story* also helped attract." It is because of language that we face the world, and it is also because of language that we enter the world. It is the language of expression that allows us to share universal truths, but this very language also empties our singularity. What remains to be thought, though, is the process that brings about the state of unconcealment and the passage from singularity to community and from voice to saying. Language, the word, empties the object and relegates it to negativity. It pushes the object aside, out of sight, and replaces it with the presentation of its property. This is either the representation of something through a symbol or the presentation of a pure negativity that, although absent, speaks to us through the medium of language (on presenting negativity through language, especially in Blanchot, see Smock 13). The latter is precisely Heidegger's understanding of language expressed by way of translation.

In the essay "Anaximander's Saying" we read these words: "does the word's literal translation pay heed to what in the saying comes to language?" (*Off the Beaten Track* 267; "Achtet das übersetzende Wort auf das, was im Spruch zur Sprache kommt?"; *Holzwege* 354). In this rhetorical question—Heidegger's preferred route to reflection—Heidegger not only illustrates what he believes to be the principal task of translation (that is, the process that he himself implements in discussing Anaximander's saying) but he also comes to express clearly and explicitly the coming to language of the "thing," its disclosure (unconcealment) in language. But what is put into language is not the actual thing but rather its halo. For Heidegger, translation is in this sense the processing of language, whose function is to illuminate what lies behind language. Representation and presentation can also be thought of as cohabiting, and not only as irreconcilable opposites. Language represents by presenting the symbol of negativity, by presenting an emptiness behind which lies the "thing" of representation. Are we now in a position to understand better the Heideggerian sheltering property of language? Language shelters—in Agamben's words, *custodisce* ("guards")—the singularity of the thing by not disclosing it. This is the ambiguity of language, and also its power and its wonderful poetry.

Engineer of words

On 16 May 1970, Giorgio Caproni put the finishing touches on his poem "Senza Esclamativi" ("Without Exclamatives"): "How high pain is. / Love is such a beast. / Emptiness of the words / that dig into emptiness empty / monuments of emptiness. Emptiness / of the grain that already attained / (in the sun) the height of the heart" (*The Wall* 58; "Com'è alto il dolore. / L'amore com'è bestia. / Vuoto delle parole / che scavano nel vuoto vuoti / monumenti di vuoto. Vuoto / del grano che già raggiunse / (nel sole) l'altezza del cuore"; *L'opera* 339). The poem carries an epigraph in German: "Oh, where is July / and the summer land" ("Ach, wo ist Juli / und das Sommerland") taken from the poem by Hugo von Hofmannstahl "Des alten Mannes Sehnsucht nach dem Sommer" ("The Old Man's Longing for the Summer").

In the same year, Caproni began to translate Flaubert's *Sentimental Education* and was commissioned to translate into Italian the complete dramatic works of Jean Genet. He turned down the commission at first, saying that "after the terrible experience of translating Céline" (*L'opera* LXXI) he could not face Genet's work. His friend, the critic Giacomo Debenedetti, insisted, arguing that, "you are an engineer of the word, you must do it." (*L'opera* LXXI; "sei un ingengere della parola e devi riuscirci"; my translation). The following year, Genet's complete works were published in the Italian translation of Giorgio Caproni. What interests us here are the words of Debenedetti, one of the most insightful and lucid of Italian literary critics: "you are an engineer of the word." How is it possible that Caproni, the great master of words, a passionate lover of language, could impress the mark of emptiness and void on the object of his love? The word *vuoto* ("emptiness") resounds ominously throughout "Senza Esclamativi"; the poem's syncopated rhythm and battering anaphora and its strategically placed enjambments haunt us to the extent that nothing remains but a sense of emptiness and void. And yet, this is no simple emptiness. More importantly, it is not an emptiness devoid of presence. It is rather "Vuoto / del grano che già raggiunse / (nel sole) l'altezza del cuore." It is the shelter behind which an illuminating image rests and vibrates. The poem says "emptiness" but, in representing and presenting this "emptiness," it partakes of the essential experience of the thing itself, and shares this with the reader. Caproni is the poet of small things, of glasses and tablecloths, of wine and taverns. Italo Calvino was very much aware of Caproni's fondness for day-to-day objects. But Calvino also warns us that these objects, which inhabit an apparently quotidian reality of strong textures and vivid colours, are not to be trusted (see Calvino, *Saggi* 1026-27). Calvino refers to them as "emblems": Caproni would have called them words. As early as 1946 Caproni remarked that "words dissolve the object" ("le parole dissolvono l'oggetto"; *L'opera* 1596), and pointed out—with a hint of irony—that only in 1953 did Blanchot launch his own motto "the name empties things" ("il nome vanifica le cose"; my translation). Competitive banter aside, it is clear that Caproni recognizes and acknowledges a poetic affinity, which is based not so much on the privileging of "things" as on their dissolution through language—or better still, on the celebration of poetic language as the shelter of things. Caproni offers language his unconditional trust, a trust based on nothing more than language's capacity to empty its referent. It is in this sense that Caproni turns inside out the apparent inadequacy of language, founding his entire poetic project not on the alleged incapacity of language but on the very power of this supposed incapacity. Caproni's language is a fragment, or, more precisely, a halo through which one can actually *see* the empty presence of the object.

In March 1977, seven years after "Senza Esclamativi," Caproni returned to present his poetic word with renewed clarity. Here is the poem "Le Parole" ("The Words"), published in the collection *Il franco cacciatore* (*The Freeshooter*): "Words. Of course / They dissolve the object / as fog does the trees / the river: the ferry" (my translation; "Le parole. Già. / Dissolvono l'oggetto. / Come la nebbia gli alberi, / il fiume: il traghetto"; *L'opera* 460) Two verses of two lines each, separated by a blank space, with a rhyme that summons the object by unifying it in the house of language ("oggetto-traghetto"). But it is precisely because of the power of language, its supreme sheltering and guarding prowess (emphasized here by the rhetorical construction of the rhyme), that the object disappears behind the fog and the horizon. It is not that the object is not there, it is only that we can no longer see it. Or is it perhaps that we can see it better? But only if we accept seeing its emptiness through the prism of language. The simplicity of this poem is staggering, no less so than its magisterial construction. See the engineer of words at work: Caproni breaks the syntax and flow of language by assembling words paratactically (recalling the lesson of the other great Italian poet of small things, Giovanni Pascoli, and his *Myricae*). In doing so, he simultaneously stresses their individuality and their being together, not only with other words but also, and more importantly, with the silence of the blank space, and with words' resounding emptiness. There is no continuity, but neither is there a discontinuity marked by enjambments, as in "Senza Esclamativi." There are instead walls of silence and emptiness; the undifferentiated silence that the characters in Blanchot's *L'Attente l'oubli* hear resonating in their hotel room. What resonates is nothing other than the object as it disappears, as it departs, carried away on its vessel-shelter, its object-ferry: "oggetto-traghetto."

The word protects by clothing (and sheltering) our being with an aura of existence and purposefulness, and by providing an image of what we are in the world. Being left wanting for words is a traumatic experience. There is a common expression in Italian which is used to express anguish as well as an extraordinary sense of vulnerability and futility: *sono senza parole* ("I am without words, I am speechless"). In this short colloquial saying, whose real meaning is no longer fully present and reflected upon, there is a powerful, compact sense of non-existence and of total loss. This loss is above all the loss of subjectivity. *Sono senza parole* means, in effect, "I do not exist," "I am transparent." This being translucent, without surface, is the real negativity of being and its irreducible emptiness. To be "without words" means to exist in the impossibility of self-manifestation and disclosure. It is neither the state of concealment nor that of unconcealment. It is rather the state of nothingness. The saying *sono senza parole* takes us out of the world. It is interesting that this saying and its considerable philosophical implications are used not only as a way of sharing the experience of pain but also as a way of comforting those who have suffered pain. It is as if the pain of the other is met, and thus partly dissipated, by our voluntary departure from existence. Loss is counterbalanced by loss. Once again, the loss of language equates with the loss of subjectivity. Our being without words is our non-being. It is in this sense that *sono senza parole* is synonymous with *sono senza me* (I am without me). It is also instructive that the exit from being is enacted by a linguistic expression. If it is true that we enter the world with language, it is also true that we exit it with language. Would it be possible, then, to interpret silence as the pause of subjectivity and the waiting of language? In other words, could silence be the resounding halo through which subjectivity *is*, as well as waiting to be again? Is this the halo that Blanchot and Caproni make visible in their work?

Latente...L'attente

Blanchot pairs two apparently unrelated words: *L'attente l'oubli.* There is nothing in between the two words; no punctuation, no explicative conjunction. There is only a blank space, a pause, a moment of silence. There is a halo and a fissure through which something has taken shelter by way of language. After the pause, there is another sound, perhaps without any relation to that which preceded it. The pairing of *L'attente* and *l'oubli* is not justified through language, but perhaps it is preserved in language.

It is not to be assumed that the silence between the two words stands for sameness. If *l'attente* equated with *l'oubli*, a colon would do the trick quite nicely. Nor is it a continuation of the discourse, the logical conclusion of a thought, as in a linguistic chain: *l'attente et l'oubli.* In fact, there is no explication or flow but only a waiting in the space between two words. We pause and wait to say the second word; but what exactly is the relation of our saying, and, perhaps more importantly, what do we do—literally *do*—as we wait to say the second word? Is the relation between *l'attente l'oubli*, their proximity, the cipher of a similarity or the symbol of a polarization? Is it a repetition or a refutation, an emphasis or a deferral? We must interrogate the meaning that *l'attente* and *l'oubli* have in Blanchot's writing. *L'oubli*, the "oblivion" of the English translation, is not to be understood as disappearance but, much more in keeping with Heidegger's thought, as sheltering and guarding. It is certainly not the void and the negative. Conversely, it is the emblematic experience of a present presence. For Blanchot, *l'oubli* is the forgetting that preserves and shelters the forgotten not as something missing but as something prominently present. The entire second section of *L'Attente l'oubli* is interwoven with the theme of the carefully deposited object. The care taken is so fastidious that what is cared for becomes inviolable, out of reach, eminently protected.

The very first sentence of the second section is to this end extremely instructive: "L'oubli, le don latent" (*L'Attente l'oubli* 87; "Forgetting, the latent gift"; *Awaiting Oblivion* 45). The similarity between this significant sentence and the title of the book must be considered. The sound of *latent* recalls immediately *l'attente*. The assonance establishes a direct link between the two words, simultaneously re-enacting a relation with *oubli*. But again, as in the title, the two concepts are not explicated or explicitly fused. This time a comma separates them. But what is a comma if not an intimation to suspend language? We are again confronted with a pause and thrown into an interstitial space between oblivion and latency, and, accordingly, between oblivion and waiting. But what is it that Blanchot's saying says in language? The answer is found a few pages later when, with a great leap of faith in the power of poetic language, Blanchot defines oblivion as action, as event: "The event that they forget: the event of forgetting. And thus, all the more present insofar as it is forgotten. Giving forgetting and giving itself forgotten, but not being forgotten. Presence of forgetting and in forgetting. The ability to forget endlessly in the event that is forgotten. Forgetting without the possibility of forgetting. Forgetting-forgotten without forgetting" (*Awaiting Oblivion* 78; "L'événement qu'ils oublient: événement de l'oubli. Et ainsi, d'autant plus présent qu'oublié. Donnant l'oubli et se donnant oublié, mais n'étant pas oublié. Présence d'oubli et en l'oubli. Pouvoir d'oublier sans fin en l'événement qui s'oublie. Oubli sans possibilité d'oublier. Oubliant-oublié sans oubli"; *L'Attente l'oubli* 147).

The latent gift, whose powerful presence and special value are loved more than anything else, is protected and guarded (sheltered) by oblivion. Oblivion becomes the guardian and savior of a precious existence that one treasures by allowing it to remain latent, and therefore present in its apparent not-being-there. Language is oblivion and oblivion is language that empties the singularity of the thing by preserving it. We can now see more clearly the link between Caproni and Blanchot. Yet there remains something to be thought further in relation to oblivion and latency. Blanchot says: "le don latent." The choice of the word *don* is not without significance. Would Blanchot say the same by saying: "The latent thing"? Is there a difference between "gift" and "thing"? A gift is something that comes from outside and that is given as a tribute. It is the most sacred and precious of things, and because of this preciousness must be protected. The gift needs to be cared for. The best way of caring for it is, paradoxically, to "forget" it. We "forget" that we possess the special gift out of our love for it, out of our special rapport with it. In order to preserve the gift we have to leave it in forgetfulness. This does not mean to remove it from our mind, to destroy it or cancel it. It might simply mean to remove it without hiding it: "That which escapes without anything being hidden" (*Awaiting Oblivion* 42; "Ce qui se dérobe sans que rien soit caché"; *L'Attente l'oubli* 82).

This act of love is the opposite of taking possession of something. The difference between possessing and loving resides in the considerably different degrees of care that we take to preserve the object of possession and of love. A possession is jealously taken care of either by hiding it from everyone else or, by contrast, flaunting the object of possession so as to make it one with us. If the first is fetishist possession, the second is the spectacularization of possession. Yet fetishism and spectacularization share the same purpose, which is the total osmosis of the object of possession with the self that possesses it. That which we love, on the contrary, lives independently from us in the space of the halo, and at a distance from the waiting created by its latency. The precious gift Blanchot narrates in *L'Attente l'oubli* is located, precisely, in the blank space between the oblivion that preserves it and the waiting. Waiting: it is now time to turn our attention to it. Language again leads us to a clearer understanding of the meaning that *l'attente* ("waiting") takes in Blanchot's *L'Attente l'oubli*. In French, a strong assonance links "waiting" to "attention"—*attente* and *attention*. Blanchot allows language, the great preserver in unconcealment, to take him further in his epistemological exploration of the depths of the relation between the said and the saying. The density, the texture, indeed the physicality that language acquires in Blanchot's writing is extraordinary. In Blanchot's work, language speaks itself, assuming a luminous presence that must be followed. Blanchot's language leaves visible traces, moves around, defining borders and marking out territories.

It is, to paraphrase Chrétien's thought (especially 31-43), a language that sees and a language that can be seen. In *L'Attente l'oubli* we read: "There must be no turning back. To wait, to make oneself attentive to that which makes of waiting a neutral act, coiled upon itself in tight circles, the innermost and outermost of which would coincide, attention distracted in waiting and returned all the way to the unexpected. Waiting, waiting that is the refusal to wait for anything, a calm expanse unfurled by steps" (*Awaiting Oblivion* 8; "Il ne faut pas revenir en arrière. Attendre, se rendre attentif à ce qui fait de l'attente un acte neutre, enroulé sur soi, serré en cercles dont le plus intérieur et le plus extérieur coïncident, attention distraite en attente et retournée jusqu'à l'inattendu. Attente, attente qui est le refus de rien attendre, calme étendue déroulée par les pas" *L'Attente l'oubli* 20).

A few pages earlier Blanchot writes that the two characters in *L'Attente l'oubli* are "enclosed...in the great shifting circle of waiting" (*Awaiting Oblivion* 5; translation modified; "enfermé...dans le grand cercle mouvant de l'attente"; *L'Attente l'oubli* 14). Circularity, the neutral: these appear to be the main characteristics of waiting. A space, that is, in which there are no openings, no exits, no doors to be slammed shut or crashed down; a space, moreover, in which time is in a state of suspended movement, denied, as it were, the possibility of going either backward or forward. Time moves here in circles, continuously folding back on itself, responding to its own action rather than to external actions and events. The characters in *L'Attente l'oubli* are locked in this suspended enclosure—this neutral confinement. The natural response to this apparent state of confinement would be to sharpen the senses, to remain vigilant, exceptionally attentive in order to discover a possibility of escape. Yet, the opposite is true of both the language and the characters' action in Blanchot's *L'Attente l'oubli*. Language, and with it the characters, becomes attentive to the neutral act of waiting and to the possibility of waiting for nothing. They just wait. It is literally true that their waiting is a waiting for nothing, but this is simply because what they are waiting for is already with them. The concept of waiting is here turned inside out to the extent that the experience of waiting is no longer projected into the future and is no longer linked to the arrival of a presence from outside. The space that language inhabits is not to be filled by further, not yet present, presences. On the contrary, *everything* language looks for, *everything that it is*, is already with it and in it. But it is precisely because of this that language must experience what is said in language by forgetting it and waiting for it. Language's hope is only a "present hope" and a "pure hope" (on the notion of "present hope," see also Andrew Benjamin, *Present Hope*).

We can best understand the meaning of waiting and oblivion in Blanchot's writing in the sense of a presence that can only be given in its latency: "The movement of waiting: he saw her as if she were turned away from him by waiting, unless, turning back to see her, he had to turn away from himself, no longer seeing her except in this detour" (*Awaiting Oblivion* 51; "Le mouvement de l'attente: il la voyait comme détournée de lui par l'attente, à moins que, se retournant pour la voir, il ne dût se détourner lui-même, ne la voyant plus qu'en ce détour"; *L'Attente l'oubli* 98). Waiting is simultaneously concealment and unconcealment. The only possibility of seeing in the space of pure waiting is that of abolishing the thing to be seen, placing it in the indeterminate and indistinct site between the oblivion that preserves it and the waiting which grants it the luminosity of a latent presence.

It is now possible to read with greater clarity one of the most significant and beautiful passages about waiting in *L'Attente l'oubli*: "Waiting takes things away from him without his losing them and without his being able to hold on to them through the feeling of having lost them" (*Awaiting Oblivion* 59; "L'attente lui retire les choses sans qu'il les perde et sans qu'il puisse les garder par le sentiment de les avoir perdues"; 114); and also the emblematic last sentence of the book: "Between them, like this place, with its great fixed stare, the reserve of things in their latent state" (*Awaiting Oblivion* 85; translation modified; "Entre eux, comme ce lieu avec son grand air fixe, la retenue des choses en leur état latent"; 162). "Des choses en leur état latent" are retained between the two characters, and between the space they have occupied, and that has occupied them; between, that is, oblivion and waiting.

The irreparable

In 1987, three years before his death, the seventy-five year old Caproni wrote the poem "Res amissa" ("The Amissed Thing"). In an interview with the Roman daily *Il Messaggero*, Caproni said that "'Res amissa' will provide the theme for my next book of poetry"; and continued: "the *res amissa* ("the missing thing") embodies goodness. Since poetry often springs from a quotidian and even banal incident, this idea [the idea of the *res amissa*] came to me after a letter from a dear friend went missing ("questa idea m'è venuta dalla perdita di una lettera di un carissimo amico"): I put it away so carefully that I can no longer find it" (*L'opera* LXXVI; "l'ho così gelosamente riposta che non riesco più a trovarla"; my translation). The last three lines of this craftily structured poem read: "Non spero più di trovarla /.../ L'ho troppo gelosamente / (irrecuperabilmente) riposta" (*L'opera* 779; "I no longer hope to find it /.../ too jealously (irrecoverably) / did I hide it," trans. Joseph Falsone).

"Res amissa" is a vertiginous vertical poem comprising forty lines, of which eleven consist of just five suspension marks. Its architecture is at one and the same time highly symmetrical and jagged, with frequent indentations and blank spaces. The feeling is that of a syncopated language and movement whose rhythm and pattern, still visible in the carefully constructed rhyme and anaphoric composition, is broken, interrupted, and suspended by detours, silences, and the insistent voice of waiting, whose presence (announced by the suspension marks) is not only obvious but also commanding and imperious. In this engineered house of language, built of waiting and oblivion, the missing thing, the *res amissa*, lives a pulsating existence in the midst of its absence (in the blank spaces, in the suspension marks)—Blanchot would say in the halo of its latent presence. There is no doubt that the book Caproni wished to write on the "missing thing," the book he never saw in print, is a powerful testament to the very "thingness" of language and its purity. Language is not here a tool that communicates, a mere instrument, it is instead language as such, behind which takes shelter what Agamben has called "the being-in-language of the non-linguistic" (*La comunità* 76; "l'essere-nel-linguaggio-del-non-linguistico"; *The Coming Community* 103).

There is no doubt, however, that this deliberately poetic and philosophical project is prepared, announced, introduced, and indeed nourished by Caproni from the 1960s onwards, starting with *Il muro della terra*. Caproni's poetry is a journey in language. But this is a language that, as Caproni writes in "L'ónoma" ("The Name"; 1984), a poem included in the collection *Il conte di Kevenhüller* (*The Count of Kevenhüller*), leaves no traces—"The name leaves no trace / It's purely grammatical: / a beast without shape, / erratic, ungraspable" (my translation; "L'ónoma non lascia orma. / È pura grammatica. / Bestia perciò senza forma. / Imprendibilmente erratica"; *L'opera* 569) It is therefore a language that travels carrying forward forgetfulness and oblivion and leaving behind it empty spaces. And yet it travels, it moves, it has been *there*; but its being there, that is, the naming of a presence (even its own presence), is precisely what language misses as it unravels itself in space. There are no footsteps, no visible signs on the page, it is true, except that, in the silence of the non-presence of language, an indistinct echo of the very thing that is not there continues to resonate. The thing has been taken away by language as language itself takes away its own existence as it proceeds. The halo—the very essence of the thing—is preserved and rests in this space vacated by everything.

Let us read now a series of poems from *Il franco cacciatore* the paradoxical language of which might seem at first glance to result from a mere game, an ironic play with words. "Indicazione" ("Direction"; 1976): "Quit tormenting yourselves. / If you want an encounter, / Look for me where I am not. / I can't point you to any other spot" (trans. Joseph Falsone; "—Smettetela di tormentarvi. / Se volete incontrarmi, / cercatemi dove non mi trovo. / Non so indicarvi altro luogo"; *L'opera* 406); "Note left before not leaving" (1975; "Biglietto lasciato prima di non andar via"): "If I happen not to return, / know that I never / departed. / My going / was always my staying / Here, where I never was" (trans. Joseph Falsone; "Se non dovessi tornare, / sappiate che non sono mai / partito. / Il mio viaggiare / è stato tutto un restare / qua, dove non fui mai"; *L'opera* 427); "Apostrophe to one impatient to embark" (1978; "Apostrofe a un impaziente d'imbarco"): "—Calm down. Where on earth would you go? / One thing is certainly known. / Believe me, you'll never be able to get / to where you've already gone" (trans. Joseph Falsone"—Si calmi. Dove vuol mai andare? / Un punto è assodato. / Lei non potrà mai arrivare, / mi creda, dov'è già arrivato"; *L'opera* 429).

This is a language that speaks against itself. It first asserts something and a moment later refutes it. It is not only that the subtraction of two exactly equivalent terms equals zero; it is also, and more importantly, the explication of a process whose graphic sign is a circle delimiting an empty and vacant space. The circular movement is provided by language, busying itself to devour its own being as it proceeds forward. Yet this movement is not in vain. On the contrary, it creates a space, an enclosure where the *non-linguistico* can deposit itself. In this space delimited by an indistinct, indeterminate language (a language in continuous denial of itself is potential) something lies which is simultaneously there and non-there; it is a presence whose existence is predicated upon its very "irreparable" invisibility. "Irreparable" is used in the sense that Agamben gives to it in *La comunità che viene* (*The Coming Community*). "The Irreparable," writes Agamben, "is that things are just as they are (L'irreparabile è che le cose siano così come sono), in this or that mode, consigned without remedy to their way of being (89; "consegnate senza rimedio alla loro maniera di essere"; *La comunità* 63).

The thing that language preserves in a woven circle is *as such* and cannot be anything other than itself. It is not the becoming or the potential, and its existence is incorporated in its very essence. It is in this sense that we *cannot have it* and *will never have it*, but will keep on missing it within its own irreparably impossible presence. It is the *res amissa*, the thing in between oblivion and waiting, the thing in which existence and essence coincide and become indistinguishable. It is the point at which philosophy and literature commence (the Platonic idea) and finish (the metaphysical aporia), and which language and subjectivity inhabit without ever being there. The proximity between Blanchot and Caproni could not be more evident. Let us read from *L'Attente l'oubli*: "That he could leave: he knew that he owed his ability to stay to this assurance. But he felt that his leaving, which was something that could be accomplished most easily on a personal level, possessed on another level all the characteristics of a decision that could never be carried out. He would leave, but he would, nevertheless, stay" (*Awaiting Oblivion* 12; "Qu'il pût partir, il savait que c'est à cette assurance qu'il devait de pouvoir rester. Mais il pressentait que ce départ qui était ce qui pouvait se faire le plus facilement sur le plan personnel, avait sur un autre plan tous les caractères d'une décision irréalisable. Il partirait, mais cependant il resterait"; 28). This last sentence is not only an emblematic definition of potentiality, it also encompasses the very meaning of poetry and the locus of subjectivity in language.

Potentiality, as Agamben has clearly articulated in *La comunità che viene*, is the power to suspend not so much the possibility as the certainty of an event (*The Coming Community* 103-04; *La comunità* 76-77). The potential being is the result of the actual being and, accordingly, the potential and indistinct language is the outcome of actual and factual language. I can decide not to speak only if I know for a fact that I could speak, and I can say *sono senza parole* ("I am without words") only when I inhabit words. Our vulnerability as "being potentially reinscribed within the isolation of concealment" stems from our "being made for exposure." This is the great vulnerability but also the great power of humans, their ability to travel along the route of ambiguity and indistinction. It is, in one word, their ability to be potential. Awaiting and oblivion are the thresholds leading to the site of potentiality and as such they implicate each other. This is to say that they are not the same and do not take place interchangeably. In fact, they are different yet reciprocal. This is why the title of Blanchot's book could not be *L'Attente et l'oubli*, "this and that," with the "and" determining spatial as well as temporal differentiation. And this is precisely why the title of the English translation, *Awaiting Oblivion*, is misleading, in that nothing is waited *for* in Blanchot's book, least of all oblivion. The space between the two words is the only possible declaration of their reciprocity, and also the only possible allusion to the auratic space defined by the coming together of waiting and oblivion.

If it is true that being potential is only possible in relation to being actual, it is also true that being in the presence of an apparent negativity originates from being in the presence of a tangible entity. The presence of the missing object is the powerful reminder and example of the etymological and aesthetic existential *habitus* of potentiality. And so are the frequent spatial and temporal incongruities scattered throughout Caproni's poetry and Blanchot's *L'Attente l'oubli*. We already know this to be true of Caproni. Let us now take a few samples from Blanchot's book. "'You will not enter this place twice.'—'I will enter it, but not even once.' Keeping watch over that which is not watched over" (*Awaiting Oblivion* 46; "'Tu n'entreras pas deux fois dans ce lieu.'—'J'y entrerai, mais pas même une fois.' Veillant sur l'insurveille"; *L'Attente l'oubli* 89); "He asked her: 'But don't you have the feeling that I came to look for you here and that I found you? What, then, does all the rest matter?'—'You found me again, perhaps, but without finding me'" (*Awaiting Oblivion* 55; "Il lui demanda: 'Mais n'avez-vous pas le sentiment que je suis venu vous chercher ici et que je vous ai trouvée? Alors, à quoi bon tout le reste?'—'Retrouvée, peut-être, mais sans m'avoir trouvée'"; *L'Attente l'oubli* 106); "'There is still a long road ahead.'—'But not one that will take us far away.'—'One that will lead us to what is nearest.'—'When everything that is near is farther away than any far-off place'" (*Awaiting Oblivion* 60; "'Il y a encore un long chemin.'—'Mais non pas pour nous mener loin.'—'Pour nous conduire au plus proche.'—'Quand tout ce qui est proche est plus loin que tout lointain'"; *L'Attente l'oubli* 115).

The door of language

A few pages earlier I asked a question which has not yet been answered: "what do we do—literally *do*—as we wait to say the second word?" The reference was to *l'attente* and *l'oubli* and the gap created by the blank space (the not-being of language and grammar), separating the two words. What is it, then, that we do as we enter the space of potentiality? It is what we do whenever we produce language, in that infinitesimal moment of pure magic and mystery, the small pause and the stopping of language from which language springs out again, magically and yet so naturally, so effortlessly. We do not merely wait for language to come to us or pledge with language to wait for us as we move toward it; we do not wait at all. Waiting is, as we have seen, the resounding being in language, a circling around, a process of creating the locus in which the missing object rests. Its rest is jealously guarded and preserved by oblivion, which is also, like waiting, a product of language; a language that protects the special object of our love and sustains it in its existence as *res amissa*. What we actually do in those instants between words—*l'attente l'oubli*—is to open the door of language. As we speak, we open doors and pass from one room of language into another room of language. We journey through language and in language. We are in language, we are language, but our being in language and our being language is predicated on our continuous departing from it and re-entering it. And this is why language, being, and time are intricately interconnected and clearly metaphorical, anaphoric, and analogical. There is no escape from this dynamism, and there is no escape from this incessant march that takes us where we already are: in language, in time, in ourselves. Caproni has provided a compelling and excruciatingly beautiful testimony to this journey. In the collection of poems *Il conte di Kevenhüller* we find the poem "La porta" ("The Door"; 1984). It reads: "...The white / door.../ The door / which, from transparency, opens / on opacity.../ The door / condemned.../ The door, / blind, which leads / where you already are, and torn / from its hinges remains / whitewalled, / intransitive.../ Amorphous / door that ushers obtuse / and labyrinthine (closed / in its bursting open) there / where no entrance / can give access.../ Where / no room or city / unfolds to the eye, and in / the torpor of vagueness / there moves / no semblance of branch / or thought.../ A single / eye of light (or of needle) / in the mind.../ Morganic door: / the Word" (trans. Joseph Falsone; "...La porta / Bianca.../ La porta / che, dalla trasparenza, porta / nell'opacità.../ La porta / condannata.../ La porta / cieca, che reca / dove si è già, e divelta / resta biancomurata / e intransitiva.../ L'amorfa / porta che conduce ottusa / e labirintica (chiusa / nel suo spalancarsi) là / dove nessun entrata / può dar àdito.../ Dove / nessuna stanza o città / s'apre all'occhio, e non muove /—nel ristagno del vago—/ ramo o pensiero una sola / parvenza.../ Una sola / cruna di luce (o d'ago) / nella mente…/ La porta / morgana: / La parola"; *L'opera* 609-10).

The blindness of language, our blindness, the conscious knowing of not knowing is also language's only—our only—possibility to communicate the incommunicable, the great epistemological potency that allows us to be in the presence of what we deliberately remove for the sake of love.

Indistinction is not only a linguistic and cultural experience, it is also—as glimpsed in Caproni's work—a mental space, a locus, a geographical mapping of the "I" of poetry. In Caproni's work, and not only in *Il muro della terra*, gates, doors, walls, and the acts of opening and trespassing occur time and time again. The very title *Il muro della terra* refers explicitly to a wall; more specifically, the wall separating the inside from the outside of the city of Dis in Canto X of Dante's *Comedy*. The separation formulated by Dante as a way of introducing one of his many poetic visions of Hell (this is the sixth circle, the circle of the heretics) is reconfigured by Caproni as the wall dividing the rational from the irrational, and the point at which the poetic decision whether or not to venture behind the wall must be taken. Indeed, the principal challenge of poetry, a challenge that can no longer be eluded or delayed, is precisely that of entering the space on the other side of the wall. There is nothing new about a metaphysical or existential journey beyond the rational. This is the very stuff of the Western literary tradition. What is radically new is that the journey upon which both Caproni and Blanchot embark takes place within the impossibility of its very taking place. With the poems "Return" and "Experience" from *Il muro della terra* in mind, let us read again a passage from Blanchot's *L'Attente l'oubli*: "That he could leave: he knew that he owed his ability to stay to this assurance. But he felt that his leaving, which was something that could be accomplished most easily on a personal level, possessed on another level all the characteristics of a decision that could never be carried out. He would leave, but he would, nevertheless, stay. This was the truth around which she, too, was circling stealthily" (*Awaiting Oblivion* 12; "Qu'il pût partir, il savait que c'est à cette assurance qu'il devait de pouvoir rester. Mais il pressentait que ce départ qui était ce qui pouvait se faire le plus facilement sur le plan personnel, avait sur un autre plan tous les caractères d'une décision irréalisable. Il partirait, mais cependant il resterait. Voilà la vérité autour de laquelle elle rôdait, elle aussi"; *L'Attente l'oubli* 28). This is a movement simultaneously going somewhere and nowhere, that is and is not: a movement whose essence and identity is predicated upon its very indistinction.

Conclusion

The hotel room

I find it fitting that Blanchot chose to set *L'Attente l'oubli* in a hotel room. Of course, many other settings might well complement a narration of suspension and indeterminacy, but the hotel room is particularly apt.

Giorgio Caproni said that the idea to write the poem "Res amissa" occurred to him in a hotel room in Germany. Caproni was looking for a letter that he knew he had with him, but he could not find it. The philosophical and literary significance of what is near in its remoteness came to him when a very courteous and diligent room attendant tried to help him recover the lost object. Their combined search proved futile and the missing letter remained missing, only to be found again in poetry as that which resides on the unsayable side of language. Was it a coincidence that Caproni encountered such a central philosophical concern in a hotel room? The hotel room appears again in my account of exile, and the making of memory as a metaphor for potentiality and life on the threshold. I also have alluded to thresholds and waiting rooms in my many references to Kafka's "Before the Law." Kafka never speaks explicitly of waiting rooms in his story, and yet that place just a few paces removed from the first door to the Law, furnished with only a stool and never fully described, is tantalisingly similar to a waiting room. Waiting rooms, hotel rooms—rooms that we inhabit only temporarily, marginally, often distractedly—they may in fact catch something of us that is kept and not released for the simple reason that we have *forgotten* this something in them. Perhaps involuntarily, we deposit something in these rooms of passage, which are also potential living spaces in between life and non-life, reality and unreality, purposefulness and *flânerie*. These rooms accumulate things which only in hindsight we realize we have jealously secured within them. What we have left behind are pieces of an irreparable originality, our originality in pieces. And yet, this loss is in reality a presence that touches us through its proximity, and that remains with us in its irreparability.

Poetic language resembles our amissed, or misplaced, life. In saying, language remembers what has been lost in memory; it remembers, that is, what can never be found or said. But as this book has attempted to indicate, our very creativity may well depend on that something which is in its *non-being*. Potentiality, suspension, and the threshold are spaces in which we deposit our being as beings and where, at times, we observe our own astonishment in the face of life. Does creativity equate with life? Perhaps, but certainly not with life understood as the Plotinian or Romantic flight of one into one. It is rather a life whose productivity depends on incessantly meeting other voices and presences which often remain unseen and unheard, lost and yet securely hidden in the folds of life. Translation—understood as event—may well be the place where a possible experience with the missing thing eventuates, and where the splinters of our originality might, even if only for a moment, resurface. This emergence is also a process of a distillation through which different voices—the bits and pieces—are allowed to speak as one by remaining many. The example I have provided, however partial and limited, is the conjunction of Leopardi's voice with the voices of two of his English translators.

While translation is not the mode or the *melos* that finds the missing thing, it can be thought of as a process that illuminates our potential condition, a process ultimately guided by the presence of, and experience with, the other. The important thing—and I hope to have made this clear—is not so much to discover what is missing as to learn that it is missing. It is within this learning that our life with others might commence yet again.

Works Cited

Agamben, Giorgio. "Friendship." Trans. Joseph Falsone. *Contretemps* 5 (December 2004): 2-7. Original title: "Amicizia."

Agamben, Giorgio. "Politica dell'esilio." *Derive e Approdi* 16 (1998): 25-27.

Agamben, Giorgio. *Il linguaggio e la morte: Un seminario sul luogo della negatività*. Turin: Einaudi, 1982.

Agamben, Giorgio. *Infancy and History: The Destruction of Experience*. Trans. Liz Heron. London: Verso, 1993.

Agamben, Giorgio. *Infanzia e storia. Distruzione dell'esperienza e origine della storia*. Milano: Einaudi, 2001.

Agamben, Giorgio. *La comunità che viene*. Milano: Einaudi, 1990.

Agamben, Giorgio. *Language and Death: The Place of Negativity*. Trans. Karen E. Pinkus and Michael Hardt. Minneapolis: U of Minnesota P, 1991.

Agamben, Giorgio. *Potentialities: Collected Essays in Philosophy*. Trans. Daniel Heller-Roazen. Stanford: Stanford UP, 1999.

Agamben, Giorgio. *Stanzas: Word and Phantasm in Western Culture*. Trans. Ronald L. Martinez. Minneapolis: U of Minnesota P, 1993.

Agamben, Giorgio. *Stanze: la parola e il fantasma nella cultura occidentale*. Turin: Einaudi, 1977.

Agamben, Giorgio. *The Coming Community*. Trans. Michael Hardt. Minneapolis: U of Minnesota P, 1993.

Aristotle. *Ethics*. Trans. J.A.K. Thomson. London: Penguin, 1976.

Augustine, Saint. *Le Confessioni*. Trans. Carlo Vitali. Milano: Rizzoli, 1999.

Augustine, Saint. *The Confessions*. Trans. Henry Chadwick. Oxford: Oxford UP, 1991.

Bartoloni, Paolo. *Interstitial Writing: Calvino, Caproni, Sereni, and Svevo*. Leicester: Troubador Publishing, 2003.

Bataille, Georges. *On Nietzsche*. Trans. Bruce Boone. New York: Continuum, 2004.

Benjamin, Andrew. "The Absolute as Translatability: Working through Walter Benjamin on Language." *Philosophy's Literature*. Manchester: Clinamen, 2001. 105-22.

Benjamin, Andrew. *Present Hope: Philosophy, Architecture, Judaism*. London: Routledge, 1997.

Benjamin, Walter. *Arcades Project*. Trans. Howard Eiland and Kevin McLaughlin. Cambridge: Belknap P of Harvard UP, 1999.

Benjamin, Walter. *Briefe*. Frankfurt: Suhrkamp, 1966. 2 vols.

Benjamin, Walter. *Ein Lesebuch*. Leipzig: Suhrkamp, 1996.

Benjamin, Walter. *Illuminations*. Trans. Harry Zohn. London: Fontana, 1973.

Benjamin, Walter. "On the Program of the Coming Philosophy." *Selected Writing 1913-1926*. Trans. Mark Ritter. Cambridge: Harvard UP, 1996. Vol. 1, 100-10.

Benjamin, Walter. *Reflections*. Trans. Edmund Jephcott. New York: Schocken Books, 1978.

Benveniste, Emile. *Problèmes de linguistique générale*. Paris: Gallimard, 1966-1974.

Benveniste, Emile. *Problems in General Linguistics*. Trans. Mary Elizabeth Meek. Coral Gables: U of Miami P, 1971.

Blanchot, Maurice. *Awaiting Oblivion*. Trans. John Gregg. Lincoln: U of Nebraska P, 1997.

Blanchot, Maurice. *L'Attente L'oubli*. Paris: Gallimard, 1962.

Blanchot, Maurice. *La Part du feu*. Paris: Gallimard, 1949.

Blanchot, Maurice. "Traduire." *L'Amitié*. Paris: Gallimard, 1971. 69-73.

Blanchot, Maurice. "Translating." *Friendship*. Trans. Elizabeth Rottenberg. Stanford: Stanford UP, 1997. 57-61.

Blanchot, Maurice. *The Work of Fire*. Trans. Charlotte Mandell. Stanford: Stanford UP, 1995.

Britt, Brian. *Walter Benjamin and the Bible*. New York: Continuum, 1996.

Brod, Max. *Franz Kafka: A Biography*. Trans. G. Humphreys Roberts and Richard Winston. New York: Schocken Books, 1960.

Brodersen, Momme. *Walter Benjamin: A Biography*. Trans. Malcolm R. Green and Ingrida Ligers. London: Verso, 1996.

Brooks, Peter. *Reading for the Plot: Design and Intention in Narrative*. Oxford, Clarendon, 1984.

Bruns, Gerald L. *Heidegger's Estrangements: Language, Truth, and Poetry in the Later Writings*. New Haven: Yale UP, 1989.

Bruns, Gerald L. *Maurice Blanchot: The Refusal of Philosophy*. Baltimore: Johns Hopkins UP, 1997.

Calvino, Italo. *Eremita a Parigi*. Lugano: Edizioni Pantarei, 1974.

Calvino, Italo. "Hermit in Paris." *Hermit in Paris: Autobiographical Writings*. Trans. Martin McLaughlin. London: Jonathan Cape, 2003. 167-75.

Calvino, Italo. *Lezioni americane*. Milano: Garzanti, 1988.

Calvino, Italo. *Saggi*. Ed. Mario Barenghi. Milano: Meridiani Mondadori, 1995. Vol. 1.

Calvino, Italo. *Six Memos for the Next Millennium*. Trans. Patrick Creagh. Cambridge, MA: Harvard UP, 1988.

Caproni, Giorgio. *L'opera in versi*. Ed. Luca Zuliani. Milano: Meridiani Mondadori, 1998.

Caproni, Giorgio. *La scatola nera*. Milano: Garzanti, 1996.

Caproni, Giorgio. *The Wall of the Earth*. Trans. Pasquale Verdicchio. Montréal: Guernica, 1992.

Carruthers, Mary. *The Craft of Thought: Meditation, Rhetoric, and the Making of Images, 400-1200*. Cambridge: Cambridge UP, 1998.

Carter, Paul. *Baroque Memories*. Manchester: Carcanet, 1994.

Carter, Paul. *Material Thinking*. Melbourne: Melbourne UP, 2004.

Carter, Paul. *Repressed Spaces: The Poetics of Agoraphobia*. London: Reaktion Books, 2002.

Castoriadis, Cornelius. "Time and Creation." *Chronotypes: The Construction of Time*. Ed. John Bender and David E. Wellbery. Stanford: Stanford UP, 1991. 38-64.

Cavarero, Adriana. *A più voci*. Milano: Feltrinelli, 2003.

Cavarero, Adriana. *For More than One Voice: Toward a Philosophy of Vocal Expression*. Trans. Paul A Kottman. Stanford: Stanford UP, 2005.

Caverero, Adriana. *Relating Narratives: Storytelling and Selfhood*. Trans. Paul A. Kottman. New York: Routledge, 2000.

Cavarero, Adriana. *Tu che mi guardi, tu che mi racconti*. Milano: Feltrinelli, 1997.

Celati, Gianni. "Mio zio scopre l'esistenza delle lingue straniere." *Narratori delle pianure*. Milano: Feltrinelli, 1985. 102-04.

Chrétien, Jean-Louis. *The Call and the Response*. Trans. Anne A. Davenport. New York: Fordham UP, 2004.

Chrétien, Jean-Louis. *L'Appelle et la réponse*. Paris: Les Éditions de Minuit, 1992.

Clark, Timothy. *Derrida, Heidegger, Blanchot*. Cambridge: Cambridge UP, 1992.

Colish, Marcia L. *The Mirror of Language: A Study in the Medieval Theory of Knowledge*. Lincoln: U of Nebraska P, 1983.

Deleuze, Gilles. *The Fold: Leibniz and the Baroque*. Trans. Tom Conley. Minneapolis: U of Minnesota P, 1993.

Deleuze, Gilles. *Le Pli. Leibniz et le baroque*. Paris: Les Éditions de Minuit, 1988.

Derrida, Jacques. "Aphorism Countertime." Trans. Nicholas Royle. *Acts of Literature*. Ed. Derek Attridge. New York: Routledge, 1992. 414-33.

Derrida, Jacques. *Dissemination*. Trans. Barbara Johnson. Chicago: U of Chicago P, 1981.

Derrida, Jacques. "From Traumatism to Promise." *Points...: Interviews, 1974-1994*. Ed. Elisabeth Weber. Trans. Peggy Kamuf and others. Stanford: Stanford UP, 1995.

Derrida, Jacques. "L'Aphorisme a contretemps." *Psyché*. Paris: Galilée, 1987. 519-33.

Derrida, Jacques. *La Dissémination*. Paris: Éditions du Seuil, 1972.

Dillon, Brian. "The Carcass of Time." *Oxford Literary Review* 19.1-2 (1997): 133-47.

Fóti, Véronique M. *Heidegger and the Poets: Poiesis/Sophia/Techne*. New York: Humanities Books, 1992.

Freud, Sigmund. "Creative Writers and Day-Dreaming." *Art and Literature: Jensen's Gradiva, Leonardo da Vinci and Other Works*. Trans. James Strachey. London: Penguin, 1985. 129-41.

Freud, Sigmund. *The Interpretation of Dreams*. Trans. James Strachey. London: Allen & Unwin, 1954.

Freud, Sigmund. *On Aphasia*. Trans. E. Stengel. London: Imago, 1953.

Freud, Sigmund. *Zur Auffassung der Aphasien: Eine Kritische Studie*. Ed. Paul Vogel. Frankfurt: Fischer, 2001.

Fynsk, Christopher. *Language and Relation:...that there is Language*. Stanford: Stanford UP, 1996.

Gadamer, Hans-Georg. *Gesammelte Werke*. Ed. Paul Siebeck. Tübingen: J.C.B. Mohr, 1986. Vol. 8.

Gadamer, Hans-Georg. *The Relevance of the Beautiful and Other Essays*. Trans. Nicholas Walker. Cambridge: Cambridge UP, 1986.

Gargani, Aldo Giorgio. "La copia e l'originale." *Filosofia '91*. Ed. Gianni Vattimo. Rome: Laterza, 1992. 51-65.

Gombrich, E.H. "Psychoanalysis and the History of Art." *Meditations on a Hobby Horse and Other Essays on the Theory of Art*. London: Phaidon, 1963. 30-44.

H.D. "Eurydice." *Selected Poems*. New York: New Direction Books, 1988.

Hart, Kevin. *The Dark Gaze: Maurice Blanchot and the Sacred*. Chicago: U of Chicago P, 2004.

Hegel, G.W.F. *Jenenser Realphilosophie I, Die Vorlesungen von 1803-1804*. Ed. J. Hoffmeister. Leipzig: 1932.

Hegel, G.W.F. *Phenomenology of Spirit*. Trans. A.V. Miller. Oxford: Oxford UP, 1977.

Hegel, G.W.F. *Werke in zwanzig Bänden. Frühe Schriften*. Ed. Eva Moldenhauer and Karl Markus Michel. Frankfurt: Suhrkamp, 1971. Vol. 1.

Heidegger, Martin. *Being and Time*. Trans. John Macquarrie and Edward Robinson. Malden: Blackwell, 1962.

Heidegger, Martin. *Holzwege, Gesamtausgabe*. Band 5. Ed. Friedrich-Wilhelm von Herrmann. Frankfurt: Vittorio Klostermann, 1977.

Heidegger, Martin. *Kant and the Problem of Metaphysics*. Trans. Richard Taft. 5th ed. Bloomington: Indiana UP, 1997.

Heidegger, Martin. "Lettre à Monsieur Beaufret (23 novembre 1945)." *Lettre sur l'humanisme*. Trans. Roger Munier. Paris: Éditions Montaigne, 1964. 182.29-30.

Heidegger, Martin. *Off the Beaten Track*. Trans. Kenneth Haynes. Cambridge: Cambridge UP, 2002.

Heidegger, Martin. *On the Way to language*. Trans. Peter D. Hertz. San Francisco: Harper and Row, 1982.

Heidegger, Martin. *Sein und Zeit*. Tübingen: Verlag, 1957.

Heidegger, Martin. *Unterwegs zur Sprache*. Stuttgart: Verlag Günther Neske Pfullingen, 1975.

Heidegger, Martin. *What is Philosophy? Was ist das—die Philosophie?* Trans. W. Kluback and J.T. Wilde. London: Vision, 1963.

Heidegger, Martin, and Eugen Fink. *Heraclitus Seminar*. Trans. Charles H. Seibert. Evanston: Northwestern UP, 1993.

Heidegger, Martin, and Eugen Fink. *Heraklit. Seminar Wintersemester 1966/1967*. Frankfurt: Vittorio Klostermann, 1970.

Heller-Roazen, Daniel. *Echolalias: On the Forgetting of Language*. New York: Zone Books, 2005.

Hill, Lesley. *Bataille, Klossowski, Blanchot*. Oxford: Oxford UP, 2001.

Husserl, Edmund. "Die Frage nach dem Ursprung der Geometrie als intentional-historisches Problem." *Revue Internationale de Philosophie* 1 (1939): 203-25.

Husserl, Edmund. "The Origin of Geometry." *The Crisis of European Sciences and Transcendental Phenomenology*. Trans. David Carr. Evanston: Northwestern UP, 1970. 353-78.

Husserl, Edmund. *The Phenomenology of Internal Time Consciousness*. Trans. James S. Churchill. Bloomington: Indiana UP, 1964.

Jacobs, Carol. *In the Language of Walter Benjamin*. Baltimore: Johns Hopkins UP, 1999.

Jacobson, Roman. *Child Language, Aphasia, and Phonological Universals*. Trans. Allan R. Keiler. The Hague: Mouton, 1968.

Kafka, Franz. *The Diaries of Franz Kafka*. Ed. Max Brod. London: Penguin, 1972.

Kafka, Franz. *Zur Frage der Gesetze und andere Schriften aus dem Nachlass. Gesammelte Werke*. Ed. Hans-Gerd Koch. Frankfurt: Fischer, 1994. Vol. 7.

Kant, Immanuel. *Critique of Pure Reason*. Trans. Norman Kemp Smith. London: Macmillan, 1963.

Kierkegaard, Søren. *Repetition: An Essay in Experimental Psychology*. Princeton: Princeton UP, 1946.

Leopardi, Giacomo. "The Infinite." *The Canti*. Trans. J.G. Nichols. Manchester: Carcanet New P, 1994. 53.

Leopardi, Giacomo. "L'infinito." *Canti*. Ed. Giovanni Getto. Milano: Mursia, 1977. 103.

Leopardi, Giacomo. "L'infinito." Trans. Lorna de' Lucchi. *Translating Leopardi 1* (2007): <http://www.textetc.com/workshop/wt-leopardi-1.html>.

Leopardi, Giacomo. *Moral Tales*. Trans. Patrick Creagh. Manchester: Carcanet New P, 1983.

Leopardi, Giacomo. *Operette morali*. Milano: Rizzoli, 1976.

Malpas, Jeff. "Death and the Unity of Life." *Death and Philosophy*. Ed. Jeff Malpas and Robert C. Solomon. London: Routledge, 1998. 120-34.

McClennen, Sophia. *The Dialectics of Exile: Nation, Time, Language, and Space in Hispanic Literature*. West Lafayette: Purdue UP, 2004.

Plato. *Phaedrus and Letters VII and VIII*. Trans. Walter Hamilton. London: Penguin, 1973.

Plato. *The Symposium*. Trans. Christopher Gill. London: Penguin, 1999.

Plotinus. *Enneads*. Trans. Stephen MacKenna. London: Medici Society, 1917-1930.

Ricoeur, Paul. "On Interpretation." *Philosophy in France Today*. Ed. Alan Montefiore. London: Cambridge UP, 1983. 175-97.

Ricoeur, Paul. *Temps et récit*. Paris: Éditions du Seuil, 1983-1985. 3 vols.

Ricoeur, Paul. *Time and Narrative*. Trans. Kathleen McLaughin and David Pellaur. Chicago: U of Chicago P, 1984-1988. 3 vols.

Saussure, Ferdinand de. *Cours de linguistique générale*. Paris: Editions Payot, 1922.

Saussure, Ferdinand de. *Course in General Linguistics*. Trans. Wade Baskin. London: Owen, 1974.

Sereni, Vittorio. *Tutte le poesie*. Milano: Mondadori, 1986.

Smock, Ann. *What is There to Say? Blanchot, Melville, des Forêts, Beckett*. Lincoln: U of Nebraska P, 2003.

Stewart, Susan. *Poetry and the Fate of the Senses*. Chicago: U of Chicago P, 2002.

Tötösy de Zepetnek, Steven. *Comparative Literature: Theory, Method, Application*. Amsterdam: Rodopi, 1998.

Tötösy de Zepetnek, Steven. "From Comparative Literature Today toward Comparative Cultural Studies." *Comparative Literature and Comparative Cultural Studies*. Ed. Steven Tötösy de Zepetnek. West Lafayette: Purdue UP, 2003. 235-67.

Tötösy de Zepetnek, Steven, ed. *Comparative Literature and Comparative Cultural Studies*. West Lafayette: Purdue UP, 2003.

Ungaretti, Giuseppe. *The Buried Harbour*. Trans. Kevin Hart. Canberra: Leros, 1990.

Ungaretti, Giuseppe. *Il porto sepolto*. Ed. Carlo Ossola. Milano: Il Saggiatore, 1981.

Valéry, Paul. *Cahiers 1894- 1914*. Paris: Gallimard, 1997. Vol. 6.

Vattimo, Gianni. *Essere, storia e linguaggio in Heidegger*. Genoa: Marietti, 1989.

Vattimo, Gianni. *Oltre l'interpretazione*. Rome: Laterza, 1994.

Virno, Paolo. *Quando il verbo si fa carne*. Turin: Bollati Boringhieri, 2003.

White, Hayden. "The Value of Narrativity in the Representation of Reality." *On Narrative*. Ed. W.J.T. Mitchell. Chicago: U of Chicago P, 1981. 1-23.

Wittgenstein, Ludwig. *Philosophical Occasions: 1912-1951*. Ed. James C. Klagge and Alfred Nordmann. Indianapolis: Hackett, 1993.

Young, Julian. "Death and Authenticity." *Death and Philosophy*. Ed. Jeff Malpas and Robert C. Solomon. London: Routledge, 1998. 112-19.

Index